THE STORY OF PAUL II

THE MIDDLE YEARS.

BY TREVOR GALPIN

Copyright 2020

The Story of Paul II: The Middle Years
by Trevor Galpin

Published by TLG Mins (US) Inc

Design and Layout by Tom Carroll

ISBN: 978-1-8380570-0-8

All rights reserved. No part of this publication may be reproduced, stored in a retrieval system or transmitted in any form or by any means - for example, electronic, photocopy, recording - without the prior written permission of the author or publisher. The only exception is brief quotation in printed reviews.

All Scripture quotations, unless otherwise indicated, are taken from The Holy Bible, New International Version®, NIV® Copyright ©1973, 1978, 1984, 2011 by Biblica, Inc.®. Used by permission. All rights reserved worldwide.

For more information and resources by Trevor and Linda Galpin please visit: **www.trevorlindafhm.com**

INTRODUCTION

it unfolding. To not focus on theology but go for the story, not a biography or a novel, but a story. Others far more competent and eminent than I have opened up the mind and explored the theology of Paul to great effect, not least N.T. Wright whose scholarship has inspired me in my journey.

I procrastinated; I did not have time to write. Well, all of that changed at the beginning of March when COVID-19 confined us to our home and I had time on my hands.

This is what emerged. It is a fictive historical narrative, a biographical story. It is therefore part fiction, but a fiction based on true events involving real people encountered in the New Testament, in the Acts of the Apostles and in the Letters of the Apostle Paul. The main characters in the story are well known, people like Paul, Timothy, Aquila, Priscilla, and Silas. The minor characters who appear in the story we know very little about. This is where my imagination comes into play. Some of the characters are historical, mentioned in the Roman writers Tacitus and Suetonius. A few are fictitious. One key character is completely fictitious, but he represents someone or a group of people who dogged Paul's footsteps throughout his journeys. You will meet him on and off throughout the narrative. I have called him Matthias.

This is a story, hopefully a gripping one inspired by true events. As in all historical narratives, it contains much truth and will hopefully have thought provoking moments which will stir you, the reader, to dig deeper into the source material in the New Testament. It is a story about one of my favourite biblical characters, the Apostle Paul and how he brought amazing revelation to us.

Trevor Galpin
July, 2020

CONTENTS

Introduction	V
MAP - Key cities visited by Paul in his Middle Years	XII
Prologue	XIII
Antioch AD 47 - 49	**18**
Chapter I	18
Chapter II	27
Rome AD 49	**32**
Chapter III	32
Jerusalem AD 30	**36**
Chapter IV	36
Rome AD 49	**48**
Chapter V	48
Lystra AD 50	**57**
Chapter VI	57
Troas AD 50	**69**
Chapter VII	69
Philippi AD 51	**81**
Chapter VIII	81

CONTENTS

Thessalonica, Berea and Athens AD 51	**94**
Chapter IX	94
Corinth First Visit AD 51 - 53	**105**
Chapter X	105
Chapter XI	119
Chapter XII	125
Chapter XIII	135
Ephesus AD 52	**149**
Chapter XIV	149
Jerusalem and Antioch AD 52	**153**
Chapter XV	153
Ephesus First Visit AD 53	**165**
Chapter XVI	165
Corinth Second Visit AD 53	**182**
Chapter XVII	182
Ephesus Second Visit AD 53	**195**
Chapter XVII	195
Chapter XIX	209
Chapter XX	217

CONTENTS

Chapter XXI	232
Macedonia AD 56	**241**
Chapter XXII	241
Chapter XXIII	251
Corinth Third Visit AD 56	**267**
Chapter XXIV	267
Chapter XXV	275
Chapter XXVI	287
Macedonia and Asia AD 57	**299**
Chapter XXVII	299
Jerusalem AD 57	**307**
Chapter XXVIII	307
Dramatis Personae	325
Biblical References	349
Other Books by Trevor Galpin	354

KEY CITIES VISITED BY PAUL IN HIS MIDDLE YEARS.

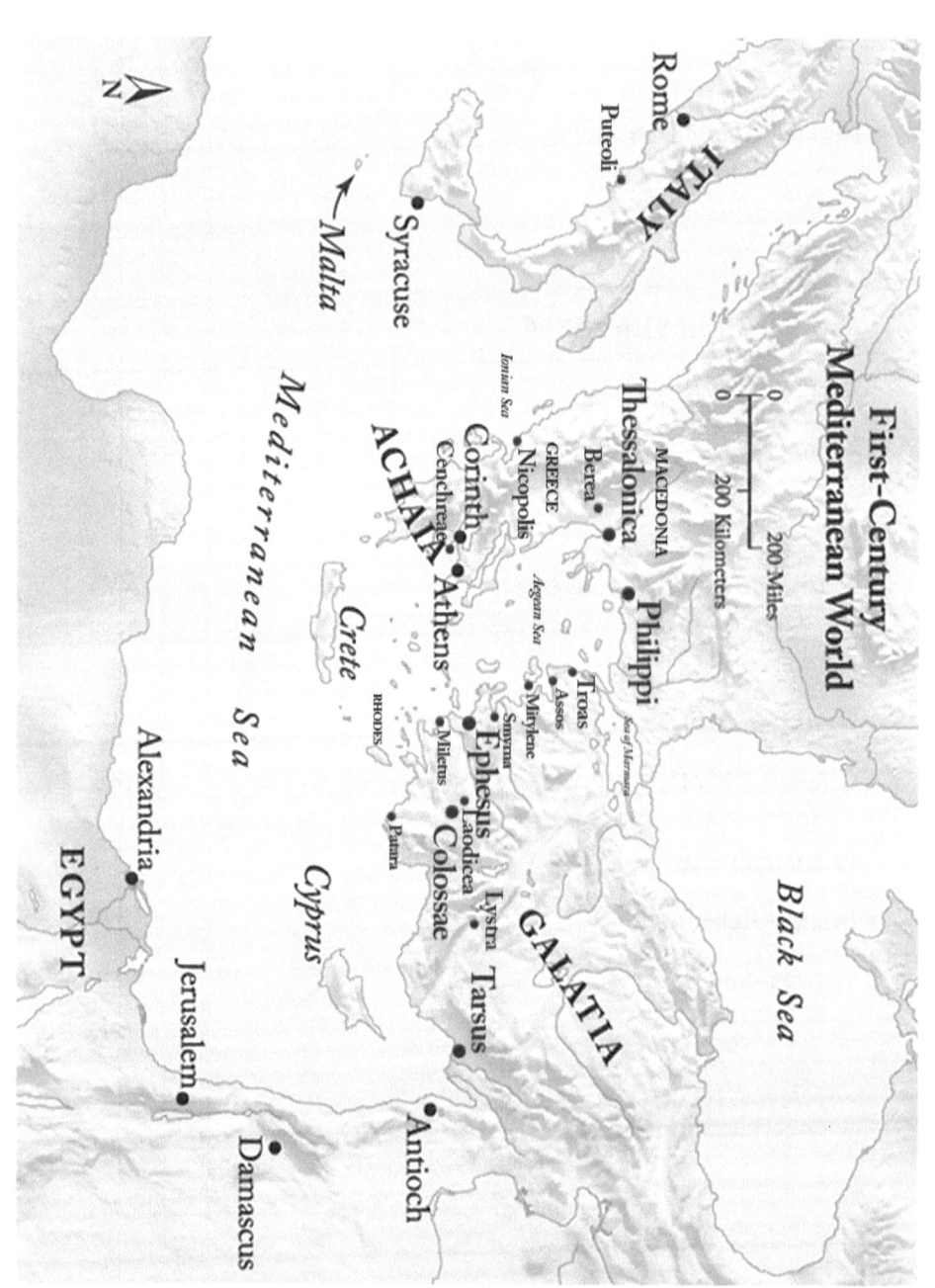

A NIGHT AND DAY IN THE OPEN SEA

PROLOGUE

"Hold on, boy." The man shivered as he clung to the remains of the mast of the ship along with a terrified young man who had also managed to swim to the flotsam. It was late summer, and the water of the Aegean Sea was still warm. The young man moaning and spluttering groaned,

"I don't know if I can hold on much longer. My muscles keep cramping and I feel my strength is failing."

"It certainly was a ferocious storm but the Lord has spared us," replied the older man. The shipwreck had taken a heavy toll sapping most of their energy and strength.

The older man was a passenger who had boarded at Cenchreae, the eastern port of the city of Corinth. He was bound for Ephesus across the Aegean Sea in the province of Asia. The boat was a small merchant ship with a cargo of high-quality Greek olive oil bound initially for Ephesus and then for Alexandria in Egypt. The crossing in late summer would normally have taken three days. At the start of the trip the favourable winds took them out of the Gulf of Saroniki along the coast, bypassing Piraeus, the port of Athens, passing to the north of the island and port of Delos, out into the open sea. This time, however, having barely lost sight of Delos over the horizon, there was an unexpected shift in the wind from the south. Very quickly a storm caught the ship by surprise and drove it northwards into a dangerous area of reefs and exposed rocks. The ship breached on the rocks and foundered within minutes. The passenger hardly had time to rush up on deck as the ship, listing heavily, keeled over, and capsized. He was thrown into the sea and swimming for his life managed to grab the broken mast that was bobbing in the water nearby.

"Help! Help! I can't swim. Poseidon save me!" screamed a young man thrashing about in the water. He kept going under the waves. Hanging on to the mast with one hand, the older man reached out and grabbed the boy by his hair pulling him to the mast. The young man grasped the broken spar.

"Poseidon has saved me!"

"It wasn't Poseidon who saved you, my lad, but the God and Father of our Lord Jesus Christ, with a bit of help from me!" said the passenger.

"I don't know this Jesus of whom you speak, but I'm grateful to your god and to you. My name is Onesiphorus, and I promise you. If I live to see the dawn I will follow your God for the rest of my days and do whatever I can to help you, just as you have helped me today."

The two men clung desperately to the mast as night drew on. In the early hours of the morning, a full moon rose. A light shone from afar, then a sail but it disappeared below the horizon soon after sunrise. Onesiphorus alternated between sleep and panic. The day dragged on with no sign of any other survivors or floating wreckage. They were alone.[1]

Towards the late afternoon after virtually twenty-four hours adrift

A NIGHT AND DAY IN THE OPEN SEA

in the sea, Onesiphorus thought he saw another sail considerably closer and heading in their direction. Indeed, a Roman naval ship with two banks of oars on each side sailed towards them. As it became clearer what sort of ship this was, Onesiphorus began to wail.

"What is it now, boy?" demanded the other survivor.

"It's a b-b-bireme," Onesiphorus choked out.

"This is good news, we will be saved. It's coming our way."

"No! It's not good news at all," sobbed Onesiphorus. "They will take us and make us slaves. I am not a Roman citizen. They will capture us and force us to spend the rest of our wretched lives rowing as galley slaves. I'd rather die."

"Stop it right now," said the passenger sternly. "They will not. I am a citizen of Rome and I will say you are my servant. Don't worry, we will be saved. My God, who is the Father of the Lord Jesus has rescued us. I haven't finished what the Father has given me to do yet. And as far as being a galley slave is concerned, I am his 'under rower' already and I am sure he has a plan for you too."

The young man looked at the other survivor in astonishment.

"When I met God's son Jesus, many years ago," continued the man, "he called me to be his servant, his under rower though not in a Roman bireme and that is what I have been doing ever since. But that is another story which I'll tell you some other time. Take heart, for now we need to attract their attention. Come on, lad, wave a bit of torn sail cloth as hard as you can."

Onesiphorus had no idea what the man was talking about, but somehow he started to feel maybe things were not as bad as they had felt in the last few hours. Perhaps if he had escaped the grip of

Poseidon, the god of the sea, and if he evaded becoming a galley slave, then this God who the other survivor called his Father may be able to help him too. It was worth a try. Onesiphorus started to frantically wave as hard as he could and shouted at the top of his lungs.

As the galley came closer, sailors on deck spotted them in the water. They heard the drum master slow the rhythm to let the ship reduce speed until it drew near. A group of sailors were hanging over the gunwale of the ship waving and gesturing to them as a rope was thrown over the side. An officer joined the sailors. Onesiphorus could hear him commanding the sailors to hang on to the rope as he and the other man were hauled, one by one, upwards onto the deck.

Onesiphorus fell on the deck grovelling at the feet of the officer. The other passenger, stood upright, dripping in his wet clothes in front of the captain who was now surrounded by a group of curious sailors.

"What have we here? Who are you?" demanded the captain.

"I am Paul, a Roman citizen from the noble city of Tarsus. Thank you for rescuing us. I seek your help. Two days ago I took ship at Cenchreae bound for Ephesus until the storm overwhelmed us."

"Well, you are in luck. The gods are with you, as we are bound for Ephesus ourselves and expect to dock there tomorrow."

"Take this man and his slave below and get them water, food and dry clothes," the captain ordered one of his men.

"He is not my slave," said Paul. "He is my son. His name is Onesiphorus."[2]

The boy stood up blinking and stared at the man who had introduced himself to the captain as Paul. Who was he? Why had the gods spared his life at the hands of this man? Was it indeed the gods or was it this God he called his Father? Who was the Lord Jesus Christ he talked about? And why did Paul call him his son? He had so many questions.

They took them below and gave them dry clothes and food. Sitting beside each other on a bunk quietly eating, Onesiphorus broke the silence.

"So, Paul is it? Who are you and why have you saved me from Poseidon's grip and from being chained to an oar in the bowels of this ship? Tell me your story. I need to know if I am going to follow your God who you call Father."

"It's a long one, but we have plenty of time," Paul answered.

ANTIOCH AD 47 - 49

CHAPTER I

The story Paul told Onesiphorus was indeed a long one. It began twenty years before. As a young man he was a member of a Jewish sect called the Pharisees. He lived in Jerusalem and was known by his Jewish name, Saul. A group of people known as 'Followers of the Way' had emerged who believed a Galilean rabbi, Jesus of Nazareth, was the promised Messiah. Jesus had been arrested and crucified by the Roman occupiers of Judea. What happened next changed everything. The Followers of the Way believed Jesus had risen from the dead and was none other than the Son of God who had come into the world to reconcile man to God as their Father.

Following the stoning to death of one of their leaders, a Hellenistic Jew named Stephen, Saul became a vehement persecutor of the Followers of the Way and accelerated the persecution. He was personally responsible for the deaths of several of them in Jerusalem.[3]

On a visit to Damascus to arrest more of the believers, he had an astonishing conversion experience resulting in him also becoming a follower of Jesus.[4]

He dropped out of sight for three years in Arabia. When Saul returned to Jerusalem, he attempted to join the group of Followers of the Way in the city. Not surprisingly many were afraid of him, not believing that he really was a changed man who was now like them a follower of Jesus

One of them called Barnabas, brought him to the 'apostles', which was the name given to the leaders of the believers.

"I have talked with Saul. I believe he has had a genuine conversion. He claims to have met the risen Jesus, as many of us have. He is not the same man who was here three years ago. He really has changed," said Barnabas.

Barnabas' words carried great weight with them. One of their leaders however said, "It would be best for him to get as far away from Jerusalem as possible since so many remember him as a persecutor." They agreed and sent Saul back to his home town, Tarsus, where he stayed for several years.[5]

Originally from Cyprus, Barnabas' real name was Joseph. The apostles in Jerusalem had given him the nickname Barnabas which meant 'son of encouragement'. He was a generous hearted man who sold a field and gave the proceeds to the apostles to help with the poor in the Jerusalem community.

One of the consequences of Stephen's death and the subsequent persecution was many of the believers fled Jerusalem and went back to their home cities and provinces scattered across the eastern part of the Roman empire. As a result, communities of believers sprang up. Wherever they went, they spread the message among the local Jewish communities. Some of these early converts who were from Cyprus and Cyrene in North Africa, went to Antioch, the capital city of the province of Syria, and began to speak to the Gentile population of the city, telling them about Jesus. Many people believed and were baptised and became followers of Jesus.[6]

When news of this filtered back to the believers in Jerusalem,

ANTIOCH AD 47 - 49

they sent Barnabas to Antioch to assess the situation and find out the full extent of what was happening. On his arrival he saw for himself what God was doing among them. The believers were very much of the same heart, excited and eager to share their newfound faith with their neighbours and friends. Barnabas was very happy with everything and true to his character encouraged them all to remain committed to the Lord. They recognised him to be a good man, full of the Holy Spirit and faith and looked to him as a leader among them. As Barnabas worked among them, many more became believers in Jesus, were baptised and filled with God's Holy Spirit.[7]

One of Barnabas' greatest gifts was knowing his own limitations. As the numbers grew, he realised he needed help in teaching the new converts. He remembered meeting Saul ten years previously and had been impressed with him. So he decided to go to Tarsus which was about a ten-day journey around the coast to look for Saul. On finding him he explained what he had in mind. Saul enthusiastically agreed to go with Barnabas.

Together they began to teach and work among the believers in Antioch. The people of the city were beginning to refer to the believers as 'Christians', which literally meant 'little Christs'. It was supposed to be a way of ridiculing them, but the name stuck and began to be their preferred description for themselves. For a year, Barnabas and Saul stayed with them teaching and encouraging them.[8]

Sometime later, the community in Antioch commissioned Saul and Barnabas to take the message beyond the confines of the city to other cities and regions. They decided to take Barnabas' young cousin, John Mark with them. Mark was from Jerusalem where his mother Mary had a large house in the city which was used as a gathering place by the believers. This had been the house where Jesus had celebrated his last Passover meal with his band of disciples immediately before his arrest and crucifixion.[9]

Their journey took them first to Cyprus. After connecting with the believers already on Cyprus, they established a number of new communities on the island. From this point on Saul began to be known as Paul. Leaving Cyprus they crossed back to the mainland to Pamphylia. But soon after arriving, John Mark decided to leave them and go back home to Jerusalem. Barnabas tried to persuade him to continue with them but Mark refused. Paul was very unimpressed with the young man's lack of commitment.[10]

Paul and Barnabas, however, pressed on inland. On their travels around the mainland, they spoke in Jewish synagogues wherever they were given a hearing. Many small communities were established made up of Jewish believers and a growing number of Gentiles. After some time, the two men returned to Antioch in order to report on all their activities to their friends in the city.[11]

One day, some months after Paul and Barnabas returned, visitors arrived from Jerusalem who told the gathered community they needed to adopt Jewish customs. In particular, they said Gentile men needed to be circumcised in order to be true Christians. This caused great consternation among them not least among the male converts.

"This is a level of commitment I had not bargained on when I became a believer," said a young convert man named Titus. Paul and Barnabas argued strongly against this teaching on the basis it was not good news but was man made rules and regulations.[12]

To try to resolve the issue, the believers in Antioch decided Paul and Barnabas, and Titus, should go to Jerusalem to raise the issue with the apostles and leaders.(13)

In Jerusalem they met in Mark's mother's house. At the gathering, Peter who had been one of Jesus' closest friends and a leader among the apostles spoke very powerfully. They felt he was speaking under the influence of the Holy Spirit in his role as an apostle. He had an authority and an anointing on him recognised by everyone.

As Peter addressed the assembly he reminded them of his own experience with a group of Roman Gentiles. It happened following a vision in which God told him to preach the message about Jesus to non-Jewish people as well as to Jews. Almost immediately visitors arrived, sent by a Roman centurion from the nearby garrison in Caesarea requesting Peter come and speak to them. The centurion and his whole household declared themselves to be believers and were baptised. This was the first significant group of non-Jewish people to become believers.

As the assembly carefully listened, Peter emphatically declared they should not try to go against God by putting on the necks of Gentiles a yoke that neither they nor their ancestors had been able to bear. He summed up his argument by saying,

"We believe it is through the grace of our Lord Jesus that they are saved, just as we are."

Peter's statement succinctly summarised the process of being saved which was being taught by the apostles and by Paul. It was suggested by James, the brother of Jesus, that a letter be sent to the Gentile believers. His intention was to not make it difficult for them, but also to encourage them. It was distinctly pastoral in tone but did not address the theological issue at the root of the problem. Paul and Barnabas returned home with a copy of the letter. They were also accompanied by two other men from Jerusalem, Judas and Silas.(14)

On returning to Antioch, they gathered everyone together and read the letter. They felt it was an encouraging message and might resolve the difficulty. Judas and Silas said much to encourage and strengthen the believers. These two were considered prophetic. When they spoke under the influence of the Holy Spirit, they spoke words as if from God himself to encourage, comfort and build people up. After some time, they returned to Jerusalem but Paul and Barnabas remained in Antioch, where they continued to teach and preach.(15)

All went well in Antioch and the community continued to grow with a steady flow of Gentile converts joining their ranks. Relationships between Jewish and Gentile converts were warm and harmonious. Peter visited and would regularly eat with both Gentile and Jewish believers. At times it wasn't clear whether Peter even had a Jewish background. John Mark returned to Antioch with Peter. Since his return to Jerusalem after leaving Paul and Barnabas in Pamphylia, Mark connected with Peter and accompanied him on his travels.

Barnabas was delighted to see Mark again and took him to Paul who was surprised to see him.

"So, what are you doing here, young man?" asked Paul.

"I came here with Peter. I'm helping him."

"Are you indeed, and how might that be?"

"Well, I am writing down the stories he talks about when he preaches."

Paul raised an eyebrow. "Stories? What stories are you talking about?"

"The events Peter witnessed when he was with Jesus. The things Jesus said and did, the miracles, the healings, the parables, everything. I haven't finished it yet though."

"Why are you doing this? Didn't Jesus say he would be coming back soon? When he returns we shall all see him and we won't need to read your stories, will we?" Paul remarked dismissively.

Mark became very quiet and didn't know what to say in response to Paul's lack of enthusiasm for his writing. Barnabas tried to ease the tension. "Well, that's interesting, Mark. I'm sure it will be useful one day."

Another group of visitors arrived from Jerusalem. They refused to eat with Gentile believers and criticised the Jewish believers for mixing with Gentiles. They claimed to have come with the support and backing of James and the leaders in Jerusalem and insisted circumcision was a requirement for salvation. These men had been Pharisees before becoming believers and were skilled at arguing. They intimidated those who did not agree with them. Peter drew back and separated himself from the Gentiles. In reality, he was afraid of them. Other Jewish believers joined him in his hypocritical response, including Barnabas.[16]

Once again, the community in Antioch faced the same crisis as before. Paul decided to confront Peter first and foremost because of his apostolic role in the wider community of believers. Paul did not hold back and challenged Peter to his face about his compromising behaviour, accusing him of hypocrisy.

"You are a Jew, Peter, yet you live like a Gentile and not like a Jew. How is it, then, that you force Gentiles to follow Jewish customs?"

It was a very tense moment which resulted in hurt and great

sadness. Many tears were shed as they realised the terrible effect this teaching was having on the believers. No one wanted this division. Finally, they recognised Paul was right. It was indeed the grace of God in Jesus which led to their salvation not the works of man or obedience to rules and regulations. A time of repentance and reconciliation followed which did much to rebuild trust. The community recovered the harmony which had been stolen from them.[17]

Not long after this, news reached Paul from Galatia. After leaving Antioch these men from Jerusalem had travelled to Galatia to further spread their teaching. They specifically accused Paul of not preaching the whole truth and questioned his authority and message. They insisted true followers of Jesus needed to be circumcised and adhere to the Mosaic laws of the Old covenant. Their message caused great confusion as most of the converts were Gentiles.

Their teaching was completely contrary to the message Paul had taught in Galatia. Consequently, Paul decided to write to them. In the letter he described the teaching by these 'Judaisers', as they were being called, as 'another gospel'.

When telling his story to Onesiphorus years later, his passion and love for the Galatians spilled out. "You foolish, Galatians! Who has bewitched you?" he wrote.

This was the first letter Paul had written and it included the revelation that a believer was 'in Christ'. He explained how being 'in Christ' resulted in a new identity for believers as sons of God.

Paul knew the wrong teaching had not just impacted the believers in Galatia but also in Antioch. He imagined they would also be discussing these things in Jerusalem. He wondered if perhaps he should send a copy of his letter to Peter, the other apostles and James in Jerusalem. Just in case, he instructed his scribe Tychicus, to make a copy before sending the original to Galatia.

CHAPTER II

Many weeks passed after Paul sent his letter to his friends in Galatia. He eagerly awaited news to hear how they were and how the letter had been received. Paul knew there would be discussion about what he had written and he also knew one day he would go back to Jerusalem and his teaching would again be on the agenda. There were many in Jerusalem who had been Pharisees prior to becoming 'Followers of the Way.' He wondered if they were calling themselves 'Christians' in the same way as the believers in Antioch. Was this too much? Would it suggest an acceptance of the more Gentile flavour of the Antiochene community? Time would tell.

One former Pharisee, called Matthias, was one of those who came to Antioch to challenge the believers in the community. He grew up in Jerusalem and heard Jesus speak in the temple on a number of occasions. He was sympathetic to his message. When Jesus was arrested, tried and crucified, Matthias was deeply disturbed. Not long afterwards, rumours circulated that Jesus had risen from the dead, and Matthias was both shocked and excited. When he heard people were following Jesus and he decided to become one of them. All went well for Matthias until a Pharisee called Saul led a violent assault on members of the community.

ANTIOCH AD 47 - 49

When Saul attacked them in Jerusalem some of these former Pharisees were caught up in the persecution and suffered greatly. Matthias, along with a number of others, had been arrested and thrown into prison. Saul personally supervised their torture and efforts to get them to recant and return to a more orthodox expression of Judaism. People were maimed and killed at Saul's instigation. He was feared and hated. Matthias' younger brother became a believer and Follower of the Way and was arrested.

Saul went to the prison where Matthias and his brother were being held. Matthias would never forget that day and the events were deeply seared in his heart. Saul actively participated in the abuse and beatings inflicted on them. Several died under the intense torture including Matthias' young brother.[18]

As Matthias looked at Saul, a deep hatred exploded in his heart. He vowed if he survived he would get even with Saul one day. Then as suddenly as it began, the persecution ended and no one heard any more about Saul. Eventually Matthias was released from prison and re-joined the Followers of the Way in the city.

All was quiet in Jerusalem for about three years. Then one day a report emerged about Saul himself becoming a follower of Jesus. Many were sceptical and suspicious. When they heard he had returned to Jerusalem and met with Peter and James, they were appalled. Why had he not been punished by the community? Instead, they heard he had effectively been exiled and was not heard of for many years until he reappeared in Antioch with Barnabas.

As the years went by Paul, as he was being called, seemed to be the new golden boy. All the reports filtering back to Jerusalem were about Paul's glittering success and the number of new believers, but alarmingly many were Gentiles. Some former Pharisees were not happy about these developments. On their own initiative, they decided to visit Antioch and find out for themselves what was going on. Matthias was part of this group.

Listening to Paul teach, Matthias was furious. He tried to speak to Paul but quickly realised Paul did not even remember him. However, Matthias remembered the vow he had made all those years ago in prison as a young man and decided he needed to stop what Paul was doing and saying. He believed this was what Yahweh wanted him to do. He reasoned Jesus, who was Yahweh's Son, had been sent to Israel. Therefore all the followers of Jesus, to be acceptable to Yahweh, including Gentiles, needed to practice Jewish customs and obey the Laws of Moses including circumcision.

The confrontation with Peter put a strain on Paul's relationship with his friend and fellow leader in Antioch, Barnabas. His compromise greatly distressed Paul who never expected his friend to succumb in the way he did. Paul was disappointed. At times he felt isolated, a lone voice holding out for what he saw was the truth about Jesus' death and resurrection and how this brought salvation to the world. He maintained there was no need to do anything to earn salvation, least of all circumcision. It was God's gift.

Finally, Paul decided he wanted to revisit the communities in Galatia and he approached Barnabas. However, the tension between Barnabas and Paul remained on the surface. Paul owed so much to Barnabas but there was now a feeling of distance between them. He told him his plan.

"I would like to go back and visit the believers in all the towns where we preached and see how they are doing. Let's go overland to see them as soon we can. What do you think?"

Barnabas liked the plan, but he wanted to take John Mark along even though on their first journey he had given up and gone home.

True to his character as an encourager who saw the good in people, Barnabas wanted to give John Mark a second chance. Paul was adamant he did not want the young man with them based on his previous experience. Barnabas refusing to be put off pressed his case with Paul.

"He was young and had not travelled before. Don't you remember? He wasn't feeling well. He kept getting sick and was missing his home and his mother. But he has grown up, and I am confident he has changed. He's a man now and we could do with his help."

Paul scowled, "I'm not convinced. Nothing I've seen about him convinces me he has changed. We don't need another hanger on who is going to give up at the first sign of pressure. No, Barnabas, he's not coming with us."

"But, Paul, I think you are being unfair and hard on him. I think you need to give him a second chance."

"Frankly, Barnabas, I'm surprised at you. I can't run the risk of having two dead weights with me."

"What are you saying, Paul? Two dead weights? Oh, I get it, this isn't about John Mark at all. It's about me, isn't it? Come on, be honest. You've never forgiven me for what happened a few weeks back, have you? Admit it. Just because I struggled under pressure and intimidation from those Pharisees, you think I will give in again sometime. Well, I won't."

"Yes, it's true, I do. How do I know the two of you won't walk away when it gets difficult?"

"That's enough, Paul! Don't say anymore. I'll show you I know how to stand up to pressure and intimidation. I don't want to come with you if you won't let John Mark come. In fact, I have a better plan. He and I will go to Cyprus together. At least we have friends there and will be welcome. As for you, Paul, you do what you like. I'm through with you."

"Barnabas, please don't be like that. It's not what I meant. I just want to be sure."

Barnabas stood and walked out of the room slamming the door as he left.

"Barnabas! Don't go! Please! Barnabas!"

A few days later, Barnabas and John Mark left for Cyprus without speaking any more to Paul. Paul was saddened by the way they parted. It was not what he wanted and he knew it would need to be resolved. He had just written a letter to the friends in Galatia about being reconciled and now here he was having argued with a dear friend. It was one thing to tell others about reconciliation, but who was going to tell him? It was not loving or kind and he did not want to keep a record of wrongs. He believed there was a better way of treating each other and this was not it. He felt ashamed of himself, his own behaviour had been harsh and unloving. He decided he would do all he could to put things right.[19]

ROME AD 49

CHAPTER III

A light breeze gently moved the sheer silk curtains hanging across the open window. The Emperor Claudius sat at his desk and yawned. He stood and threw his stylus down among the scrolls and parchment littering his desk and the floor. Shuffling across the room in his usual awkward way, while scratching his backside, he went to the window. He had been emperor for eight years and it had not got any easier. His physical disability was a continual challenge. He knew he should walk more, but the relentless demands of state never let up. He pulled back the silk drapes and looked out across the city stretched out below him. His vantage point was the vast sprawling imperial palace on the top of the Palatine Hill in the very centre of the city, Rome, the largest city in the world; the city that ruled the world, the world he ruled. He was lost in his thoughts.

Behind him, he heard a gentle cough. He knew it was Pallas his chief secretary and freedman. He knew he had silently entered his study, and he knew his arms would be full of yet more reports and papers he needed to deal with.

"Wha…wha…what is it now, Pallas?" said Claudius in his usual stammer. He turned around and to his amazement, Pallas had no papers in his arms.

"My Lord," Pallas said bowing deeply, "it is nothing new. You have to make decisions about these Jews. The head of the Praetorian

Guard is here again wanting an audience and the city Tribune is with him. There have been more riots in the Jewish quarter. They report today it has spilled out of their district into the Forum itself. There were fights along the Via Sacra right next to the house of the Vestal Virgins and some thugs threw stones over the wall into their gardens. The last thing we need is the Vestals marching up here demanding we slaughter all the Jews in Rome."

Claudius shuffled back to his desk and sat heavily in his chair.

"Remind me, what it is all about? I presume they are arguing about some complicated matter of their ridiculous theology. I wish my friend Herod Agrippa was still alive instead of dying inconveniently in Caesarea. He would know what to do. They are his countrymen after all."

Pallas offered the emperor an obsequious smile before clearing his throat, "I am sure my lord remembers it has to do with some new sect that has arisen in recent years. There is now a large group of Jews in the city who follow the teachings of someone we think they call Chrestus or something like that. Not all Jews agree with this new teaching and now they are fighting about it among themselves."

"Who is this Chr...Chr...Chr... estus?" Saliva dribbled down his chin.

"We think he was one of their so-called Messiahs who keep appearing over in Judea. This one was executed some years ago by the then governor of Judea, Pontius Pilate during the reign of your illustrious uncle, the late emperor Tiberius."

At the mention of Tiberius, Claudius spat into a large spittoon strategically placed by a slave.

"There was n...n... nothing illustrious about that dr...dr...

dreadful man. He was a sex crazed per...per...per... pervert, as you well know, Pallas! But he was n...n...n... nothing compared to the vile m...m...m... monster, my nephew Caligula." Saliva was shooting everywhere.

Pallas knew the more agitated Claudius became, the worse his stammer would become and there would be an explosion of frustration. He had learnt from bitter experience he would end up the butt of his anger. He also knew he had to get Claudius back onto the issue in question otherwise he would be subjected to a long account of the previous two emperors' more salacious crimes, all of which he had heard numerous times.

"If I might remind you about the Jews, sire. May I suggest we expel them all from Rome? Forbid them to enter the city," said Pallas. This was always Pallas' strategy. Advise something extreme then let the Emperor suggest a softer option, thus making him appear to be gracious and merciful. It nearly always worked with Claudius.

"Wh...wh...wh...at? All of them! We can't do that, they run half the b...b...banks in the city. They can't all be rioting," said Claudius.

"Well, sire. We could round up known trouble makers and the ringleaders of this new sect if we can find them and expel them as a token gesture. That way the Jews will be happy this sect has been dealt with and its leaders made an example of and expelled. Their businesses will be saved and their homes not looted. The last thing we need in the city is the mob burning, looting and killing. It would be a bloodbath."

"Exactly what I had in mind, Pallas! It's a g...g...good plan. We will announce the expulsion of all the Jews in the city to start with to give them something to worry about. Then when things have quieted down, we will tell their leaders to give us a list of anyone they want to get rid of including some of the followers of this Chr…Chr…Chrestus fellow, at least a couple of thousand in total and tell them they have two days to be gone. Also, levy a special tax on the whole community to pay for all the damage their rioting has caused."

He raised his hand and continued, "Oh and give some of the cash to the Vestal Virgins to keep them quiet while you are about it. I don't want any of those sacred crones harassing me."

"Excellent plan, Sire. As usual, your wisdom and divine insight can be relied on to resolve this situation. I never cease to be amazed, sire." Pallas bowed low and began to back out of the room in his most obsequious manner.

"Oh, shut up, P…P…Pallas!" Claudius hurled the spittoon across the room towards him. "Get out and get on with it. I don't want to hear about this again."

JERUSALEM AD 30

CHAPTER IV

Eighteen years earlier some Jews who were residents in Rome went on a pilgrimage to Jerusalem. The group, which included a small number of God-fearing Roman converts to Judaism, travelled to Judea in order to celebrate the Jewish Passover. Their plan included staying in the city to experience some of the major festivals beginning with Passover and ending with the festival of Pentecost. One Jewish couple who joined the group, Andronicus and his wife Junia, had a young relative in Jerusalem who was a Pharisee called Saul and they stayed with him while in Jerusalem.[20]

They celebrated the Passover and went to the temple. In the middle of the festivities their relative Saul announced he was very happy about the arrest of a young rabbi from Galilee who had caused a lot of excitement in recent months. This rabbi was arrested and dragged before the Roman Procurator Pontius Pilate who after pressure from the High Priest Caiaphas condemned him to death. Andronicus and Junia, however, did not take much notice of what was going on. Later in the day Saul returned and announced to his guests the problem was resolved. The rabbi was dead having been crucified. He appeared very satisfied with this outcome. The Sabbath began an hour or so later and they spent the day resting at Saul's house.

The day after the Sabbath, the first day of the week began as normal except there was a very strong earth tremor about dawn which woke everyone up. There was no damage to Saul's house so they did not think anything more about it. Mid-afternoon Saul went out to meet with friends. He returned later in the evening very agitated.

"Whatever is the matter, Saul?" asked Junia.

"You won't believe it! Those idiots who are supposed to be temple guards have completely messed up. Someone will swing for this." His agitation grew as he spoke and his breathing became difficult.

"Slow down, Saul," said Junia, "take deep breaths. That's better. Now, what are you talking about?"

"It's the disciples of the rabbi who was executed last Friday. They are saying the body has disappeared from the tomb. Apparently, the man had predicted he would rise from the dead and to make us think this has happened they have stolen his body. Everybody up at the High Priest's house is talking about it. The guards claim the earthquake we had this morning was caused by angels! How ridiculous is that? They are also claiming angels opened the tomb and the corpse came out alive. They'll be corpses by the end of the day, mark my words. They are covering up the fact the rabbi's followers came in the night and stole the body while they were sleeping." Saul's anger increased as he shared what he had heard.

Andronicus and Junia looked at each other in bewilderment as Saul ranted on. Soon, he left and didn't return until late that night. In the following days, the rumours became more and more bizarre. By the end of the week the followers of the rabbi, a man called Jesus of Nazareth, were claiming he had risen from the dead and was seen in person. Not just a revived corpse or a ghost but a healthy normal human being who walked, talked and ate.

They had never heard anything like this before. Everyone was talking about it. One evening Saul confided in his relatives he knew it was impossible for this Jesus to be alive.

"I know he is dead, beyond any shadow of a doubt," he said, "you see, I went out to have a look at what was going on outside the city up near Skull Rock. It was late afternoon, getting close to the Sabbath. There were a few women all bawling and carrying on and to my amazement I recognised one or two Pharisees, Nicodemus and Joseph of Arimathea were there. This Jesus had died some while earlier and they had just taken his body down from the cross. I saw him, I know a dead body when I see one. There was no way he was alive. What in the world Nico and Joseph were doing, goodness only knows! I went off and left them to it. All this talk about being alive again is absolute nonsense."

Rumours continued to circulate about Jesus, but generally things went quiet. They were now beginning to anticipate the Feast of Weeks as the Jews called Pentecost. Andronicus had been out on his own most of the day and came back looking mysterious. He gestured to Junia and the two of them went up onto the roof of Saul's house and sat under an awning to talk.

"You will never guess who I bumped into today!" he said to his wife.

"What have you been up to, husband? Who did you bump into?" she smiled at him.

"Nicodemus!"

"What? Do you mean the man Saul is angry with?"

"Exactly! You won't believe it. Apparently, Nicodemus was one of this Jesus' followers, a secret one. But it gets better. He apparently helped bury the body and was convinced he was dead too except, wait for it, he claims to have seen him alive!"

"You are making this up! It can't be true, can it?"

"Well, I don't know. Nicodemus is convinced and he is no fool. He says it happened about a week ago outside the city somewhere. He reckons there may have been about five hundred people and in the middle was Jesus. I asked him if he really saw him and was he sure it wasn't a ghost. He said he actually spoke to him. Then just a few days ago he told me Jesus was taken up to heaven. A whole group of them saw him go up in the air, as if he was flying, but not before telling them to go back here to the city and wait for the Holy Spirit to come and tell them what to do next."

"It all sounds very strange to me. What do you make of all this, Andronicus? Should we ask Saul?"

"He is the last person I want to talk about this with at the moment. I know where Nicodemus lives, maybe we could both go and see him together. What I haven't told you yet is Nicodemus and all his friends believe Jesus is none other than the Messiah, and also the Son of God!"

"No! That's not possible," said Junia. "The Messiah is one thing, but how can the Lord God have a son? You say they claim to have seen him?"

The couple talked all afternoon about what Andronicus had heard from Nicodemus. By the end it was clear to Junia her husband was almost as convinced as Nicodemus. They decided since it was the Feast of Weeks they would go and meet with him the next day.

Saul was not at home when they got up and broke their fast together before heading into the city. The streets were beginning to fill up with visitors to Jerusalem. As Andronicus and Junia walked through the streets, they heard a curious noise coming from a large two-story house along the street. There was a strange sound of wind swirling around the house, and a large crowd of curious onlookers was straining to see what was going on, anxiously looking for the source of the noise.

Suddenly, the doors flew open and a large group of men and women tumbled out of the house into the street looking as if they had just come out of a wild all-night party. They sounded drunk and some staggered like drunkards. What was particularly strange was a fiery glow which seemed to hover over them. Many people laughed at them, thinking them drunk but others sensed something very different was happening.

To everyone's amazement, these apparently drunk people started talking to the crowd in all sorts of different languages. To Andronicus and Junia's absolute astonishment, a man approached them and started speaking to them in a Roman dialect which they had spoken in their childhood homes. They were really surprised at this as so few people spoke this dialect. They saw Nicodemus among them, and he spotted Andronicus and came over to him and addressed them in Latin. Hardly anyone used Latin in Rome these days, but they understood him.

"When did you learn Latin, Nico?" asked Andronicus.

"Numquam enim! I never have!" said Nicodemus in perfect Latin. "I wondered what language it was. The Holy Spirit has fallen on us just as Jesus promised and everyone seems to be speaking unknown or at least unlearnt languages."

A huge commotion was going on. Some people were laughing, others crying. Some looked totally shocked and confused as more people spilled out of the house into the street. Soon the street was so crowded people could hardly move. Then a man came out onto a balcony above the street and called out for silence. When the noise subsided, he addressed the crowd.

"People of Judea and all of you who live here in Jerusalem, I want to tell you to what is happening so listen very carefully to my words. These people are not drunk, as some of you are thinking, it's only nine in the morning. Rather this is what the prophet Joel said would happen." He then quoted Joel's prophecy.

"'And in the last days it shall be, God declares, that I will pour out my Spirit on all flesh, and your sons and your daughters shall prophesy, and your young men shall see visions, and your old men shall dream dreams; even on my male servants and female servants in those days I will pour out my Spirit, and they shall prophesy. And I will show wonders in the heavens above and signs on the earth below, blood, and fire, and vapour of smoke; the sun shall be turned to darkness and the moon to blood, before the day of the Lord comes, the great and magnificent day. And it shall come to pass that everyone who calls upon the name of the Lord shall be saved.'"

Julia turned to Andronicus, "This is what we have been longing for, and it seems to be happening before our very eyes."

"Men of Israel, listen to these words," continued the man speaking from the balcony. "Jesus of Nazareth, a man who God has acknowledged by performing mighty works and wonders and signs through him in your midst, as you yourselves know. This Jesus delivered up according to the definite plan and foreknowledge of God, you crucified and killed by the hands of lawless men." The speaker paused and let those words sink into the ears of the crowd who were hanging on every word.

"God raised him up, loosing the bonds of death, because it was not possible for him to be held by it."

Nicodemus gripped Andronicus by the arm. "This is what I have been telling you, my friend. This Jesus is the one we have been longing for."

They listened intently to the man's words, their hearts pounding in their chests as he continued pointing out from their Scriptures how all these events had been predicted. Finally, he drew everything to a close and shouted,

"Let all the house of Israel therefore know for certain that God has made him both Lord and Christ, this Jesus whom you crucified."

This stunned the crowd. Some people were openly weeping. One man towards the back of the crowd called out, "Brothers, what shall we do?"

Nico whispered to Andronicus and Junia. "That's Peter, one of Jesus' closest friends," pointing to the speaker on the balcony.

Peter said to them, "Repent and be baptized, every one of you in the name of Jesus Christ for the forgiveness of your sins, and you will receive the gift of the Holy Spirit. For the promise is for you and for your children and for all who are far off, everyone whom the Lord our God calls to himself."[21]

Andronicus turned to his wife and said, "We need to talk." Then turning to Nicodemus said, "Please, can we talk more with you? I have many questions."

"Of course, my friends, do you want to come to my home and

we can talk together in peace. We can eat together. I'd love to share more with you."

They edged their way through the crowd and walked a few streets to Nicodemus' home in the city. It was a large spacious house with a courtyard and, like many houses in the city, a roof garden. He instructed a servant to prepare food and they went up and sat together under an awning on the roof.

"Will you tell us when you first met Jesus? How did that come about?" asked Andronicus. Nicodemus paused and looked at them both.

"It's a long story. About three years ago Jesus was here in Jerusalem and I heard him speaking in the temple. I knew there was something different about him. I wanted to hear what he had to say. He spoke with great authority. He gave me such hope but as you know I am a Pharisee and many of my colleagues here in the city were not remotely interested in what he had to say. So I sent him a message and asked if I could have a private meeting with him. Two days later we met here in the evening under this very awning where we are sitting now. We talked for hours. It was as if he knew everything about me." Nicodemus paused and tears filled his eyes. "He spoke right into my heart."

Andronicus and Junia listened intently to everything Nicodemus had to say. Nicodemus continued.

"He told me I needed to be born again. I didn't really understand what he meant. I thought he was talking about physical birth. But he meant something completely different. He was talking about being born from above, from Yahweh."

He paused for a few moments then said, "When he talked about

Yahweh, he spoke as if he knew him. He had a relationship with him in a way completely unlike anything I'd ever heard before."

Nicodemus paused again. Then looking directly at them both said, "He called Yahweh his Abba! His own Father."

There was a long silence before he continued. "He came to show us what Yahweh is really like, how he loves us like a father loves his children. I began to see Jesus knew the Father unlike anyone else. Now I see by his death he has reconciled us to the Father so that we can know him as our real Father too. That's what he meant by being born again."

"What do you mean by being born again?" asked Junia.

"I mean it is as if we are born a second time as we become his sons and daughters in the same way as Jesus is his son. God the Father has come to us in Jesus. This is such good news."

They talked together all day and as the sun was going down, Junia said to Nicodemus, "I believe every word you have said. I want to know this Father too. I want to be a follower of Jesus. I want to be filled with his Spirit."

"Me too!" said Andronicus.

Andronicus and Junia joined Nicodemus in the small room that was set aside for ritual bathing; there they were baptised by Nicodemus and the Spirit of God filled their hearts as they rejoiced in what happened. This was the beginning of a completely new day for this couple from Rome.

Later that evening they went back to Saul's house. They decided not to say anything to him at this point, instead they wanted to let things settle in their hearts. They went back to Nicodemus' house on a number of occasions and found out everything they could about Jesus of Nazareth. They believed he was the Messiah, the son of God who was now their saviour and Lord.

On one occasion they met one of the leaders of the group, the Peter who they heard speaking in the street at Pentecost. They quickly warmed to him and a friendship developed between them.

Meanwhile back at Saul's house he was growing increasingly angry at the developments happening in the city. Finally, one day Andronicus sat down with him and said they needed to talk. They carefully explained the events that had happened over the previous few weeks up to the point where they told him about their baptism. At this point Saul who had listened quietly finally exploded.

"No! No more! Not another word! You are insane. No, worse than that, you have been deceived. This is all lies and what's worse it is blasphemy. I cannot allow you to stay another minute defiling my house. Go right now. Pack your bags and to go back to Rome. You are no longer any family of mine. I disown you both."

Astonished and upset, they left Saul's house and went straight to the home of Nicodemus. They explained what had happened, and without hesitation he invited them to stay as long as they wanted. Their original plan had been to stay in Jerusalem from Passover to just after Pentecost and then return to Rome. Instead, they stayed many weeks longer. After some discussion with Nicodemus and their new friend Peter, they decided to remain in Jerusalem for a few months more. In their hearts they wanted to stay and be part of the new community in Jerusalem but their family and their ties were back in Rome. They also had a growing desire to return to Rome in order to tell their friends and family the amazing truth they had discovered about Jesus. They spent as much time as possible with the leaders in Jerusalem. They discussed their future with Peter and Nicodemus and one or two others, including James the brother of Jesus who appeared to be the main leader.

After discussion and prayer between them, they concluded it was best for Andronicus and Junia to return to Rome. They didn't want to go back to Rome on their own initiative, they wanted to return with the full backing of the believers in Jerusalem. Peter speaking on behalf of many of them, acknowledged they had a special place in the Father's plan.

"I believe our God and Father of the Lord Jesus wants you to be his messengers to take this good news to our brothers and sisters in Rome itself," said Peter. There was a murmur of approval from the others in the room.

Peter continued. "Therefore, we are sending you to Rome. You're not just returning. We want you go with our blessing. We want to appoint you to be the carriers of this revelation of the love of the Father poured out through his son Jesus to that great city. Will you accept this commission? Will you be apostles of the good news for Rome?"

The whole room went silent as Peter spoke. Andronicus and Junia looked around at their friends and then Junia said, "We can only do this if we know that you are with us and one day, as soon as you can, you will send help. Maybe, Peter, you will come and visit to help us. We do not feel equipped for this task but we have learnt the Holy Spirit of the Father and his Son Jesus who is within us, will go before us."

All the believers gathered around and prayed for them. They placed their hands on them to bless them and to appoint them to the work they believed God had called them to.

They tried to contact Saul but he refused to speak to them. A few days later Andronicus and Junia said their farewells amid many tears and left for Rome.

Two months later they landed at the port of Ostia and took the road that follows the River Tiber inland to Rome. Within a few days of arriving back in the city, they gathered their friends to their home to tell them all they had experienced while away in Jerusalem. After a few months there was a small gathering of believers in the city who believed Jesus was the Messiah, the Christ, the Son of God.

ROME AD 49

CHAPTER V

Years went by and the number of people calling themselves followers of Christ in Rome had grown considerably. People gathered regularly in homes across the city. Andronicus and Junia's closest friends were a couple about the same age as them, called Priscilla and Aquila. They were Jewish by birth. Aquila originally came from Pontus in the East. Priscilla was from a wealthy Jewish family who had lived in Rome for many generations. They had established a successful tentmaking business. This couple quickly embraced the message and joined Andronicus and Junia in the leadership of these groups. When the other two were away from Rome, Aquila and Priscilla looked after the various groups in the city. They were gifted teachers and had encouraged many people within the community. Among the followers of Jesus in the city, they were probably the most well-known, respected and loved.

During those years Peter kept his promise to Andronicus and Junia and visited Rome several times. On a number of occasions, they travelled to cities around Rome including the large city to the south, Puteoli. Located down on the coast on a beautiful bay not far from the city of Herculaneum and across the bay from Pompeii, it was the major port that handled all the grain imported by Rome from Egypt. A community of believers had been established there and Andronicus and Junia regularly travelled to the city to meet and encourage the brothers and sisters in Puteoli.

While Andronicus and Junia were making a visit to Puteoli on one occasion, trouble broke out among the Jews in Rome. Animosity intensified towards those who believed Jesus was the Messiah, the Christ, the 'Christos' or Chrestus, as Jesus was mistakenly called among Jews who did not believe and serious riots broke out. This resulted in the Emperor Claudius' decree expelling large numbers of Jews from Rome. When the announcement was made, Aquila and Priscilla, as prominent leaders of the Christ followers in Rome, found themselves on the top of the list for expulsion. Large numbers of people from both sides of the divide were included in the upheaval. When news reached Andronicus and Junia, they decided to stay in Puteoli and wait for all the trouble to subside before slipping quietly back to Rome at some later date.[22]

Priscilla and Aquila hardly had any time to gather their belongings before soldiers were hammering on their door demanding they go straight to the Campus Martinus and await instructions. From all across the city and the Jewish Quarter, people were rounded up by the Tribune of the city's soldiers with only the bags they could carry. Hundreds gathered in the Campus Martinus, standing there through the heat of the day. No one knew what was happening. All they knew was they had to leave. Some even wondered if they would be sold as slaves as had happened to many of their forefathers who had been brought to Rome as slaves a hundred years before.

A large troop of Praetorian guards appeared armed with swords and spears. Terror gripped many of them as they thought they were about to be slaughtered. Finally, the Tribune of the city himself arrived flanked by more soldiers. He climbed onto a dais dressed in his senatorial toga looking flustered. He was carrying a scroll in his hand. Calling for silence he unrolled the scroll and started to read, shouting at the top of his voice so that all could hear his words.

"By order of his Imperial Majesty the divine Emperor Tiberius Claudius Caesar Augustus Germanicus, it is hereby decreed that all Jews assembled here on the Campus Martinus are immediately expelled from the city of Rome. You shall not be permitted to return to your homes but exit the city forthwith through the nearest gate of the city. You will leave immediately. Furthermore, you will not be permitted to reside within five hundred stadia of the city until further notice."

This announcement caused great consternation among the people. Some tried to escape to the nearest side streets only to find their way blocked by Praetorians. If that wasn't bad enough, crowds of the Roman mob had gathered, alerted by the day's events. Carrying the few belongings they had gathered, Aquila and his wife made their way out of the city. They tramped along in silence, long lines of Jews leaving their homes behind them, a scene repeated countless times in the centuries to come. As they left the city, looters and robbers were already breaking into their abandoned houses.

Priscilla and Aquila walked for about five days until they arrived exhausted in Puteoli where they sought out Andronicus and Junia. They talked together about the future. Neither couple had any sense that Aquila and Priscilla should remain at Puteoli or indeed in Italy. They discussed going east by ship from Puteoli. Finally, Andronicus spoke.

"There is something I have been thinking about, and I have a feeling it is from the Lord."

"Tell us, we are open to anything."

"I have a relative who is a believer in Jesus and is based in Antioch in Syria. We stayed with him before he became a believer back in Jerusalem at the time when Jesus was crucified and raised from the dead. He threw us out of his house when we became 'Followers of the Way'. We were called this before we became known as Christians. In those days our relative was called Saul. But today, he goes under the name of Paul of Tarsus."

"Are you talking about *The* Paul of Tarsus, the one Peter told us about? The one they call the apostle to the Gentiles?" asked Priscilla.

"The very same, Prisca," said Junia. "After we came back to Rome, we heard how Paul, as we now call him, had become a Christian. He had a dramatic encounter with the risen Lord Jesus when he was going to Damascus to try to arrest many of our friends there. Everything changed for him overnight. He had been a very high-profile Pharisee in Jerusalem and his conversion caused a great stir."

"How was he received among the Followers of the Way in Jerusalem?" asked Aquila.

"Initially, there was great suspicion, which is no surprise really as he had been instrumental in many deaths. He went to ground for a few years. Eventually he went home to his family in Tarsus," continued Junia, "where we caught up with him again."

"You met him there?" asked Priscilla.

"Yes," said Andronicus who took up the story. "Peter, on one of his visits to Rome, spoke to us about Paul because he knew we were related to him. He said if ever we were travelling east and were passing through Tarsus to make a point of visiting the family and try to connect with him. Well, some years ago we made a point of it. We went to Ephesus first where we know people, then took the overland route to Tarsus. When we got to Tarsus, we found him. He was in a very bad way."

"Why? What happened to him?" asked Aquila.

"He had virtually been disowned by his family because of his newfound faith and belief in Jesus as the Messiah," explained Andronicus.

"His father had been so proud of his son's position in Jerusalem, being such an eminent Pharisee. To them, he appeared to have thrown all that away and embraced what they saw as a blasphemous new belief system. To make matters worse their son had started mixing with Gentiles and Greeks, which in their minds made him ritually unclean. They had thrown him out of the house."

Junia took up the story, "Then there was the issue of his wife. She was a lovely local girl whom he had married when he was a Pharisee. You know, it goes with the role. They had a child, a little boy, who had died in childhood and they were heartbroken. When he returned to Tarsus, the tensions between them became extreme and she refused to accept his faith. She went home to her parents and effectively they were divorced. Every attempt he made to reach out to her was rebuffed."

"Saul had been very enthusiastic in talking to people about Jesus and many small groups of believers were established in the countryside, in Cilicia and even north of Syria. He told us about them and how he would often go and visit them. He would sometimes take a boat along the coast of Cilicia and he told us that on two occasions he was shipwrecked. It is a miracle that he is still alive." Andronicus paused and reflected on these things as he thought about Aquila and Priscilla who were about to take a ship east.

"When we arrived, as I said, he was in a bad way," said Andronicus. "We actually found him at his father's home. Even though his family had disowned him, he was there recovering from a ritual whipping because, as you know, the law required them to care for him."

"Oh no! 'The forty lashes less one' ritual whipping from the Synagogue rulers?" exclaimed Priscilla covering her face with her hands. "I have seen that before or rather seen the effect on a human body. Poor man!"

Andronicus spoke softly as his voice cracked. "The Synagogue rulers in Tarsus were so angry with him, accusing him of many breaches of the law of Moses, they decided to discipline him. They used the sanction permitted by the law to correct him and purge him of his offence in order to allow him to be accepted back in the Synagogue. He was dragged before them all and accused, but he refused to go back on what he had been saying. Later he told us it was no surprise as he had been warned when he became a follower of Jesus in Damascus he would suffer many things for the sake of Jesus." Andronicus became distressed and gazed into the distance to gather himself before continuing.

"They tied him between two pillars and stripped him to the waist. Then thirteen lashes to the chest, thirteen over his right shoulder and thirteen over his left." His words hung in the room as the four thought about the pain and agony of this punishment.

"However, that was just the first time," said Junia. "It seems his refusal to change his teaching brought down even more severe punishment on him. Not long after his wounds had healed, they did it again. They took the letter of the law to the extreme and repeated the whipping time after time. We have no idea how he survived. He has endured great suffering for the sake of Jesus." Junia stopped as tears ran down her face.[23]

"We arrived in Tarsus while he was still recovering from his most recent whipping. He was in such bad shape," said Andronicus. "His family gave us hospitality as was their duty, but when it became apparent we believed the same things as Paul it became difficult. We cared for Paul as best we could. Then one day the local Synagogue rulers came to the house and arrested us along with Paul and we were all thrown into prison. After some time, we were released and told we were not welcome in the synagogue, and they made it very clear if we stayed in the city our lives would be at risk.

"The three of us went out into the countryside to a place where Paul said there were some believers who would give us shelter. We stayed for many days while he regained his strength. One day he took us up into the Taurus Mountains to the north of Tarsus and led us to a cave. He had often gone there to pray and spend time alone with Jesus. He said it was a special place where he had many encounters with the Lord and he was shown things by Jesus."

"What sort of things?" asked Priscilla.

"He couldn't really say," replied Junia. "He called them mysteries, inexpressible things. He hinted he was even taken up into heaven. He said one day he may be able to explain more but he had wanted to show us the place to encourage us and reassure us his time in Tarsus, while it was hard, was also a place of great revelation for him."[24]

The two couples sat and looked at one another as the light began to fade in the room.

"Before we left him he said one day he would come to Rome and visit us. He didn't know when it would be but he promised to do so. He encouraged us to continue to do the work the Father had given us to do."

Andronicus paused then becoming animated said, "You know he is a tent maker by trade just as you are. If you were able to find him, you might be of help to each other. I have a strong sense the Father is in this and your departure from Rome at this time is more than coincidence. The last we heard was he eventually left Tarsus and went to Antioch in Syria for some time. Then he apparently travelled around in Cyprus and some of the provinces in the East including Galatia. He was also in Jerusalem for a gathering of the leaders which we heard about earlier this year. There have been glowing reports of his teaching and how he has opened the door to the Gentiles to hear the truth about Jesus.

"My suggestion is you go east and see if you hear news of him," said Andronicus. "If you find him, greet him for us. I am sure the Father is going before you and will show you where to go and where to live. We will miss you, and we will send word when we feel it is safe for you to come back to Rome. Let us know where you end up as soon as you can."

They were encouraged by this news and decided to board a ship bound for the East just as soon as they could. Aquila and Priscilla stood on the deck hand in hand waving at their two friends standing on the quay, wondering when they would see them again and what adventures lay ahead.

After many days at sea they landed at Cenchreae, the port of Corinth. Their plan had been to go further to Ephesus or maybe even Antioch but as they set foot on the shores of Achaia, they both felt they needed to stay there. They made their way up the road from the port to the city of Corinth with a distinct feeling the Father had gone before them. Somehow in their hearts, they sensed this was a new day.

LYSTRA AD 50

CHAPTER VI

About the same time Aquila and Priscilla arrived in Corinth, Barnabas and Mark left for Cyprus. Silas returned to Antioch from Jerusalem and found Paul feeling very low and miserable after the falling out with Barnabas. He sat down with Paul to talk with him.

"Paul, I had a strong prompting from the Lord to come back to Antioch, and I want to share with you what's in my heart."

"Yes, Silas. By all means, dear friend, please share."

Silas nodded. "I sensed Father wanted me to come to find you and tell you I am meant to work alongside you. To go with you wherever Father leads you and support you in whatever he has put in your heart to do." Silas wrung his hands together and looked down at the floor. "I am just saying… I am available if it would be a help to you. But, please don't feel you have to."

Tears welled up in Paul's eyes. "Oh, Silas! You have no idea what this means to me. I wanted to go and visit the believers in Syria and Cilicia and beyond into Galatia. I asked Barnabas to come with me as he had done before, but he emphatically said no. Therefore, we have decided to go our separate ways."

Silas stared at him and Paul looked away. Silence hung in the air between them until Silas said. "And?"

"Well," Paul turned his attention back to Silas, "actually, he and I have fallen out, or rather we have not parted on good terms." Paul rubbed his eyes. There was a long silence before he continued, "No, let me tell you how it really is. We have had a serious disagreement. It was horrible and I feel upset about it all. I sometimes get so passionate about what I think the Father wants me to do I get impatient with people who don't see it my way. I lose my temper and end up alienating them. This is what has happened here between Barnabas and me. It's entirely my fault. It's not what I want to do at all. But the good I want to do I don't do and I end up feeling wretched. It is like a war going on inside of me."

Silas reached out his hand and put it on Paul's shoulder.

"You remind me of the prophet Elijah after his great triumph over the prophets of Ba'al on Mount Carmel. What did he end up doing? Running off and hiding from King Ahab feeling very sorry for himself."

"Ouch!" said Paul.

"I heard you say once you thought in all things God works for the good of those who love him, who have been called according to his purpose," said Silas. "Both you and Barnabas love God and have both been called to serve him. Somehow Father will work this out."

He waited for this to sink in then added, "I think too, Father is teaching you something about how his grace works in you in the middle of your weakness. After all, you have said yourself there is nothing we have to do to please God. He accepts us as we are in all our weakness and brokenness." Silas paused and let his words land.

"Maybe what you are going to learn in these coming days is all about your weakness rather than your strength. Also, you may find he is going to teach you something about receiving his comforting love, Paul. He loves you not for being a great teacher and revealer of truth or the success of your ministry. He loves you because he loves you! In all your weakness and strengths and in your successes and failures, he loves you, Paul, even before you knew him, when you refused to believe he was risen and when you persecuted his followers."

Paul wept openly, and Silas put his arms around him and hugged him.

"Father wants to comfort you, Paul. You don't have to be strong all the time. The old Saul tried to do all those things for God and what a mess he made! But you are Paul now, forgiven and loved by the Father. Open your heart and let him love you, my friend."

Paul sobbed deeply as Silas held him in his arms representing the Father to him. Paul opened up his heart and Father's love flowed into him.

After a while, Paul said to Silas. "You know, my friend, I can speak in tongues, prophesy, preach, work miracles, do all sorts of things for God but without his love I see those things are just noise, like a clashing cymbal. I have been like a banging gong, especially in the way I have treated Barnabas. In my desire to be right, I have neglected love. If ever I meet him again I will ask him to forgive me and to bless him in his travels. Who knows, maybe someday we can work together again. I even dismissed the account of Jesus' life Mark is writing. I was very rude to him too."

"Oh, an account of Jesus' life?"

"He is writing down everything he hears about what Jesus said and did, especially the memories and reminiscences of Peter. I rather poured cold water on it by saying Jesus was coming back any day now and we wouldn't need it. But who knows, Jesus may not come back before all those people who met him have died and we will lose a great treasure if we do not record the stories. Yes, if I meet Mark again I will encourage him to continue."

"A good idea, Paul."

"You know, Silas," continued Paul thoughtfully, "John Mark was there on the last evening before Jesus' arrest. His mother owns the house where the believers often gather in Jerusalem. Jesus celebrated Passover there and Mark helped serve. When Jesus and his disciples left for the garden on the Mount of Olives, Mark followed them, hid in the garden and watched. He even heard Jesus pray and call Almighty God, Abba! He told me this when we were together in Cyprus.

"I tell people we have become his sons and daughters, and we can all call God our Father, Abba. Mark told me he nearly got caught by the soldiers but he managed to escape by wriggling out of his tunic and running home naked." Paul chuckled at the thought, then added, "Maybe if I meet Mark again…" His words trailed away into the silence.

After a few moments, he turned to Silas and looked him in the eyes. "Your words are life to me, Silas. Thank you. You have a wonderful gift of encouragement and building people up. You are a true prophet."

A few days later, Paul talked with Silas about his idea to go on another journey to visit the believers. He wanted to return to the believers in Galatia who would have received his letter. Silas readily agreed to accompany him. Titus, the young Gentile believer who had been with Paul in Jerusalem for the council, asked if he might join them on the journey.

"We will be passing through Greek speaking areas and a young man like you, Titus, would be a great asset. You can help carry my bags too!"

All the believers gathered together to pray for them and commend them to 'the grace of the Lord' as they called it.

"Come back when you can and tell us how you get on, won't you?" said Manaen, one to Paul's fellow leaders, as he said farewell to them.[25]

They took the main coastal road from Antioch which heads west from Syria into Cilicia strengthening the small groups of believers they encountered along the route. The road was busy with endless carts and pack horse trains carrying goods from the east to the west. This was a major overland trade route from lands beyond the borders of the empire. Vast amounts of exotic goods and products flowed westward towards Rome. As Paul looked at these traders from the east in their strange clothing with their flat round faces, he wondered how the lands from which they came would hear the good news he and Silas were preaching.

"Look at these traders, Silas, I wonder if they understand our language. How can they be reached with the good news about Jesus?"

"Yes, I was thinking that too. When I was last in Jerusalem, there was talk about Thomas, who was one of the original twelve disciples of Jesus. Did you ever meet him?" Paul shook his head.

"Well, I heard he travelled far to the east beyond the lands even Alexander the Great had conquered. A year or so ago news came back from some merchants from India that he has established a number of community of believers there. But it was all a bit vague and nobody seemed to know much about it," Silas paused and looked again at the traders on the road. "Do you think we should go to the east after this trip?"

"No, Silas, my heart is set on taking the good news to Rome itself and then one day even on to the far reaches of the west to Spain, if God gives us the strength and grace and a long life!" Paul laughed.

Silas shook his head. "Sometimes I can't imagine what living a long life would be like."

Within a few days they came to Tarsus. Paul went straight to his family home where he had been born and some family members still lived.

There was a group of believers in the city, which now included some of his family members. After talking with them, he discovered his sister and her husband and son were about to leave Tarsus and move to Jerusalem in order to expand the family tentmaking business to Judea. He told them he would make a point of seeking them out next time he was in the city and blessed them in their new enterprise.

After staying two weeks, Paul and Silas decided to move further into Pamphylia and then up into the southern part of Galatia to revisit the believers in Derbe, Lystra and Iconium. They came first to Derbe, and the believers in the city were delighted to see him again and quickly gathered as many of their number as possible. They all reported how Paul's letter had been very well received and had helped resolve the conflicts between the Jewish believers and the Greek believers. The name of a young man from Lystra called Timothy came up several times. This young man had written to Paul and reported the situation to him, alerting him about the seriousness of the problems stirred up by the teachers from Jerusalem. The main teacher of the group was Matthias of Jerusalem. He fiercely criticised Paul declaring him to be a self-appointed false apostle and not a true apostle. Paul could not recall meeting him or recognising his name.

They were told Timothy lived in Lystra, about a day's journey further west. He had regularly visited the believers in Iconium and also Derbe helping to explain Paul's letter and bring people back together. Everyone spoke well of him. Paul sent word to Lystra that he planned to visit them and sent a message to Timothy to ask if they could stay with him when they were in the city. As soon as Timothy heard Paul was in the area, he came in person to greet him and bring him back to Lystra.

"Paul! I am so glad you have come back to us. How long can you stay?" Timothy bounced up and down like an excited puppy. "There is so much to tell you and so many things I want to know."

"It is good to see you too, Timothy, but calm down. There is plenty of time," said Paul as he reached out and hugged the young man. "Let me first introduce you to my friends. This is Silas from Jerusalem, and this is Titus from Antioch." All three greeted each other and embraced as if they were brothers. Timothy and Titus were about the same age.

Paul and his companions stayed some time in Derbe encouraging and teaching people. And during those weeks, many more people became believers.[26]

They decided to move on to Lystra. They chatted animatedly on the road as each man shared his story. Timothy described his background; how his mother Eunice was Jewish and a believer as was his grandmother Lois. He spoke about his deceased father who had been Greek.

"Do you consider yourself a Jew or a Greek?" asked Titus.

"Well, it is a bit complicated," Timothy explained. "I'm Jewish by birth, born of a Jewish mother but my father raised me as a Greek, so culturally I'm more Greek. But now I prefer to see myself as neither Jew nor Greek. Neither slave nor freeman, male or female but in Christ! Isn't that how you say it, Paul?"

Paul grinned, "I'm glad something I wrote has sunk in."

"Much more than that, Paul, believe you me." He turned to Titus, "What about you, Titus?"

"Me? Oh, I'm Greek through and through. In fact, my Greek or rather Gentile background caused quite a stir when those former Pharisees turned up in Antioch demanding we all get circumcised to prove we were proper Christians. There was no way I was going to agree to having it done, thank you very much! I told them it was none of their business either!" Titus laughed at the memory of it all before continuing.

"I went to Jerusalem with Paul and Barnabas for the council to resolve the issue of whether we Gentiles needed to be circumcised to be considered true Christians. The issue of, 'Was I? or Wasn't I?', came up again. It was embarrassing, everyone looking at me, discussing the nature of my manhood! Honestly, it was ridiculous and laughable at the same time. It was all I could do to not hoist up my tunic to settle the matter!"

"And were you or weren't you?" laughed Timothy.

"Was I what?" asked Titus.

"Did they force you, you know, to be done?" asked Timothy blushing.

"Absolutely not," said Titus. "It was the whole point. Nothing we do makes any difference. Jesus has done it all and we are in him reconciled to the Father by his death on the cross, not by our works or circumcision or anything else for that matter. Though I have to say, I am heartily glad Paul's explanation won the day!"

The two young men laughed and continued chatting.[27]

Paul and Silas listened as the two of them walked and talked. They let the boys get further ahead a bit.

Then Silas asked Paul, "A Greek father and a Jewish mother? Interesting! I presume his father raising him as a Greek means he is more Greek than Jew if you know what I mean. I wonder how he is treated by the Jews?"

"I have been considering this too," said Paul. "I've been thinking it would be good for him to accompany us as we go west, but every time we enter a synagogue, you know what will be asked don't you?"

"Exactly!" said Silas. "What do you think we should do, Paul?"

"The issue is straight forward to me. It is not about his salvation. For Titus, the issue was about his salvation as a full Gentile, consequently there was no need. But for Timothy, it is different. All the local Jews know his father was a Greek and some of the doors to the synagogues have been closed to him as a result. The Gentiles won't care, but our Jewish brothers will. Frankly, it will be a hinderance to the spread of the message among our Jewish people," said Paul. "It seems to me we need to be able to be all things to all men in order that one might be saved. I see great potential in young Timothy, and it would give him a far wider sphere of influence."

"I am not sure he will be too excited when he hears about this, and I am not going to tell him either. You can. And who will do the deed?" asked Silas looking at Paul.

"Well, it will have to be me I suppose. After all I am rabbinically trained. I've performed the ceremony a number of times before," said Paul rather sheepishly.

"But they were week old babies," said Silas, "not adult men!" He grimaced and looked away. "Rather you than me, Paul!" Silas stifled a laugh and Paul went slightly pale.[28]

Two days later in Lystra, Paul, Silas and Titus were sitting at Lois' table enjoying a meal together. Eunice came into the room and sat down at the table.

"How is he?" asked Titus.

"Oh, he is groaning and whimpering still. I told him to lay still and eat his food. He will be fine in a week or so," said his mother.

Titus had great difficulty not laughing.

Paul looked at him. "That will do, Titus. Enough or you will be next."

All the men at the table were laughing now.

Lois stood and gathered the dishes, "You men!" she said. "You are behaving like a bunch of adolescents. It is no laughing matter."

Even Paul could not hold back his laughter.

Lystra held many memories for Paul. He remembered the excitement that followed the healing of a lame man, how the locals assumed he was the god Hermes and Barnabas, Zeus. He also remembered the way the town quickly turned on him after being stirred up by Jews from Iconium and Pisidian Antioch. His time in the area was difficult and plagued by those who opposed him and his message. He had nearly died in Lystra the last time when he was attacked, stoned, dragged out of the city and left for dead. This time, he was keeping a low profile but regularly meeting with the believers and spending time encouraging them.

About a week after Timothy's *operation*, Titus, who had been in the main market square, returned to Lois and Eunice's house greatly agitated. As a Greek, he blended into the background and was able to listen to the gossip and the news. On this day he heard a commotion in a portico of the main hall of the forum and wandered over to join the crowd. Climbing onto the base of a column he got a better view of what was happening. A group of men were talking animatedly in Greek. He heard Paul's name mentioned. These men were stirring up the crowd; he heard them say Paul was a subversive who did not believe in the divinity of the emperor. This was a new and dangerous accusation. He reported to Silas what he had just seen.

"This is serious. They were in a very ugly mood. It's just a matter of time before they find out where we are staying and come for Paul," said Titus.

Silas called them all together. "We must be careful, and we need to protect Lois and Eunice as well as ourselves. Lois, is there anywhere you can go to be safe for a few days? We need to leave immediately and get out of the city. We don't want another situation like the last time Paul was here."

"We can go to my other daughter's home; her family has a farm outside the city. I agree we must all go immediately." Lois answered.

They gathered their things. Timothy was still finding walking somewhat uncomfortable. However, he looked at Paul.

"I'm coming with you, Paul. Mother and Granny will be safe at my aunt's. I am going with you, Paul." Timothy said.

Paul looked at Timothy. "As long as you are sure you are able to travel. We will help you as much as we can." Turning to Titus, he said, "I want you to go with the women and ensure they get to a place of safety. Stay with them and when things have settled down, I would like you to come back to Lystra and encourage the believers. If this turns nasty against them, they will need to be built up and supported. They need a good man with the heart of a shepherd to watch over them. Will you do this for me, Titus?"

"I will, but will you send word when you are safe? If I can do anything else, you only have to say. But quickly, all of you, there is no time to lose."

Titus opened the door into the street and looked about. All was normal but he could hear shouting coming from a few streets away.

"Quickly, they are coming. It is better if we go out the back through the courtyard gate. There are less people that way." Titus said.

They hurried to the back of the courtyard where there was another door. Just as they opened it, they heard loud banging on the door at the front of the house. There was angry shouting and then the splintering of wood as the door was broken down. As an angry mob broke into Lois and Eunice's house, all of them escaped into the back street. They ran through the streets not looking back and went out through one of the gates of the city.

TROAS AD 50

CHAPTER VII

With information received from the believers in Lystra and Iconium, Paul and his companions sought out other groups of believers scattered throughout the region of Phrygia and Galatia. As they travelled from town to town, Paul passed on the news from Jerusalem and the decisions reached by the apostles and leaders in Jerusalem for the people to follow. They taught and shared the great revelation of how being in Christ brings them into their true identity and position as sons of God. The believers were encouraged and many joined them.[29]

Paul's intention was to head west into the province of Asia hoping eventually to reach the great city of Ephesus. However, news of their activities had spread ahead of them and their presence in the region had become known among the leaders of synagogues. Wild rumours were circulating about what they were teaching. Particularly, Paul was accused of teaching Jews to turn away from Moses, telling them not to circumcise their children or live according to Jewish customs. This was sufficient of a threat to make them try to frustrate the work Paul, Silas and Timothy were doing.

In one city they met a group who claimed to be believers and followers of Jesus. As they talked Paul heard how they had been visited by some men from Jerusalem led by a certain Matthias. Paul recognised this name and realised this was the same man who had stirred up troubles in Antioch, recalling how he had been at the heart of the conflict over circumcision. He had spoken ill of Paul and warned them to avoid any contact with him or his colleagues.

One evening over dinner with these people, local city guards suddenly burst in and seized them. Betrayed by these false brothers, Paul and his companions were marched off and thrown into prison in the town. The next morning, they were dragged before an unauthorised tribunal led by leading Jews in the city who accused Paul in particular of all manner of wild excesses. Paul was singled out for special punishment and to the horror of many, he was stripped and whipped. Terribly wounded, his back yet again was a mass of bloody weals. Paul was beginning to lose count of the number of times he had been beaten, whipped and imprisoned.

Some of the believers who had not been part of the conspiracy came to their aid. They negotiated their release and took the three of them to a safe house just outside the city. Paul spent many days recovering from the whipping and was given food and comfort.

Laying on his stomach as his back healed, Paul cried out to God in his despair. He pleaded with the Lord to stop these people who were following him and trying to frustrate the work to which he had been called. He felt their continual attacks on him were like a thorn in his foot that just wouldn't go away. Every step he took, it pained him. He knew it was an attack from Satan and he cried out for deliverance.

Paul was depressed and frustrated. He was so sure they were to go to Ephesus and Asia, but it was proving almost impossible. Silas, always more upbeat than Paul, finally said to him, "Paul, I'm convinced the Spirit doesn't intend for us to go to Asia."

Paul had learnt to listen to Silas, and he recognised the voice of the Spirit through him. As soon as they were able to travel, they headed north. When they came to the border of Mysia, they tried to enter Bithynia which spread eastward along the shores of the Euxine Sea, but again it was Silas who said he felt the Spirit of Jesus did not want them to go there.[30]

Before turning back, they spent a few days resting. One evening Paul had gone to bed and Silas and Timothy sat staring into a fire together. Timothy had been thoughtful all day. He looked at Silas intently.

"What is it? What are you thinking about, Timothy?"

"Well, it's something you have said twice now. You said the Spirit doesn't want us to go to Asia, now Bithynia. How does it work? How do you know this is the Spirit of Jesus? How can you be so sure? Paul obviously believes you and here we are again turning around and heading in the opposite direction because of it. It is not that I don't believe you. I'm just interested to know how it works."

Silas stared into the fire, reflecting. "It comes out of my relationship with God. I sense his pleasure and joy when we are in the right place. There is an ease about things even if it is hard work. The more I relate to him as my Father and as his son, the easier it becomes."

"But how do you *hear* him?" asked Timothy.

Silas poked the fire and turned and looked at Timothy. "I'm learning to walk as Jesus walked. I heard John, Jesus' cousin, say this once. He said we know we are in him, because we walk as Jesus walked."

"But how do we do it?"

"Well, John told us how Jesus constantly said he only did the things he saw his Father doing, he only said the things he heard his Father saying. It's the same for us."

"It sounds good but how does it actually work? The reason I am asking is because when Paul was with us back in Lystra teaching, we heard the Spirit speaking through him. There was a sense of his presence in Paul's words. When he was with us we felt it; but when he left and went back to Antioch, it was hard. Others came from Jerusalem claiming they were speaking under the anointing of the Spirit. You know, they told us all these things Paul had neglected to tell us."

"Did it feel any different to you, Timothy?"

"Yes, very different. It was like a heavy burden being put on us. It did not give life or joy."

"Exactly! The Spirit of God who is within you was witnessing to what sort of spirit they were speaking in. One thing we are learning is to trust the inner witness of the Holy Spirit. There is always an abiding sense of peace and ease even if what he is saying is going to be hard or difficult. As you grow like this, take heart and learn to trust your own walk with Jesus. The more room we give him in our lives, the easier it gets."

Timothy sat in silence for some time then said, "That was how it was with us. As we were trying to get into Asia, it was very hard. There were many obstacles. Each step we took was painful and stressful. The resistance we were feeling through the circumstances, was it the clue you were looking for? Is that right?"

"Yes," nodded Silas. "Did you notice, once we realised we were on the wrong track and turned north there was a sudden lifting of the heaviness even though the road was hard? Did you notice the joy came back? It is something I am learning. You can live like this too, Timothy. Trust what Father has put in your heart and he will walk with you and you will learn to hear his voice too."

"I want others to learn this too, especially these small groups of believers we have been visiting. It will help them to discern what is true and what is not," said Timothy.

"I think this is why Paul wanted you to come with us. You can learn how to live like a son and experience the Father's Spirit and abiding presence in every circumstance. I see your young heart is open and teachable and you long to see others come into this revelation too. So be encouraged, young man. Watch Paul closely, follow his example, even how he handles his weaknesses and failures. We learn more in our failures and questions than we do in our own strength and ability."

Silas yawned and rubbed his eyes. "Now, no more questions tonight. We head west again tomorrow and it's a long walk. You need your beauty sleep, you ugly mutt!" Timothy grinned, stuck his tongue out at Silas and ducked as Silas pretended to throw a punch. Both of them laughed and went off to bed.

The next day they began the journey west. They walked for several days in deteriorating weather conditions. Autumn, without warning, turned to winter. They were in desperate need of shelter. Seeing a light burning they assumed it was an inn. As they approached, a gang of bandits attacked them out of the darkness. In the struggle they were robbed and Paul was even stripped of his clothes by one of the brigands and left for dead on the ground naked. Timothy ended up with a black eye and a split lip. Silas lost a tooth and was convinced his nose was broken. The furore roused the owners of the inn who came out with torches and swords and drove off the bandits. They took the three of them in and gave them some clothes. The next morning, the men headed for the coast road that skirted along the southern shore of the Seas of Marmara.

They trudged on at a very slow pace. Never had Paul felt such despair. He had reached far beyond his ability to endure. The road they had taken led them to a river. Close to exhaustion they struggled through the swollen river. The recent incessant rains had washed away the bridge and travellers were forced to cross the dangerous torrent holding on to a rope the locals had managed to attach to broken timber work on the far bank. The early winter storms made travel virtually impossible.

Timothy had eaten something that gave him endless stomach cramps and the frequent need to disappear behind the nearest rock or tree. The rigours of the recent weeks had taken their toll on Paul also. His eyes had become infected and sore. Only Silas seemed to have strength left. Sometimes he needed to lead Paul as he could hardly see. Other times he was forced to virtually carry Timothy.

The Sea of Marmara narrowed and they were able to see the shore on the other side. They continued west passing a small settlement where they stopped for rest and food. The locals told them this was the site of the ancient city of Troy which had been destroyed many centuries before by the Greeks. Paul sat on a rock resting, looking out across the plain where once Achilles was killed by an arrow, shot by the Trojan prince Paris. He thought about the struggle he was facing as he journeyed throughout the eastern provinces of the empire.

In his physical weakness he knew his strength came from the Lord and from his mighty power. He pictured Achilles and his armies dressing for battle each day putting on their armour. As he imagined the scene, he felt the Spirit speaking to him to put on the full armour of God, so he could take his stand against the devil's schemes. For he recognised his struggle was not against flesh and blood, but against the rulers, against the authorities, against the powers of the dark world in which he lived. It was against the spiritual forces of evil in the heavenly realms. As he reflected on these things, he sensed the Holy Spirit say to him personally,

"Paul, I want you to put on the full armour of God, so when the day of evil comes, you may be able to stand your ground, and after you have done everything, to stand. Stand firm with the belt of truth buckled around your waist. Cover your heart with the breastplate, which is righteousness, and put on shoes ready to spread the gospel of peace. Take up the shield of faith, it will extinguish all the flaming arrows of the evil one. Put on the helmet of salvation and hold the sword of the Spirit, which is the word of God."

With these words flooding his heart and mind he felt encouraged and finally he stood up and walked back to where Silas and Timothy were sitting on the ground wrapped in their cloaks sheltering from the gusty wind.

"Is everything okay, Paul?" asked Silas.

"Yes, I'm fine. Well, I'm not fine physically. I'm exhausted and my eyes are really bad today. But in my heart, I am strong and I am seeing things about the true nature of our struggle. I'll tell you about it when we get to Troas. Come on, let's get going. It's not far now."

Finally, the city and port of Alexandria Troas lay ahead of them. It sat on a peninsula jutting out into the Aegean Sea. To the north, a narrow waterway separated the Roman province of Asia from the province of Macedonia, with Greece and Italy many, many miles to the west. Crossing over to these provinces would involve a sea journey from Troas but from then on it would provide a continuous land route, albeit a very long road, which would lead all the way to Rome. The weary travellers stood on a hill looking down to the city and its port. They could smell the salt of the sea as the cold wind blew in their faces. Paul looked at the angry sea and contemplated more sea hazards. He had already survived two previous disasters at sea and did not relish another.

As was their custom, they entered the city and made enquiries about a synagogue. All three of them were Jews which gave them an opening among the Jewish community. This place was no different. Without hesitation, the leader of the synagogue welcomed them and recognised their need for food, rest and assistance. There were no hints of any ugly rumours preceding them. As they talked, it became apparent they were in the right place.

The ruler of the synagogue in Troas was known by his Greek name Carpus. He explained to Paul their synagogue included a number of God-fearing Greeks who were deeply interested in Judaism. Together, they all spoke Greek rather than Hebrew or Aramaic as the majority understood the language. He quickly saw Timothy and Paul needed medical attention.

"We have a man in our congregation who practices as a doctor in the city as well as across in Macedonia, in Philippi where he is from originally," he said. "He is not a Jew but he is a God-fearer and is often with us on the Sabbath. Would you like me to contact him and ask him to come and attend to you and see if he has some remedy?"

"That would really help," said Paul whose eyes were inflamed and encrusted with unsightly scabs oozing a noxious liquid. "They have never been as bad as this before. What is his name?"

"Lucas. He is a good man and we all think he is a good doctor too. He doesn't follow those ungodly remedies the Greeks typically employ. There will be no dead frogs or making you drink cat's pee. He mostly uses herbs. I'll send my son to see if he can come."

"Eutychus!" he called, "Eutychus! Where are you?" A spotty young boy aged about thirteen appeared from behind a door where he had been listening. He was struggling to make both his feet go in the same direction at the same time and his arms seemed to have a mind of their own.

"This is my boy Eutychus," Carpus said proudly. "He is on the brink of manhood as you can see."

Paul couldn't see, but he got the general idea. Silas grinned and Timothy remembered. Eutychus was sent off with very clear instructions to find and bring this doctor Lucas to their house. About an hour later they were back. Eutychus was visibly at ease with Lucas. As they entered, it looked as if they had been sharing a joke.

"Ah! Here you are, Lucas. Thank you, my son, now go off and see if you can get on with some of your studies," said his father.

"Oh, I wanted to stay and watch Lucas do his thing. We caught a cat on the way and we got all the pee we needed," the boy said in a rather squeaky voice.

Timothy went pale and looked with panic at Lucas who smiled warmly.

"Hello, everyone; I am Lucas. Eutychus, you rascal! Off with you." There was a huge sigh of relief from Timothy and everyone relaxed.

"Now, who shall we start with?"

Lucas spent the rest of the day with them. He checked Silas first and recommended a healthy feast at Carpus's table. For Timothy, he commended the opposite, a few days without food except some chicken soup and bread until his stomach and digestion had settled. He told him not to drink water, anywhere, unless he saw it coming out of the ground in a clear stream.

"Ideally," Lucas said, "boil it and let it cool. I don't know why, but water which has been boiled doesn't cause the same stomach problems. Failing that, drink wine, but not too much."

Then turning to Paul, he carefully examined his eyes. He looked concerned.

"Paul, your eyes are in very bad shape. I need to bathe them first. Carpus, a bowl of clean hot water please, oh, and some honey and olive oil too. I have a number of herbs I will need to crush and make into a poultice. Do you have a pestle and mortar?"

Lucas got on with his art. The others left him to it and went off to arrange for a place to sleep. After some time, Paul's eyes felt better than they had in weeks. Lucas had bandaged them and asked Paul to lay down.

"Right. You need to keep the bandage on for about a week, and every day I will come and change it and apply more ointment to your eyes. Don't touch or rub your eyes even over the bandage." Lucas paused, then said, "So what brings you to Troas, Paul?"

"I came here to find you!" said Paul.

"What! We have never met before. How do you know me?"

"I have been asking my heavenly Father to send me a doctor to help me with my wretched eyes for a long time, and now here you are, Lucas. You are indeed a God send," said Paul.

Lucas came as promised every day to attend to Paul, change his bandages and check his progress. He was very pleased with his patient. Each day, it gave him a chance to talk with Paul and find out what sort of man he was.

He discovered Paul was not a God-fearer as was he, rather he seemed to know God personally and had an intimate relationship with him. Paul spoke easily and unselfconsciously about his relationship with God. He talked about Jesus of Nazareth who he explained was the promised one the Jews had longed for. He was the hope of Israel. Lucas had been many times to the synagogue in Troas and saw the longing in the hearts of the Jews for their Messiah. Here was Paul telling him the hope of Israel had come, and this Jesus was the Son of God who had come as a man yet was the eternal son. Paul's words transfixed Lucas. His treatment times became longer every day. Initially, Silas and Timothy were concerned but then they understood.

After a week, Paul's bandages were removed and he was very excited to report he could see almost perfectly. There was great rejoicing and some said it was a miracle. Paul said, "It is a miracle of God's kindness and love administered through the hands of our beloved physician Lucas. Man's skill and God's kindness and healing power going hand in hand."

They stayed in Troas at Carpus's house and each Sabbath Paul was invited to speak at the synagogue. Carpus finally said to Paul one day,

"Paul, there are a number of us here who have listened to you week after week talking about Jesus, and they have asked me to speak on their behalf. It is not everyone, but there are many for whom I speak. We want to become followers of Jesus because we believe what you say is true. We want to demonstrate this by being baptised and becoming his sons and daughters. Can we do this please?"

Paul, Silas and Timothy were delighted at this news and they asked Carpus to gather this group together after the next Sabbath meeting of the synagogue. Two days later, at Carpus' house, a group of nearly two dozen men and women met with them. Eutychus was there with his father and mother. The last one to walk in the door was Lucas. Paul looked at him and tearfully embraced him. "My dear doctor, my dear brother, I am so happy."

During the night Paul awoke suddenly. He thought he saw a Macedonian standing and begging him, "Come over to Macedonia and help us." He did not know if it was a dream or a vision, either way he was sure he recognised the man. It was none other than the beloved physician!

The next morning Paul gathered Silas and Timothy and told them about his experience in the night.

"We leave for Macedonia as soon as we can and I would like Lucas to come with us."

"This is another way the Spirit leads." Silas said to Timothy. They got ready to leave for Macedonia, having decided God was going before them.[31]

PHILIPPI AD 51

CHAPTER VIII

The four of them walked through the town accompanied by a number of believers from Troas. Eutychus lolloped along beside them helping to carry Paul's bag. At the port they bought four passages on a ship going across to the province of Macedonia. The harbour was full of merchant ships sheltering and waiting for a break in the weather to make a quick dash across the sea to the main port on the coast of Macedonia, Neapolis. It was late winter and there was always a chance of being delayed by storms. However, for a few days it had been calm and mild so they took the opportunity to take the crossing. Having boarded the ship, they gathered on the deck and waved goodbye to those who had come to bid them farewell.

The ship put out to sea and sailed straight for Samothrace. They stayed a night ashore and the next day they sailed on to Neapolis. This was the port city for Philippi, which was a Roman Colony and the leading city of that district of Macedonia. It also sat astride the Via Egnatia which was the main land route from the east to Rome. It went overland and eventually connected with the Via Appia which went all the way to Rome. The city was populated by the descendants of soldiers who had remained after the great battle between Mark Antony and Octavius who became the Emperor Augustus nearly one hundred years before.[32]

When they docked at Neapolis, Lucas went ahead to arrange

accommodation for them and the others followed at their own pace. They all met in the forum and Lucas announced.

"It's all arranged, I have found some rooms. We can stay above a friend's shop in the herbalist's street. It's full of doctors and herbal specialists. It will be fine, I know many of them. But don't let them treat you or give you anything. Most of them are charlatans, nice people trying to make a living but with no idea about medicine." Lucas enthusiastically led them through the streets and alleys of Philippi to the place where they would stay.

Paul noticed there were very few Jewish people on the streets.

"Is there a synagogue in Philippi, Lucas?"

"I only know of a handful of Jews, not enough to form a synagogue. There are some God fearing Greeks but no one to teach them. They can be found on the Sabbath outside the city gate close to the river where people meet to pray and talk. We could go there on the Sabbath if you like."

On the Sabbath, Lucas led them through the city gate to the river. Paul looked around and saw a group of women who had their heads covered in the traditional way among the Jews. They walked over to them and asked if they could join them. After a while, Paul began to share why they were there and where they had come from. Naturally, he talked about Jesus and how he was the promised one, the Christ as the Greeks called him. The morning passed into the afternoon and the women were enthralled with all Paul had to say.

One of those listening was a widow from the city of Thyatira in the Province of Asia. Her name was Lydia. She was a businesswoman and dealt in purple cloth which was expensive merchandise. She talked with Paul and described herself as a worshiper of God.

Lydia was Greek and had taken on her husband's business after he had died.

Her heart was open to Paul's message. When Paul invited them to respond to God's love and desire for them to be reconciled to him, Lydia was one of the first to speak up.

"I have been longing for this message all my life. It feels like I have finally found the reason for being alive. I feel like I am coming home, to my real home. My heart is full of joy. Please, may I be baptised? I so want to turn away from my old way of life."

"Are you saying you want to turn away from your sinful past and turn in faith towards Jesus the Christ as your saviour?" asked Paul.

"Yes! Yes! Indeed, I do. I have." Lydia could barely contain her excitement. Paul reached out his hand, led her into the river and baptised her.

As she came out of the water, Paul said to her, "Lydia, the Father says you are his beloved daughter, and he is so proud of you. Now receive the Holy Spirt of Jesus as a confirmation of this transaction and as a seal of his presence and power upon you and in you." As he said these words, Lydia was filled with joy and laughter. Her heart sang for joy and she opened her mouth and started to sing in an unknown language. Onlookers thought it was her mother tongue because it was not Greek. Paul said she was singing the song in a language of heaven and he would explain this another time.

After Lydia, a number of people eagerly responded, confessing their sins and need for salvation and were baptised. This included several members of Lydia's household. It was almost dusk by the time they finished, so she invited them to her home.

"If you consider me a believer in the Lord," she said, "come and stay at my house." Paul looked at Silas, Timothy and Lucas, and Lydia spoke again. "Please come, I have guest rooms where you can stay. You can stay as long as you like. It will be my honour to have you with us."[33]

They stayed at Lydia's home and went every Sabbath to the river where people gathered to pray. In the evenings, there were gatherings in Lydia's spacious home. Her house in the city occupied a quarter of a city block. It was a large two-story villa with several guest rooms. Her late husband's business continued to expand under her. She had a number of household slaves who managed the house and worked in the business. In the centre was an open-air atrium which let in light and rain kept a pool full of water. At the back, there was a modest garden and a covered triclinium where guests could recline to dine in the open air. There was also a small bath house for bathing. It opened onto one of the grander streets in the city. Lydia was known and respected by the city's business community.

On one occasion, when Paul and some of the others were going to the place of prayer at the river, a slave girl whose owner used her to make predictions about the future and tell people's fortunes accosted them. She earned a great deal of money for her owners by fortune-telling and as a result was kept confined as a virtual prisoner. Her behaviour indicated she was influenced by a demonic spirit of some kind. Paul had encountered her when he first arrived in the city and had seen her on a number of occasions. She would often follow Paul and his companions, shouting after them.

"These men are servants of the Most High God, who are telling you the way to be saved."

Initially, they were amused by this as she was accurate in her description of them. But every time she saw them, the demonic spirit in her reacted to the Spirit of God in them. A deeply tormented young woman, she kept this up for days. Finally, Paul became so annoyed with the demonic spirit within her he turned around and spoke directly to the spirit,

"In the name of Jesus Christ, I command you to come out of her!"

Instantly, the spirit left her. She convulsed and fell on the ground but then sat up rubbing her head and eyes. She looked around bemused but calm for the first time in years.

A crowd gathered around to see what had happened, hoping to see some mad screaming or drama unfold. Instead, they saw the poor girl calmly sitting on the ground with Lucas beside her checking her for injury.[34]

The owners of the slave girl quickly realised their way of making money through the girl was gone and were furious. They started to beat her, but Paul and Silas intervened to protect her. The men turned on them. Seizing them, they dragged them into the marketplace to face the authorities. In the uproar Lucas and Timothy were able to escape with the slave girl and took her for safe keeping to Lydia's house. Paul and Silas, however, were brought before the magistrates.

The girl's aggrieved owners presented their case to the magistrates, but in addition provoked trouble by raising ethnic issues and anti-Roman sentiment.

"These men are Jews, and are throwing our city into an uproar by advocating customs unlawful for us Romans to accept or practice."

The crowd joined in the attack against Paul and Silas, and the magistrates ordered them to be stripped and beaten with rods. After they had been severely beaten, they were thrown into prison, and the jailor was commanded to guard them carefully until the morning when their case would be reviewed. The jailor put them in a cell and fastened their feet in stocks. (35)

The two men were naked, bleeding and bruised from the beating but grateful to be alive. They sat together in the stocks doing their best to support each other. Silas, positive and upbeat as always, suggested they sing to lift their spirits. Paul slowly joined in as Silas bellowed songs with as much energy as he could muster. He chose one of his favourites, Psalm 37.

> *"Do not fret because of those who are evil or be envious of those who do wrong; for like the grass they will soon wither, like green plants they will soon die away.*
>
> *Trust in the Lord and do good; dwell in the land and enjoy safe pasture. Take delight in the Lord, and he will give you the desires of your heart.*
>
> *Commit your way to the Lord: trust in him and he will do this: He will make your righteous reward shine like the dawn, your vindication like the noonday sun."*

He particularly liked the verse that said,

> *"The wicked plot against the righteous and gnash their teeth at them; but the Lord laughs at the wicked, for he knows their day is coming."*

They repeated the verse in Greek several times for good measure. This went late into the night and the other prisoners could not help but listen to them.

Around midnight, there was a rumble and the prison violently shook as an earthquake rocked the whole city. They could hear crashes of falling masonry. The air was filled with dust and falling stones. All the prison doors were shaking and began to open. The chains holding the prisoners came out of their sockets on the walls. There were screams and shouts from terrified prisoners. After what seemed like an age, but in reality was probably less than a minute, the shaking came to an end. People stopped screaming and waited. There was another crash as a piece of masonry somewhere fell and prisoners screamed again, then there was silence.

The jailor staggered into the area of the cells sword in one hand and a burning torch in the other. He was horrified when he saw the prison doors off their hinges and open. He assumed the prisoners had escaped. This would have been the worst thing for him as he would be held responsible and punished severely if they had escaped. In a panic response, he lifted his sword to his chest and was about to kill himself, but Paul seeing this from his cell shouted,

"Don't harm yourself! We are all here!"

The jailor called for slaves to bring more lights so he could better see what had happened. Like so many, he was deeply superstitious and terrified of darkness, which was believed to inhabit the underworld. He rushed into Paul and Silas' cell and fell trembling before them. He had heard them singing earlier and concluded their god caused the earthquake to punish him for having flogged them. The jailor's worldview was, like the vast majority of people, the gods were always angry and regularly punished people by sending disasters such as earthquakes. The terrified jailor brought them out. "Sirs," he asked, "what must I do to be saved?" He had no idea if he could be saved by Paul's God. His request was driven by sheer terror of being damned.

Paul replied, "Believe in the Lord Jesus and you will be saved."

Paul and Silas were taken into the jailor's living quarters where his equally terrified family and household slaves had gathered. Silas helped calm their fears, and he and Paul explained their God was a Father who did not send earthquakes to punish them. Instead they told them about the Father's love for them, how he had sent his own Son to bring them back into relationship with him, to reconcile them to him. As they talked, the jailor and his wife washed their wounds and bandaged them. Their hearts eagerly accepted the message Paul shared.

They talked all night until dawn began to break. The jailor set a meal before them, then he and all his household were baptized in a small pool in the bath house attached to the prison. They were overjoyed because they had come to believe in God, all of them, the jailor and his whole household.

Not long after sunrise, many people were about trying to clear debris and assess the damage caused by the earthquake. An officer and some soldiers arrived from the magistrates with a message for the jailor.

After reading the message, the jailor told Paul, "The magistrates have ordered you and Silas be released. Now you can leave. Go in peace." However, Paul said to the officer, "Just one minute. We have been beaten publicly without a trial, even though we are Roman citizens, and then we were thrown into prison." At the mention of the phrase 'Roman citizens,' fear and concern filled the officer's eyes. Paul continued, "And now they want to get rid of us quietly? No! Let them come themselves and escort us out." Paul and Silas exchanged glances, and the jailor began to look worried.

"Don't worry, my friend." Paul said to the jailor. "God intends this for good; let us see what happens. You have done us no harm."

The officer reported this to the magistrates, and when they heard Paul and Silas were Roman citizens, they were alarmed. Within a few minutes, a group of anxious magistrates arrived at the prison.

"Sirs, we had no idea you were citizens. Of course, if we had known we would have acted differently. We beg your forgiveness and want to know what we can do to recompense you for this unfortunate mistake." They bowed before Paul and Silas and one of them deliberately brought a money bag he was hiding behind his back out to the front.

"Thank you for your concern," said Paul. "In the future you would be wise to get your facts straight before you take actions. Next time someone might die, and I can't imagine what the Provincial Governor would make of that. In this case, I have a request."

"Anything you want," the lead magistrate said quickly. Paul's mention of the Governor's reaction had raised the stakes considerably.

"First, I want you to acknowledge the work of the jailor here. He has treated us with great kindness and not been cruel to us. In fact, I would promote him if I were you. You need people who know what they are doing in this city. The other request I have is a guarantee of safety for our friends in this city. We have taught them nothing contrary to Roman Law as we were accused. It would be good for you all to meet with them and hear from their own lips what they believe."

"You don't want money?" asked the lead magistrate, expressing his surprise and relief. "We agree to your requests. Jailor," he said turning to him, "come to the magistrates office at the basilica later today and we will talk."

He turned back to Paul, "You have my word on safety for your friends, but my final word is you two must leave the city as soon as possible. We would not want your presence here to cause any additional turmoil. Agreed?" And with that, he escorted them from the prison. Paul and Silas left the prison and went to Lydia's house, where they were met by a few of the new believers along with Lucas and Timothy. They had been helping Lydia clear the damage from the earthquake. Lucas immediately took charge of attending to their bruises and abrasions.

"Your back! It looks terrible, Paul!" exclaimed Lucas on seeing the dark blue weals. "You really could do with resting, not leaving the city. Let me have a look at your back, Silas. Hmm, at least it's not quite as bad." He spent the day doing what he could to ease their pain and help the wounds heal.[36]

As they prepared to leave Philippi, it became clear Lucas had decided to stay in the city to be part of the small group of believers. Paul had been talking to him for some days prior to his arrest and the earthquake about this. Paul's concern was increasingly for these small communities of believers which were emerging as a result of preaching. It occupied a large amount of his thinking. He found himself constantly praying for them and listening to the Father's voice for them. He wanted them to grow, to be protected from error and the attacks coming from many quarters, not least from those trying to undermine his role as an apostle. He began to see the need for local people, known and trusted by him, whose hearts were open to God to care for them, people such as Lydia. This would help bring some cohesion and focus to their gatherings. In addition, he saw there was a need for people with freedom to travel who would represent him and carry his heart. This was his thinking when he left Titus back in Lystra those months before.

PHILIPPI AD 51

As much as Paul valued Lucas' personal care for him, he was just the right person to stay connected with the group in Philippi and the one in Troas. His personal connections in both cities and the regard in which they held him were significant. More to the point was the heart of Lucas. He loved his newfound God and Father and over the months had opened his heart to receive and drink deeply, as Paul put it, of the Father's love for him.

There had been some discussion and everyone felt this was the leading of the Spirit. The day or two before Paul, Silas and Timothy left, everyone gathered at Lydia's house. They prayed together and shared in worship of the Father. A number of new converts were baptised, and then Paul spoke to them all about how to stay close to the Lord and one another. The last thing they did was to appoint a small group to care for the group. This included Lydia and two others, Clement and Epaphroditus. Paul called them 'shepherds' to give an indication of their function. Everyone prayed for them and reached out their hands to bless them. Then he and Silas placed their hands on them in the traditional Jewish way to impart a blessing and anointing from the Father. As they did this there was a strong sense of the presence of the Spirit of Jesus among them which filled them with great joy.

Paul turned to Lucas and explained to everyone how he saw his role among them. Again, there was great enthusiasm and joy in response which seemed to confirm what Paul felt was the leading of the Spirit. They all gathered around Lucas, placed their hands on him and set him apart for the work the Spirit had called him to do. Finally, they all had a meal together which turned into a party. As the day drew to a close, a group who had been whispering in the corner came to Paul, Silas and Timothy.

"What are you up to?" asked Paul.

Clement, one of the leaders answered. "Well," he said, "Epaphroditus and I have been talking, as have Euodia, Syntyche and Lydia, all of us in fact. We agree together on this. We have decided to help you on your journey ahead and we have collected some money. Lucas told us what a mess you were in when you arrived in Troas. We don't want you to be like that again. Insofar as we can, we want to support what you are doing and provide for your needs. Travelling is not cheap, travel by sea costs money and we want to partner with you in this and help you. We want you to contact us at any time if you need help."

Lydia stepped forward and placed a leather moneybag in Paul's hands.

"Use it as you think fit, dear brothers. There will be more. We love you. How can we thank you for coming to Philippi? You have brought us life, hope and we now know how much God the Father loves us. We know we are his sons and Jesus is our brother. Thank you. Thank you."

"Just make sure you come back to us one day. There will always be a room for you in my house and in my heart." She hugged Paul and wept on his shoulder.

The following morning as they were preparing to depart, Paul and Lucas sat together in Lydia's garden reflecting on recent events.

"I have been thinking about something else, Lucas."

"What's that, Paul?"

"You remember I told you about John Mark who was with me and Barnabas in Antioch and Cyprus? He has been writing down the things he hears Peter and the others say about what Jesus said and did before he went back to the Father. Initially, I thought it was a waste of time, but I see now it would be really useful especially where nobody ever met Jesus or heard him teach like they did in Galilee or Jerusalem. I was thinking someone like you, who is educated and has a knowledge of the Greek and Roman world might be good at this too. Maybe if you met John Mark you could see what he has been doing. The last I heard was he was on Cyprus. If you are ever over there, seek him out."

Later in the morning Paul, Silas and Timothy walked out through the west gate of the city taking the Via Egnatia heading towards Thessalonica. As they did so, two travellers from the east entered through the east gate of the city. One was Matthias from Jerusalem.

THESSALONICA, BEREA AND
ATHENS AD 51

CHAPTER IX

Paul and his companions walked slowly west along the Via Egnatia. Progress was slow as the two older men were still stiff and sore following their beating in Philippi. They passed through Amphipolis and Apollonia, then finally after about a week came to Thessalonica.

Compared to Philippi, Thessalonica was a much larger city. It was the seat of regional government for this part of Macedonia. An acropolis dominated the city and there was a large modern harbour which the Romans had extended and enlarged about a century earlier.

As they began to explore the city, they enquired about the Jewish population, and quickly found a section of the city where there were many Jewish merchants and traders. Paul recognised some tent-makers he used to do business with and through conversation with them discovered there was a large synagogue made up of predominately Greek speaking Jews, and there was quite a large number of God-fearers, both men and women in its congregation.

Paul went into the synagogue on the first Sabbath they were in the city and on the two subsequent Sabbath days. As a visiting rabbi from Jerusalem, he was warmly welcomed as were Silas and Timothy. Timothy sat down and crossed his legs, thinking it was worth it after all.

Paul told them about Jesus' life and ministry in Galilee and Judea. He told them how Jesus had revealed the true nature of Yahweh being a Father. They listened intently and asked questions. He reasoned with them from their Scriptures, explaining and proving the Messiah had to suffer and rise from the dead.

"This Jesus whom I am proclaiming to you is none other than the Messiah," he said. Some of the Jews were convinced by what Paul taught. But it was more than the words he spoke. It was how he said things and the passion they saw in him and the other two. Many of them longed to have the same hope and joy they saw in Paul and Silas.[37]

At the end of the third week many asked to become followers of Jesus. Jason who was the leader of the synagogue had already invited the three of them to stay in his home, and he was one of the first to embrace the truth and revelation they brought. In addition, a large number of God-fearing Greeks and some prominent women of the city joined the group.

They stayed with them for some weeks encouraging and instructing them. They told them Jesus had promised to return one day and they should live in the daily expectation of his return.

One Sabbath, as they were meeting together, other visitors arrived. Jason approached them and warmly greeted them as was his custom. He brought the two men over to where Paul and Silas were sitting talking with some of the new believers.

"Paul, I'm sorry to interrupt you," said Jason. "There are two men here who say they are believers from Jerusalem and they say they know you."

Paul looked up wondering who these men were.

"I'm sorry, I don't think we have met before, have we?" said Paul.

"I have found you at last, Paul! Don't you recognise me? I am Matthias from Jerusalem." He paused to let his words sink in.

"You are a hard man to track. Still up to your old tricks, I see. How many have you deceived in this city?" Matthias deliberately raised his voice and looked around. His face was a cross between a sneer and a frown as he glared at Paul.

Many in the congregation looked shocked and confused.

Jason stood and placed his hand on Paul's shoulder. "Gentlemen, these men are here as our guests, and they are great teachers. We all love what they are saying and have welcomed their message of hope and good news."

Across the room a man stood. "Not all of us, Jason, some of us think this has gone too far. While you may be the ruler of this synagogue, we don't all agree with you. It would be good to hear what these newcomers have to say."

This unexpected development caused a great stir. People began talking loudly and arguing, taking sides. In the resulting turmoil, Jason ushered Paul, Silas and Timothy out of the synagogue. Jason asked two of his close friends, Aristarchus and Secundus to take them to a safe house where they would not be found. Soon a great mob of louts and ruffians from the marketplace had gathered outside the synagogue. There was shouting and the occasional smashing of clay pots thrown at the walls of the synagogue. A full-blown riot ensued.

Jason went home to secure his property and bar the windows.

THESSALONICA, BEREA AND ATHENS AD 51

But the mob, including some Jews from the congregation who were jealous of Jason, ran down the street after him. They rushed to Jason's house in search of Paul and Silas in order to bring them out to the crowd. The crowd was in an ugly mood and Jason knew their lives were at risk.

They broke down the door and burst into his house demanding Jason bring out Paul and Silas from where he had hidden them. The house was filled with men smashing furniture and stealing household goods. Jason was punched in the face and his terrified wife and children were threatened. When they did not find Paul, the mob dragged a bruised and bloody Jason and some other believers before the city officials.

"These men who have caused trouble all over the world have now come here, and Jason has welcomed them into his house. They are all defying Caesar's decrees, saying there is another king, one called Jesus."

When they heard this, the crowd and the city officials were thrown into turmoil. No one was sure who was making this accusation. The whole situation was totally out of hand. To calm things down, the city officials made Jason and the others pay in order to get out of custody and let them go.[38]

On arriving back at his ransacked house Jason looked around at the mess and found his traumatised wife and children hiding in a store room. Checking all was safe he brought them out and went to find Aristarchus and Secundus where he had sent Paul, Silas and Timothy.

The believers decided to send the three of them away to Berea as soon as it was night.

"Berea is a good two days walk from here, three if you go slowly. It is inland and we have good friends there in the Jewish community," said Jason.

"You need to get out of the city as soon as you can. My contacts tell me this man Matthias who came looking for you is spreading all sorts of ugly rumours about you, Paul. He says you are not a true apostle, whereas he has described himself as a senior or super apostle, whatever that is supposed to mean. He seems intent on undoing all God has done through you but at the same time claims to speak with the authority of the apostles in Jerusalem."

"My friend in Berea is called Sopater son of Pyrrhus," Jason continued. "If you find the synagogue in the city, they will direct you to him. Here take this, I have written a letter introducing you and commending you to them. I am sure they will be open to the message you are bringing. Don't delay you must leave first thing in the morning."

Before dawn, Paul, Silas and Timothy slipped out of Thessalonica heading southwest along the Via Egnatia.

Two days later they arrived in Berea. They went straight to the synagogue as Jason advised. Jason had a very high opinion of his Jewish friends in Berea. He described them as having a more noble character than those in Thessalonica. Berea proved initially to be a welcome respite after the troubles in Thessalonica and Philippi. Paul, true to form, immediately began to speak about Jesus being the Messiah who reconciles man to God the Father. They eagerly received the message and examined their Scriptures every day to see if what Paul said was true. As a result, many of them believed. This included a number of prominent Greek speaking women.[39]

Matthias however had stayed in Thessalonica and tried to discover Pauls' whereabouts from the Jews in the city who had opposed Jason. It was not easy, and for some days, he heard nothing. One evening as he was hanging around in the forum, he saw a group of Jewish travellers who he had not seen before. Matthias ambled over to the group, wondering if they would have information.

"Hello, friends. Where have you come from?"

"Berea. We've come for—"

"Berea, you say?" He stroked his beard. "You wouldn't happen to have heard of a noted teacher travelling through there, would you? Man by the name of Paul? Paul of Tarsus?"

Their eyes lit up at the mention of Paul's name.

"Oh, yes we have. A wonderful man! We heard him speaking recently in Berea not a few days ago. Do you know him? Has he been here? We would love to connect with people who think like him." The men looked eagerly at Matthias.

"You are sure his name was Paul from Tarsus?" asked Matthias.

"Definitely," replied one of the men.

"Thank you for this information it will be very useful." With that, Matthias walked away leaving them looking at his back with quizzical expressions.

Later that day Matthias dispatched two trusted friends to Berea to check out the report and if Paul was still there to try to stop him from preaching. Matthias' attitude had slowly hardened, particularly after the confrontation in Antioch. Driven by his own pain, anger and jealousy of Paul, he had become obsessed and lost all objectivity. Matthias had made his mission personal.

"Try to get the synagogue leaders to help you deal with Paul," he instructed them. "If that doesn't work, get the local ruffians to start a riot or something. If you need to pay them to do it, so be it. Whatever happens, stop Paul. Get rid of him if you have to. Let me know what is happening. If need be, I will come and smooth things out with the synagogue. Then maybe I can go home and be rid of this troublesome rabbi."

A few days later, the believers in Berea noticed a change in the attitude of people in Berea. Crowds in the marketplace were starting to shout about Paul. They discovered some men had come from Thessalonica who were agitating the crowds and stirring them up. There were even rumours of a plot to kill Paul.

Sopater acted quickly. Since Paul was the focus of the disturbance they felt it would be safe for Silas and Timothy to stay at Berea. So the believers decided to escort Paul as quickly as possible down to the coast and then to Athens, which they thought would be far enough away for him to be safe. No one was told of the plan except a small inner circle. By keeping Silas and Timothy in Berea they felt it would mean Paul had a better chance of escape.[40]

"As soon as I have get to Athens, I'll send you word and you can join me without raising suspicion," said Paul as he waved to them before slipping away under cover of darkness.

They escorted Paul down to the coast and put him on a ship bound for Athens. A letter was written to introduce him to some members of the Jewish community in the city. Within a few days he was in Athens.

Paul was amazed at all the buildings and monuments in Athens. He had known of the ancient city through his studies, but nonetheless he was impressed at the beauty of the architecture, the size of the temples and in particular the great Acropolis crowned by the Parthenon. The original masterpieces of Hellenistic Athens still stood even though the Romans had destroyed much of the city when they conquered Greece one hundred and fifty years earlier. The suburbs and fortifications were destroyed but the Romans, prizing the classical monuments had spared them. The city had been rebuilt and grand new monuments and temples were constructed. On the Acropolis itself stood the magnificent new temples of Roma and Augustus. Recently, a huge new market of Caesar and Augustus had been completed.

As Paul looked around, he found the religious fervour of the Athenians staggering. The temples had queues of people going in to offer sacrifices to the gods, and there appeared to be a temple for every god he had ever heard of. He found it a profoundly depressing experience. In addition to the religious fervour of the people, which he considered mere pagan superstition, he noticed many people just sitting around discussing, gossiping and philosophising. It seemed a strange city to him. What had once been the noble capital of Greece was now a backwater. The Romans had moved the capital of the province of Achaia, south to Corinth. Its original grandeur was gone, replaced by empty and hollow superstition in his opinion. Paul gazed at the beautiful many-sided Tower of the Winds called the Horologion by the locals, near the new market and smiled to himself as he wondered what wind had blown him to this city. He knew it was no wind of fate but the wind of the Spirit had led him to this place.

As he walked back to the guest house attached to the synagogue, he came across an altar where a woman was leaving some flowers.

He paused and read the inscription carved into the pedestal. It read "TO THE UNKNOWN GOD". He touched the inscription with his hand and let his fingers trace the carving which was worn and old. Then he smiled and looked up at the sky.

"This is why you have brought me here, Father!" He chuckled to himself and walked back to his lodgings.

The next day Paul continued wandering around the city and encountered some Jewish merchants. He began to talk to them. They showed little interest in what he had to say, so he sauntered through the marketplace and wherever he could he started up conversations with people. He got into a discussion with a group of Epicurean and Stoic philosophers. As he debated with them, people stopped and listened. Paul had been talking about Jesus and in particular his resurrection from the dead. This was completely foreign to their thinking, and as he would like to say, it tickled their ears.

"What is this babbler trying to say?"

"He seems to be talking about some foreign god."

"Well, in that case he should speak before the Areopagus, let them decide what he is up to."

"Oi! Somebody take him off to the Areopagus." Someone shouted.

A small crowd had gathered and they seized Paul and dragged him off to their ancient court. They brought him to a meeting of the Areopagus. This was a small hill covered in stone seats to the northwest of the city, once used as a forum for the rulers of Athens to hold trials, debate, and discuss important matters. Previously, the ancient court of Athens and the centre of political and religious life in the city, it had long lost its prestige particularly after the Roman occupation. Now, the Areopagus was little more than a place to debate where they discussed the newest philosophical and religious ideas. The members who made up this court were known as Areopagites, and the presiding Areopagite addressed Paul.

"May we know what this new teaching is that you are presenting? It is reported you are bringing some strange ideas to our ears, and we would like to know what they mean." There was no hostility in his enquiry, so Paul launched into a skilful presentation of his teaching.

Speaking of an 'unknown God' whose altar he had found, Paul tied the Athenians' search for truth to the reality of his gospel. He brilliantly alluded to their philosophical ideas and quoted from Greek poetry.

Some years later, he recounted his memories of the speech to Lucas who summarised them and wrote them down.

"As I walked around your city, I could not help but notice that you are very religious. For as I walked around and looked carefully at your objects of worship, I even found an altar with this inscription: to an unknown god. So you are ignorant of the very thing you worship and this is what I am going to proclaim to you.

"The God who made the world and everything in it is the Lord of heaven and earth and does not live in temples built by human hands. And he is not served by human hands, as if he needed anything. Rather, he himself gives everyone life and breath and everything else. From one man he made all the nations, that they should inhabit the whole earth; and he marked out their appointed times in history and the boundaries of their lands. God did this so that they would seek him and perhaps reach out for him and find him, though he is not far from any one of us. 'For in him we live and move and have our being.' As some of your own poets have said, 'We are his offspring.'

"Therefore, since we are God's offspring, we should not think that the divine being is like gold or silver or stone—an image made by human design and skill. In the past God overlooked such ignorance, but now he commands all people everywhere to repent. For he has set a day when he will judge the world with justice by the man he has appointed. He has given proof of this to everyone by raising him from the dead."

"You are crazy!" shouted one of the members of the council sneering at Paul. Another stood and started mocking Paul.

"You are a silly fool, wasting our time. No one with half a brain believes the dead rise. You are a half-brained donkey! Hee-haw! Hee-haw!" As they stood to leave, they started to bray like asses and to laugh at Paul.

"We want to hear you again on this subject," shouted one member of the Areopagus called Dionysius.

Paul slowly walked away from the ancient Council. Dionysius ran after him and caught up with him as did a woman called Damaris who had been waiting outside.

"Don't take any notice of those ignorant fools. There are some of us in this city who believe you. Please stay a bit longer," said Dionysius.[41]

CORINTH FIRST VISIT
AD 51 - 53

CHAPTER X

Paul decided to go south to Corinth and set out from Athens with a heavy heart. The ridicule of the Athenian intellectual elite was nothing more than he had expected, but nonetheless he was disappointed. He had hoped some would believe his message. The few who opened their hearts to him asked him to come back again and he decided he would find someone who might be willing to go there. He thought about Silas and Timothy back in Macedonia and his heart ached wondering how they were and if they had received his message to come and join him. He had left instructions with Dionysius and Damaris in Athens to let them know he had gone to Corinth if they turned up in Athens looking for him.

He was alone and he was weak. Paul's body was exhausted and the journey to Corinth, whilst shorter than many of his other journeys, was slow and painful. The well-maintained road led along the coast and there were many villas and inns along the way. It was a rich and densely populated part of Achaia. Stopping many times and using what little money he had to buy and eat the local seafood, which was cheap and abundant, he deliberately did not hurry. One day, he sat on a beach, allowing the sun to warm his body and heal his wounds. He took off his clothes and bathed in the warm water of the sea which soothed and refreshed him.

He could not get his concerns for the communities he had established out of his mind. He wondered how Lucas and the believers in Philippi were and Titus in Galatia. He missed their company and he longed for news of them.

As he lay on a mat in his room in one of the inns along the coast, he found himself thinking again about the man Matthias who kept following him and stirring up trouble wherever he could. His mind went back to his days in Jerusalem as a young Pharisee almost twenty years before. Suddenly, as if a light went on, he realised Matthias must have been one of those early followers of Jesus whom he had arrested and tortured. It all fell into place. Matthias had been one of those who opposed Paul over circumcision in Jerusalem, then again in Antioch. It made sense to him now. This was not about theology; it was revenge and it was personal for Matthias. A pang of fear gripped him. Would he ever be free of this man? He felt this man was truly a thorn in his flesh that irritated and made every step painful.

As Paul lay there, he found himself crying out to God his Father to take this thorn in his body away from him. He had prayed like this several times now. He felt this man was sent as a messenger from Satan himself to undermine all he was doing. He felt helpless and weak. He did not know what to do. "Father, please take this thorn away from me." Paul cried out in desperation.

In the quietness of his bedchamber Paul sensed the presence of Jesus in the room. He felt waves of peace and love fill the chamber and seep into his aching body and anxious heart. In the darkness he knew he was not alone. Gently, he heard a whisper very close to his face.

"Paul, Paul." He recognised those affectionate and comforting tones.

"I'm here; I am with you. My grace is sufficient for you. My power is made perfect in weakness." Tears spilled on to his pillow.

Paul began to see every time he felt the pain of his weakness, Jesus would be with him. He did not have to be strong, to know what to do, every time there was a problem. He was discovering how to rely everyday not on his own immense ability and strength but on Jesus. This was a major lesson he was learning.[42]

The next morning, he awoke and opened his eyes slowly. After stretching, he yawned, then gently massaged his aching bones. He felt more peaceful than he had in months.

Corinth was a short walk away. "I can easily get there before dark," he said to himself as he set out towards the city.

The city stretched before him as he came over the brow of a hill. It was the capital city of the Roman province of Achaia. Corinth was an ancient city but very little was left of its earlier greatness having been destroyed by the Romans two hundred years before. Julius Caesar had re-founded the city as a colony about ninety years before. He renamed it Colonia Laus Julia Corinthiensis and populated it with conscripted Italian, Greek, Syrian, Egyptian and Judaean freed slaves. New Corinth thrived.

Within a few years, Corinth's new settlers had filled the city with profitable commerce. It stood at a crossroads of the nations and brought thousands more eager settlers from all over the Mediterranean. The city had a ruling class of self-made women and men with great personal wealth. It was also full of slaves from all over the empire. The city Paul walked into had a large mixed population of Romans, Greeks, North Africans, Gauls and Jews.

As Paul made his way along the coast towards the city, he saw lines of slaves sweating in the noon day heat pulling a boat up from the sea. Corinth sat astride an isthmus which was narrow and there was a road cleared to enable boats to be dragged on rollers from one side to the other. This cut many days off the hazardous journey by sea from Rome to the Aegean Sea. He watched the poor wretches at their task and wondered how long they would survive doing this crippling labour.

In the heart of the city was the forum filled with temples and shrines to the emperor and various members of his family, built alongside temples to the older Greek gods such as Apollo. The city was crowned by the Acrocorinth high above the city and atop the acropolis of Corinth stood the Temple of Aphrodite, the Greek goddess of love. The marble columns of the Temple of Aphrodite dominated the skyline. Supposedly within those incense-filled, candlelit precincts, a thousand sacred prostitutes worked around the clock gathering funds for the deity. And because of them, the city was filled with all manner of vice and also became very wealthy.

The reality was Aphrodite's servants were not exactly willing volunteers. Corinth's many cosmopolitan *'pornai'* or prostitutes, were slaves purchased by wealthy Greeks and dedicated to the temple as a form of religious offering. While the Temple looked large it was too small for even one hundred women to be working in its precincts, let alone one thousand. Instead, the sex slaves received their clients in filthy back street brothels around the temple, huddled on lumpy straw mattresses in small, dark, airless stalls with illustrations painted above the booths demonstrating each girl's specialty. The male Greek culture was deeply chauvinistic. Wives were considered chattel, suitable only for raising families. Consequently, married Greek men went to prostitutes and young boys for 'pleasurable sex.'

CORINTH FIRST VISIT AD 51 - 53

Corinth had a reputation of being a particularly licentious city. Paul knew one of the Greek verbs for fornicate was '*korinthiazomai*', a word derived from the city's name. No doubt, Corinth, like other large port cities, had plenty of prostitutes to service the sailors. After landing at the Corinthian docks, sailors would wheeze up the thousand-odd steps to the top of the stunning crag of rock, the Acrocorinth, with its panoramic views of the sparkling Mediterranean. The sailors would spend fortunes there. The proverb said: 'The voyage to Corinth isn't for just any man.' After encountering Aphrodite's servants, visitors to ancient Corinth always left much poorer than when they arrived.

As Paul entered the city gates, he was immediately approached by a young woman offering her services on behalf of the goddess. Barely had he moved on a few paces when two young boys, perhaps in their mid-teens dressed in loose robes in a way that revealed their naked bodies, walked up to him.

"If you are not interested in Aphrodite's servants, maybe we can introduce you to Apollo, his temple is close by. No need to climb all those steps up to the goddess's temple." The speaker gestured suggestively to Paul, who looked at him with surprise and sadness. Politely declining, he felt love flooding his heart for them which he knew came from God the Father. Paul longed for them to know this source of love.

Paul made his way towards the Forum in order to gain a perspective of the city. He was used to big cities having lived in Tarsus and Antioch, but those cities had a flavour of the East about them. Corinth was very large and cosmopolitan and definitely less eastern. The colonnaded Forum was crowded as was the large Agora which opened out from the Forum. Paul walked under the covered porticos along the sides of the marketplace. As he looked at the traders and noticed a stall selling leather goods. There was a sign advertising tents for sale. It caught his eye and he wandered over to inspect the quality of the merchandise.

"You have tentmakers in the city?" he enquired.

"Yes. We are tentmakers. Who wants to know?" asked a gentle faced woman. Paul though she might be Jewish.

"I do," he answered. "I am a tentmaker by trade, but a bit out of practice. These are excellent quality goods you are selling. Where do you make your tents?"

"At our workshop across the city," answered the woman. "Why do you ask?"

"Well, I was just wondering if you needed any extra work as I could do with a job," said Paul.

The woman looked at him curiously, then smiled slightly. "Your name is not Paul by any chance is it, originally from Tarsus?"

"It most certainly is. How do you know that?"

"You are obviously Jewish, your accent is eastern, and we have friends in Rome who told us to look out for you. Their names are Andronicus and Junia," she said smiling at Paul.

"This is extraordinary! I take it you are believers in Jesus the Messiah as they are? They are relatives of mine, in fact they were in Christ before I was and they have even been in prison with me."

Prisca started to pack up her stall. She had a young man with her who was helping her, so she told him to finish up and then turned to Paul.

CORINTH FIRST VISIT AD 51 - 53

"Come on. We are going home. My husband Aquila is there. He will be delighted to meet you. I, by the way, am called Prisca, but most of my friends call me Priscilla." She turned to Paul and looked him in the eye. "You are an answer to our prayers."

They made their way through the streets turning off from one of the main thoroughfares into a less crowded side street where Aquila had established the workshop of their business. It was in a typical three-story tenement.

"We have our shop at the front and the workshop at the back." Prisca informed Paul. "We live above the shop and have a room where you are welcome to stay."

Aquila came out from the workshop when Priscilla called for him.

"You will never guess who this is! We just met in the Agora," said an excited Priscilla. Her husband raised an eyebrow and looked from his wife to the dusty traveller standing next to her.

"This is Paul of Tarsus whom Andronicus and Junia told us about. He has just this day arrived in Corinth. Would you believe it!"

Aquila greeted Paul warmly and they went into the back of the shop. There was such a familiar smell of canvas and Paul immediately felt at home. Prisca left Paul and Aquila talking while she hurried off to organise an evening meal for them.

So began a friendship between them that would last for many years to come.[43]

Within just a few days Paul settled into life with Aquila and Priscilla in Corinth having been invited to join them in their tent-making business. This also helped him support himself by providing income. They worked in the workshop every morning which gave them a chance to talk and hear each other's stories. It was exciting for Paul to hear how the good news of Jesus arrived in Rome and the part played by his relatives Andronicus and Junia in this. He was pleased also to hear how Peter regularly travelled to Rome and was encouraging both Jews and Gentiles to be together in the community. It seemed to Paul the struggles Peter experienced in Antioch were behind him.

Aquila and Priscilla had not been in Corinth for many months and as yet there were only a handful of followers of Jesus in the city. One man, Stephanas, and his family had embraced the message and became believers in Jesus. They were the first converts in Achaia and were active supporters of Aquila and his wife.

Priscilla introduced Paul to Stephanas and asked him to baptise the family, which he willingly did. There was a large Jewish community in the city with several synagogues. They tended to group around national backgrounds. One synagogue was mostly made up of Jews from Judea who were newcomers to the city. There were also synagogues made up of Greek speaking Jews who had been in Achaia for several generations. It was in one of these Greek speaking synagogues where Aquila and Priscilla had the most contact with people.

The ruler of the synagogue was a man named Crispus. He was well educated with a good knowledge of the Hebrew Scriptures. People spoke highly of him. On the first Sabbath after his arrival Paul was introduced by Aquila as a visiting rabbi. Crispus invited Paul to sit in the seat reserved for rabbis and then to bring a message of encouragement to the congregation.

Paul stood to speak and began to talk about the longing for hope within the hearts of Jewish people for the Lord to come and rescue them. He talked about Jesus as the promised anointed one, using the Greek term, 'the Christ'. Before long everyone in the synagogue was paying careful attention to Paul.

He preached about Jesus' death by crucifixion. For some of the listeners this was a stumbling block and it sounded like foolishness to some of the Greeks. However, there was an anointing on Paul's words. The whole place was filled with a sense of the presence and power of God and the wisdom of God. Paul explained how God raised Jesus from the dead. He continued,

"The foolishness of God is wiser than human wisdom, and the weakness of God is stronger than human strength."

He stood there before them in weakness and at times his voice was shaky and not strong but the presence of the Spirit was powerfully filling the room.

Paul was sowing in a well tilled field. Aquila and Priscilla had been preparing the soil through their example and their words and now Paul was sowing. At the end of his address a number of people gathered around eagerly wanting to know more. Crispus was weeping openly. Another man named Gaius Titius Justus who lived in a domus, a large villa, right next to the synagogue was also clearly touched. At the end of the meeting he came up to Paul.

"All my life I have been longing for this hope which you speak about. Please, will you come to my house? It's next door. I would like you to share with my whole family and household the things you have been saying."

"Certainly," said Paul, "when can we come?"

"This evening as soon as the Sabbath has ended, come and break bread with us first. Bring Aquila and Prisca too. You are all most welcome."

"Excuse me, Gaius," interrupted Crispus. "As long as you are not having to work you do not have to wait for the Sabbath to end. They can attend without breaking the law as soon as you like." Paul looked at Crispus and was surprised at his reaction. The man had a pleading look in his eyes as Paul stared at him. In his experience, this was not the usual reaction of a synagogue leader. It seemed to Paul a door was wide open in Corinth. He turned to Gaius.

"It seems our worthy friend Crispus has given us his blessing on this continuing today. Gaius, if it is no problem maybe Crispus can join us?"

"Of course! Please do come, Crispus, and bring your family too."

A little while later Paul, along with Aquila and Priscilla were being welcomed into the home of Gaius. The outer door from the street led into a hallway where a black and white tessellated mosaic depicting a dog, adorned the floor. This led into a light and airy atrium open to the sky, with a central pool filled by rain water. Various rooms led off in all directions and Paul saw a stairway leading up to a second storey. The pavements of the ground floor rooms were covered with intricate mosaics. The walls were painted in the latest styles. This was the house of a wealthy man. Household slaves hovered in the shadows wondering who the visitors were. Gaius, who was now joined by his wife and older children, stood and formally welcomed them into his house. They were all introduced one by one. Then Gaius addressed his guests.

"You are all welcome in my home this day and any day. We are honoured and also by your gracious presence, lady Prisca," he said as he bowed to her.

Paul looked at Prisca who flushed slightly and replied, "Please call me Priscilla. Prisca is very formal and whilst my family has status and position in Rome, here I am Priscilla the wife of Aquila of Pontus." She turned and smiled at her husband who looked proudly at her.

Gaius led them from the atrium, past the triclinium, where they would later recline to eat, through to the back of the domus into a lush garden which was surrounded by a colonnaded peristyle. They were invited to sit under an awning for shade. No sooner had they sat down than there was more banging on the front door. Gaius looked up, and in a moment, his chief steward came to say Crispus and his family had arrived. They were escorted into the garden, and they all sat eagerly awaiting what Paul was about to say.

Paul looked around at the faces of the people and he knew their hearts were open. He continued to talk about how Jesus was the Messiah, the Christ, the promised one, how he was risen from the dead. He shared with them his own experience of seeing Jesus die then meeting him on the road outside Damascus. He explained how through Jesus' death on the cross they were reconciled to God the Father. He said by receiving him as saviour and Lord they would be in him and become part of this wonderful new relationship God was bringing to mankind. They listened intently to what Paul had to say.

Paul explained to them how God's original intention and purpose, before time began, even before he had created the world, was to have a family of sons and daughters.

"Right now, by being in Christ we are brought back into a new and special relationship with the Father as his sons," he said. Paul told them how Jesus had forgiven all his sins. How he had been baptised and his baptism meant he was in Christ Jesus. As Paul spoke these words the truth began to come alive in them.

"You know we are all sons of God through the faithfulness of Jesus. What he did has brought us back into relationship with the Father. When we are baptised, we are baptised into him. All the Father said to Jesus at his baptism he says to us. We too are his beloved sons, and he is proud of us. He clothes us in him. Like our own sons, at the son placing ceremony, we wear the toga of sonship, we wear the ring of sonship. We are completely united with him. It's not an issue of being a Jew or a Greek, man or woman, or even a slave or freeman. In Christ we all become one in him."

Paul looked around the room. There was Gaius, the wealthy God-fearing Greek, with his wife. Standing behind him were his children, his steward and household slaves all listening to Paul's words. Next to him sat Crispus the Jew, with his wife and their sons and daughters. This mixture of people were entering into Christ, they were becoming one. Then Paul said,

"Because you are sons, you are also heirs and you receive all the promises of Abraham's descendants. Through us all the nations of the Earth will be blessed. This is a message of hope for all of humanity."

As Paul finished speaking there was a heavy silence in the garden. Crispus was the first to speak.

"I want to be in Christ. I want to know God as my Father. I want to receive him as my Lord right now." His wife nodded her agreement and his son said, "I'm with my father, this is for all of us."

"Us too!" said Gaius standing holding his wife's hand. "Paul, can we be baptised now? Can we be clothed in Christ as you've promised?" Then to his amazement his chief steward who was a slave spoke,

"Excuse me, master, but may I be baptised too? May I be included also?" Gaius nodded and turned to Paul,

"We have a bath house attached to the side of the house. Can we be baptised now? All of us?"

"Of course!" said Paul, "Yes, let's do it now." They all stood and walked through the garden back into the house led by Gaius who showed them the entry to the small bath house. There were two pools in the bath house, one was the hot room and one the cold. Paul stepped down into the cool pool and helped them into the water. Before baptising them, he prayed over them as they stood in the water.

"Do you turn from your old life of sin and do you embrace Christ? Do you embrace Jesus as your Lord and saviour so that your sins will be forgiven and you will be united with the Father?" he asked each of them. Each by turn said this was what they wanted. So, Paul baptised them one after another. Before they came up out of the water, Paul said, "The Father says to you, you are my son. I love you and I'm so proud of you."

One by one, they came out the water and felt an overwhelming sense of the presence of God in the room. The power of God came upon them, and the Holy Spirit was poured into their hearts. Joy erupted in the room, laughter and songs burst from their lips. Some started to reach out their hands to worship the Father, to thank Jesus for all he had done for them. First, one, then another began speaking languages they had never heard before. Others knelt on the floor. There was a profound sense of worship in their hearts as the Holy Spirit was poured on them just as it had on that first day of Pentecost all those years before in Jerusalem.

They were not expecting this to happen and had no paradigm

for it. Paul knew he would have to explain what was happening to them at some point but for the moment they enjoyed the wonderful presence of the power of God flowing among them.

After a while, Gaius announced there was food for anyone who would like to eat and the whole event became a party. They celebrated their newfound faith, their love for God and the realisation of who they were in Christ. As they poured wine and broke bread together Paul told them the bread spoke powerfully of the broken body of Jesus and the red wine spoke of the blood shed for them by Jesus. They celebrated together in this new way and were amazed by all they had experienced.[44]

News spread about Crispus having accepted the teaching Paul was bringing and how he was now a believer in Jesus. Other members of the synagogue followed suit and soon there was a number wanting to hear more and to be baptised. Gaius regularly opened his home for people to gather as it was spacious and gave room for people to sit and talk. Paul encouraged Priscilla and Aquila to baptise people when they became believers.

Eventually, much to everyone's amazement, Crispus resigned as ruler of the synagogue. He was replaced by another man called Sosthenes who was equally interested in what Paul had to say and continued to allow him to speak on the Sabbath in the synagogue.

CORINTH FIRST VISIT AD 51 - 53

CHAPTER XI

Soon after Paul arrived in Corinth and it became clear to him he was going to stay for a while, he sent a message to Thessalonica to Silas and Timothy. He told them of the open door in Corinth and how he needed their help. He asked them to join him as soon as they could. About one month later, Silas and Timothy arrived from Macedonia. Paul was overjoyed and relieved. He introduced them to Aquila and Priscilla and the three of them sat down together to hear all the news from Macedonia.

It was good news. After Paul's untimely and speedy departure things had settled down. Silas reported the Pharisee Matthias was briefly in Thessalonica asking if anyone knew of Paul's whereabouts. The community had continued to grow and were following Paul's example of imitating the Lord.

Timothy reported how in the midst of severe suffering there was joy which he said was given by the Holy Spirit.

"What is so good, Paul, is the eagerness they have to take the message to outlying towns in Macedonia. They talk about their faith wherever they can."

Timothy was also pleased to bring a substantial gift of money from the believers in Philippi. Lucas had organised a collection and met with Timothy to make sure Paul got the money. They wanted to stand with him and free him from financial worry so he could continue to give himself to preaching the good news.

Paul confessed to his friends how hardly a day went by when he had not been thinking about them and praying for them in Macedonia. He said he felt like a nursing mother caring for her children. He realised in spite of his worries and fears, the Lord had been watching over and nurturing them. He wanted to tell them the one who had called them was indeed faithful and would continue to watch over them.

"They have very warm memories of you and long to see you as much as you also long to see them," said Timothy.

Paul listened with great interest to all the news and how they were standing firm in the Lord. Finally, he said, "I am going to write to them. This news really encourages me. I want them to know we are well and how their faith is a blessing to people all over Macedonia and also here in Achaia. Aquila, where can I get styluses and papyrus sheets?

"We can get them easily, no problem at all. First, let us sort out somewhere for these brothers to stay and let them rest a bit before you send them back with a letter," laughed Aquila.

"Timothy will you write while I dictate please?" asked Paul. Timothy looked surprised and said, "Of course I can try, but I have never done this before."

Aquila obtained all the writing materials needed and Gaius set Paul up in a room in his house. He provided a small table as a writing desk and there was a comfortable chair for Paul to sit in. Timothy readied the papyrus sheets and ink and prepared several styluses to begin writing the letter to the Thessalonian believers when Paul was ready to dictate.

"Now remember, Paul," said Silas, "He's never done this before. Don't speak too fast."

"I'm afraid I will make mistakes and we will be wasting the papyrus," added Timothy.

"You will be fine, Timothy, don't worry about it." Paul reached out and placed his hand on Timothy's shoulder. "You are often anxious and fearful about things. The Holy Spirit is with you. He will strengthen you. In your weakness his strength will help you. I'm learning to live like this too, you know."

"Okay, I'm ready." Timothy clutched the stylus in his hand. His hand shook slightly as he waited, looking anxiously at Paul for the first words.

"Paul, Silas and Timothy," Paul paused and said, "I'm sending this from all of us." Then he continued, "To the assembly of believers in Thessalonica who are in God the Father and the Lord Jesus Christ. Grace and peace to you."

"We always thank God for all of you and continually mention you in our prayers. We remember before our God and Father your work produced by faith, your labour prompted by love, and your endurance inspired by hope in our Lord Jesus Christ."

"Have you got that, Timothy? How was the speed? Not too fast I hope." Timothy hesitated and looked at Paul. "That's fine, though the ink is a bit thin. But it will do."

Paul continued, "Timothy has come to us from you and has brought good news about your faith and love. He has told us you always have pleasant memories of us and you long to see us, just as we also long to see you. Therefore, brothers and sisters, in all our distress and persecution we were encouraged about you because of your faith."[45]

As they worked together, Silas and Timothy kept interrupting with bits and pieces of news and things they wanted Paul to know. At one point, Silas asked Paul a question.

"You know, Paul, several of our friends in Thessalonica were very badly injured in the riots. Two did not recover from their wounds and died. People are wondering what to think. What happens to people who die after they have become believers in Jesus?"

Paul reflected a while, then said, "I will say something to them to encourage them in the letter. Ready to go on, Timothy?"

"Brothers and sisters, we do not want you to be uninformed about those who sleep in death, so that you do not grieve like the rest of mankind, who have no hope. For we believe Jesus died and rose again, and so we believe that God will bring with Jesus those who have fallen asleep in him. According to the Lord's word, we tell you we who are still alive, who are left until the coming of the Lord, will certainly not precede those who have fallen asleep. For the Lord himself will come down from heaven with a loud command, with the voice of the archangel and with the trumpet call of God, and the dead in Christ will rise first. After that, we who are still alive and are left will be caught up together with them in the clouds to meet the Lord in the air. And so we will be with the Lord forever. Therefore encourage one another with these words."[46]

"How does that sound, Silas?" he asked.

"I am sure it will really help. How do you know this will happen?" asked Silas.

"Do you remember I told you I have been shown things by the Lord Jesus. Things were revealed to me long ago when I was alone in Arabia and in the hills beyond Tarsus," answered Paul. He paused and looked into the distance. "I saw things I did not fully understand at the time. But now, as I am saying these things, it is as if the Holy Spirit reminds me of them and suddenly I see their significance. As I am dictating to Timothy, I sense the stirring or prompting of the Spirit. It's as if I hear the Father speaking and bringing them to my mind."

By late afternoon the letter was almost done. Paul drew it to a close.

"Rejoice always, pray continually, give thanks in all circumstances; for this is God's will for you in Christ Jesus. Do not quench the Spirit. Do not treat prophecies with contempt but test them all; hold on to what is good, reject every kind of evil. May God himself, the God of peace, sanctify you through and through. May your whole spirit, soul and body be kept blameless at the coming of our Lord Jesus Christ. The one who calls you is faithful, and he will do it. Brothers and sisters, pray for us. Greet all God's people with a holy kiss. I charge you before the Lord to have this letter read to all the brothers and sisters. The grace of our Lord Jesus Christ be with you."[47]

Paul stopped dictating, stood up and stretched. It was getting dark and writing by oil lamp was not easy. Timothy said he wanted to check it all and read it back to Paul to make sure everything was to his liking.

"Let's leave it for the day and look at it again in the morning," said Silas.

Paul was tired but satisfied. His letter to the Galatians written over two years previously had been very different in its tone. It was an urgent appeal to the readers to return to the true gospel and not to add anything to the truth. This letter came from his pastoral concern for these believers in Thessalonica.

The next morning as they gathered in Gaius' house to finish the letter and prepare it for sending, Gaius asked if he and Crispus could listen as Timothy read the letter aloud while Paul checked its content. Paul willingly agreed.

Timothy began, and it did not take long for them to finish the reading. When he put the papyrus sheets down, they looked at one another. Crispus spoke first.

"Paul, this is so encouraging. Would it be possible for you to make a copy of it before it is sent so we can have a copy here in Corinth? In fact, we have been talking about your letter to the Galatians. Can we get a copy of it?"

Paul thought for a few moments then said, "I am going to send a message to Titus in Galatia. I want to ask him to come to us here and to make a copy of the letter to bring with him when he comes."

Three days later the letter was ready to be sent to Thessalonica. Gaius had offered the services of one of his trusted slaves to courier the letter. Silas said it had taken him and Timothy two weeks to walk to Corinth from Thessalonica so it was agreed the young man would set off the next day. A copy had been produced by Timothy for the believers in Corinth to keep. The courier was instructed to place it into the hands of Jason personally.

CHAPTER XII

The gift the Philippians had sent enabled Paul to devote himself exclusively to preaching. The synagogue had been very open to Paul and his team for many weeks. Paul particularly sought to explain to the Jews that Jesus was the Messiah. Not all were open to what he had to say, however. Over the previous few months a number of significant members of the synagogue had become enthusiastic advocates of Paul's teaching but this alarmed some of the others.

One Sabbath as Paul was invited by Sosthenes, the new ruler to address the congregation, a group of men stood and began shouting at Sosthenes and Paul. They demanded Paul be stripped and given the forty lashes less one on account of his blasphemy. They grabbed him and a scuffle broke out. They started to rip his clothes off to have him whipped. They shouted and verbally abused him. Sosthenes and a number of others managed to pull Paul away from the men. Paul picking up his torn clothes shook them out in protest. "Your blood be on your own heads!" he proclaimed. "I'm innocent of it. From now on I will go to the Gentiles."

With that, Paul, followed by a number of others, left the synagogue and went next door to the house of Gaius Titius Justus. Crispus, the former synagogue leader, and his entire household also left and joined the group.[48]

CORINTH FIRST VISIT AD 51 - 53

One of the results of leaving the synagogue was many of the pagan Corinthians who heard Paul believed and were baptized. Before very long Sosthenes also converted and became a follower of Jesus.

The expulsion from the synagogue deeply upset Paul. He vacillated between feeling militant and full of faith and feeling disappointment and great sadness over the way his own people had rejected his message. Sometimes he was concerned his opponent Matthias would arrive in Corinth and try to undo all the progress made. He found himself lying awake at night anxiously turning over various scenarios in his mind. One of those nights when he was in a half-awake half-asleep phase, he felt Jesus' presence in the room. The Lord spoke to Paul this time in a vision: "Do not be afraid; keep on speaking, do not be silent. For I am with you, and no one is going to attack and harm you, because I have many people in this city." When he awoke in the morning, he had deep sense of peace and reassurance.[49]

About that time the newly appointed Proconsul for Achaia, Lucius Junius Gallio, a high ranking Roman senator and brother of the famous writer Seneca arrived in Corinth. He was a personal friend of the Emperor Claudius.

His arrival was planned to coincide with the Isthmian Games which were held in Corinth every two years. Athletes gathered from all over Achaia and Macedonia for the Games. The prestige of these games drew athletes from Rome and other areas where there were large Greek communities. Many people travelled to Corinth to watch the games as well as to participate. Local people took time off work and many who were slaves were also allowed to attend the games. The prostitutes attached to the Temple of Aphrodite did a roaring trade.

CORINTH FIRST VISIT AD 51 - 53

The believers in Corinth saw this as a great opportunity to mix with the crowds and share the good news about Jesus. Gaius opened his home to visitors who wanted to talk in a less busy context than at the stadium. Hundreds of Corinthians were contacted during the games not least some of the infamous prostitutes from the Temple of Aphrodite. Some of the boys who were attached to the Temple of Apollo also became believers.

When the believers met together they crowded into Gaius' house along with other houses in the city. Paul looked around the room one day and saw people who had been formerly sexually promiscuous, idol worshippers, adulterers, male and female prostitutes and sex slaves, homosexuals, thieves, slaves and slave owners, drunkards and swindlers, rich people and poor people. This was the community of believers in Corinth. These people, whom the world had judged and condemned were now inheritors of the kingdom of God. They had been washed, sanctified, and were made whole and welcomed in the name of the Lord Jesus Christ and by the Spirit of God. Paul delighted in telling them nothing separated them from the love of God the Father and they were one in Christ.

Unbeknown to Paul some Jews arrived in Corinth towards the end of the Games led by Matthias from Jerusalem. He had developed an extensive network of informers and contacts across the Greek speaking Jewish world. His spies reported Paul had been in Corinth for some time, so he had taken a ship to Corinth with two young Pharisees from Jerusalem. His personal allegiance to Jesus as the Messiah was still important to him, but his judgement was coloured by his personal animosity towards Paul. He had one overriding obsession; he was determined to destroy Paul. His plan was to try to persuade the leaders of the local synagogue to expose Paul and if possible draw the imperial authorities into the mix by trying to get a judgement made that might result in a death sentence.

Matthias lay low for a few days to discover the extent of Paul's influence in the city. He started asking questions and discovered the leader of one of the synagogues, Sosthenes was very sympathetic and supportive of Paul. He also quickly learned the new proconsul of Achaia, Gallio was the sort of man who wanted to make an impression.

One evening Matthias made his way to a Jewish owned tavern and sat in a darkened corner with his accomplices listening to the chatter and banter of the drinkers. As the wine flowed and the talk became rowdier, he picked up a comment about Paul. Clearly not everyone was happy with the situation. These were not men who had much of an idea about the content of Paul's message rather they were jealous of his popularity. Matthias saw his opportunity.

"Let me buy the next round. One for everyone?" Matthias was suddenly everyone's best friend.

"How much longer are you going to tolerate this man Paul? He is a known law breaker, a Roman law breaker. Unless he is stopped we run the risk of losing our special status as Jews in this city and Gallio will punish us for tolerating this blasphemous law breaker among us."

The mood in the tavern turned ugly. Someone shouted they must get rid of Paul then and there. The man said they should go to the house of the leader of the synagogue and demand Paul be arrested. Some were eager to see him lynched, but Matthias calmed them down and said a cool head was needed rather than mob violence.

"Regroup in the morning, then go and seize Paul and take him to the Proconsul with a very specific accusation. You need to be clear as to what you are accusing him of. Clearly, he is a law breaker and the Proconsul will want to stamp that out. We need to get Gallio to condemn him under Roman law," Matthias said. There was cheering and agreement and someone ordered another round of drinks.

The next morning a large group gathered at the tavern. Matthias was there with a number of men he had met the night before. They divided into two groups. One group was sent to alert the Proconsul's staff there was trouble brewing. The second group went to look for Paul. They found him coming out of Gaius' house with Sosthenes. They grabbed both of them, dragging them into the Forum to the Proconsul's office in the Julian Basilica.

Matthias had ensured there was already a crowd gathering. It was not just Jews who opposed Paul but as was always the case, ruffians and thugs with nothing better to do than cause trouble and get into a fight. Paul and Sosthenes were dragged forward and brought to the place of judgement outside the newly built basilica at the eastern end of the Forum. Gallio finally appeared along with some other city officials to find out what was happening. He looked at the two somewhat bedraggled prisoners who stood in front of him. Blood was dripping from Paul's nose and Sosthenes nursed a cut on his head. A well-dressed man who was probably a lawyer stepped forward and asked permission to speak to the Proconsul. Gallio waved his hand for silence.

"What is this commotion about? What are these men accused of that requires my attention?"

"This man," said the lawyer pointing at Paul, "is persuading the people to worship God in ways contrary to the law."

Just as Paul was about to speak, Gallio said to them, "If you Jews were making a complaint about some misdemeanour or serious crime, it would be reasonable for me to listen to you. But since it involves questions about words and names and your own law, settle the matter yourselves. I will not be a judge of such things." He turned to his guards and commanded them to clear the hall. The guards started to drive them all out into the Forum. As they did so, the crowd of thugs, disappointed there was no punishment, turned on Sosthenes and started to beat him up in front of the proconsul. Gallio showing no concern whatsoever turned on his heel and disappeared back into his office.(50)

Two guards grabbed Paul and dragged him back inside the basilica. He thought he was about to be thrown into prison or beaten again and maybe even killed. To his surprise one of the officials who had come out with Gallio approached him.

"Quickly!" he said, "come with me, you will be safe."

"Thank you," said Paul. "What about my friend Sosthenes?"

"I have others who will get him, don't worry," said the official.

"Who are you?" asked Paul.

"My name is Erastus, I am the city treasurer."

Erastus dismissed the guards. "Follow me," he said to Paul. They went along several corridors. Erastus opened a door and invited Paul into his office. Two scribes who were in the office working stood when Erastus entered. They eyed Paul suspiciously.

"Leave us and send my slave to me with a bowl of water," Erastus said to the scribes. He turned to Paul. "Please sit down. Can I get you something to drink? Are you hurt at all? I have water coming so we can sort out your nose. I hope it is not broken."

Paul was relieved as he sat in the chair. Soon a slave arrived with a bowl and towels, and he was able to clean himself up. He looked at Erastus.

"Why are you doing this for me?" he asked.

"Well, you probably don't recognise me in my fine clothes. I have been to Gaius Justus' house a couple of times. I came with Archaicus here, my slave. I dressed as a slave because I did not want to draw attention to myself. I know Gaius and he said I could slip in the back. I wanted to hear what you had to say for myself."

"This is amazing, Erastus. I did not recognise you at all, but now I remember you being there. I just thought you were slaves!"

"You know, Paul, I am a Roman citizen. I have status and an office here as the steward of the city's finances. I am important. But after I heard you speak I realised I have been a slave all my life, in my heart! A slave to my need for recognition, acceptance, and my own struggles. But I have to say this to you, I know who I really am now. I am a son, I am in Christ and God is my Father. Both of us, Archaicus my slave and I, we are followers of Jesus. I wanted you to know this."

Paul's eyes welled up as Erastus spoke. "I had no idea! I am delighted and I understand the delicacy of your situation. Would you feel you could come and meet with us at Gaius' house? In fact it would be wonderful for you to be baptised too."

"We would love to. Wouldn't we, Archaicus?" said Erastus.

Archaicus looked at his master and nodded. He looked slightly awkward.

"What is the matter?" asked his master.

"Well, I am a slave; it will be difficult for me."

"No! Stop saying that. I have been thinking about this for some days now. As from this moment, you are no longer a slave. I have prepared a document and I was waiting for the right moment to give it to you." He walked to his desk and picked up a scroll.

"This is your certificate of manumission. From this moment, Archaicus, you are my freedman. You remember what Paul said last time we were at Gaius' house? 'We are all one in Christ Jesus, there is neither slave nor freemen.' Archaicus, you are my brother."

Archaicus could not hold back his tears and sunk to the floor sobbing. Erastus walked over to him and squatted on the floor beside him. Paul also knelt next to Archaicus and put his arms around him and held him as he wept.

"Father," said Paul as he held the young man, "let my arms be your arms around your dear son and pour you wonderful love into him. May he know the height and depth and width and length of your love."

Out in the Forum the riffraff and mob had finally dispersed after having attacked a number of the members of the Jewish community. Sosthenes had taken the brunt of their attack. Stephanas and several of the believers found him curled up at the foot of the statue of the Emperor Claudius in the forum. He had been beaten within an inch of his life and was seriously hurt. They carefully picked him up and carried him home. His jaw looked as if it might be broken and his eyes were so swollen he could not open them. Terrified, his wife had bolted the door and on peeping out through the security grill, let out a frightened cry when she saw her husband. Friends inside the house opened the door and let them in. Crispus and Gaius came along with Aquila and Priscilla to find out what was going on.

"Is Paul with you?" asked Priscilla.

"No! He seems to have disappeared. No one has seen him. The last glimpse we had of him was at the basilica and we saw him being dragged off by some guards," said a man called Fortunatus.

Priscilla took charge of the situation straight away. She instructed Fortunatus to go and fetch a physician to attend to Sosthenes' injuries. He had been taken to his bedchamber by his wife and some of the servants. Priscilla turned to Gaius and asked him to go to the basilica and see if he could find out anything about Paul's whereabouts. He was about to leave when there was banging on the street door. Everyone froze and anxiously looked at one another. One of the household servants went towards the door to carefully look out to see who was outside. He ran back and said,

"It's one of the city officials. He has guards with him!" There was more banging on the door. Priscilla said, "I'll go to the door, they will think I am the lady the house. Everyone else go and wait in the dining room." She went with the servant to the door. A few minutes later she reappeared and walked into the triclinium where the others were waiting. They all looked up in amazement. Priscilla stood there with Paul and the city treasurer Erastus and Archaicus. Two bodyguards stood behind them.

There was more banging on the door, and this time it was Timothy and Silas who had also been out looking for Paul. Soon many had gathered in the house and Paul was introducing Erastus and his newly manumitted freedman Archaicus as brothers. Among them, there was a great sense of relief that Paul had not been arrested or injured. A doctor arrived and Priscilla took him to Sosthenes and his wife while the others prayed for him.⁽⁵¹⁾

Priscilla and Aquila stayed the night with Sosthenes and his family. They all agreed to lay low for a few days but to meet again on the afternoon of the Sabbath at Gaius' house.

Across the city in a tavern sat a very angry Matthias. His carefully orchestrated plan had failed and once again Paul had slipped through his fingers. He had seen the way the Proconsul had quickly dismissed the accusations made against Paul and had virtually, by default, given Paul a free hand to continue his work in the city. Matthias was obsessively angry with Paul, yet every time he tried to act, his plans seemed to backfire and Paul lived to see another day. As he thought about things, he wondered if there was another way. Perhaps he could stop Paul's activity by getting others to do his work for him. He remembered the Pharisees he worked with in Jerusalem who had visited Antioch and Galatia and who sought to call people back to a more authentically Jewish expression of following Jesus. He realised his own personal vendetta against Paul had clouded his thinking. To stop Paul, he needed to be smarter and more careful.

A few days later, he slipped out of Corinth determined to return to Jerusalem to talk with those who felt as he did about Paul's teaching. A plan was forming in his mind. If he could catch Paul when he was in Jerusalem, he believed there was a far better chance of silencing him once and for all. It would take time, but he had time. He was sure at some point Paul would visit Jerusalem. When he did, he would be ready for him and there would be no friendly Gentiles around to protect him.

CHAPTER XIII

When the believers met on the Sabbath, there was good news. The trouble in the city had blown over. Friends in the Jewish community had reported a Pharisee from Jerusalem had been the main instigator of the trouble. They said his name was Matthias but he was believed to have left the city.

Sosthenes was considerably better and his injuries were healing much to everyone's relief. Many of the believers gathered at Gaius' house as usual. Since the weather was warm and sunny, everyone crowded into the garden under the peristyle and the awnings Gaius' servants had erected.

Erastus and Archaicus sat side by side. Fortunatus helped Sosthenes in as everyone clapped and welcomed him and his wife. Aquila and Priscilla were welcoming newcomers when Paul, Timothy and Silas walked in eagerly talking with a young Greek man who was new to the group. Paul called for silence.

"Friends, I am delighted to introduce you to our very dear friend and co-worker from Galatia. This is Titus."

Everyone turned to look at the young man who was grinning from ear to ear. Under his arm he clutched a scroll. People welcomed him and he found a seat.

"Titus has had a long journey and has come all the way from Lystra on the overland route. He comes with news from Troas, Philippi and Thessalonica. And he has brought with him a copy of the letter I wrote some time ago to the believers in Galatia. You are most welcome, my dear friend." Paul embraced Titus warmly.

Priscilla stood in the middle of the garden and everyone looked towards her. She invited Titus to share news of the other communities. When he finished speaking, the whole gathering spontaneously broke into worship and praise on account of the news. One after another prayed or sang. After some time, Priscilla brought a prophetic message to the group which she believed God had given her. Then she explained what was in her heart and how it was reflected in a section of one of the Psalms in the Jewish Scriptures. Everyone listened intently as she spoke to the group. They recognised there was a weight of authority in her words. Paul said nothing throughout the meeting, but at the end he stood up and went to her and hugged her affectionately.

During the following week Titus was able to share with Paul in detail the news from the communities he had visited. Whilst stopping in Thessalonica on his journey he heard talk about the return of the Jesus which Paul had mentioned in his recent letter to them.

"At one of their gatherings someone shared a teaching suggesting Jesus had returned already. The speaker said the source of his teaching was a prophetic word he had received from God and had been sanctioned by you, Paul. It was confusing and didn't sound at all like anything you would say."

This news so concerned Paul, he decided he would write another letter to them to address this and a number of other matters Titus had reported. As before, he dictated the letter to Timothy who acted as the amanuensis. He began writing about the day of the Lord's return.

"Concerning the coming of our Lord Jesus Christ and our being gathered to him, we ask you, brothers and sisters, not to become easily unsettled or alarmed by the teaching allegedly from us, whether by a prophecy or by word of mouth or by letter, asserting that the day of the Lord has already come.

"Don't let anyone deceive you in any way, for that day will not come until the rebellion occurs and the man of lawlessness is revealed, the man doomed to destruction. He will oppose and will exalt himself over everything that is called God or is worshiped, so that he sets himself up in God's temple, proclaiming himself to be God.

"Don't you remember that when I was with you I used to tell you these things?" He paused to allow Timothy to catch up and checked a word with him.

"I remember you saying these things when we were there. Who do you think the 'man of lawlessness' is? Do you think it's the emperor?" asked Silas.

"I am not sure at all," said Paul. "I saw a vision one time. I was seeing things in my spirit, mysteries I could only glimpse what they might mean. They were about the end times just before Jesus returns. I felt at some time in the future there would be a great final confrontation between we followers of Jesus and the world system, the kingdom of darkness, Satan's realm. What I saw gave me great hope and a longing for Jesus to return. I was not shown any sense of when this would happen. Barnabas once told me Jesus said his return would be when least expected, like a thief in the night. So as far as our friends in Thessalonica are concerned, I want them to be encouraged and know God's eternal kingdom and his sovereign rule will ultimately triumph."

Paul carried on dictating and sharing his perspective on these events which he saw unfolding in the future. Finally, he drew the letter to a close and went over to Timothy. He looked at the characters on the page in front of him and lifted them close to his eyes to read them. He took the stylus out of Timothy's hand and squinted at the sheet of papyrus as he tried to focus.

"I want to write something in my own hand." Bending over, he spoke aloud and began writing,

"I, Paul, write this greeting in my own hand, which is the distinguishing mark in all my letters. This is how I write. The grace of our Lord Jesus Christ be with you all."

As before Timothy carefully copied out the letter so it could be left with the believers in Corinth. In a couple of days, it was ready to be sent off. Titus requested copies of both Paul's letters written to Thessalonica for Galatia.

"Our friends in Thessalonica would benefit from a copy of your Galatian letter as well," Silas added. Paul had thought carefully about this, and he asked Silas to sit with him.[52]

"My good friend, I have been thinking about you and our dear friends up in Macedonia and particularly Thessalonica." He paused and looked closely at Silas.

Silas looked at him, "No need to say anything. I have been feeling for some time I should carry this letter to Thessalonica and stay there and help them. Father has been speaking to my heart about this. I was going to talk to you about it, but it appears he may have been talking to you already."

Both men had a sense this was the Father's plan.

A few days later Silas packed up his things and with the newly written letter set off for the long journey north to Macedonia and Thessalonica. There were tearful partings for the group of friends.

"I will see you again soon, Silvanus," said Paul as he waved him off. "Tell the brothers and sisters I will come again myself as soon as I can."

The increase in numbers of believers in Corinth necessitated meeting in several homes across the city. Gaius Justus' house was too small to hold all those who wanted to gather. One of the groups met in the home of a wealthy woman named Chloe.

After Silas left, Paul walked one afternoon through the city. He had been in Corinth for a year and a half, teaching the word of God at every opportunity. In almost every street someone stopped and greeted him. A youth came up to him and greeted him warmly. He told Paul he was a follower of Jesus. Paul did not know him by name, and the boy started to tell Paul his story. Purchased as a child slave by a rich Greek merchant, he did not remember where he came from. His fair hair and complexion suggested he was from Germania beyond the border of the Empire in the north. Soon after entering puberty, his master recognising his value as a pretty boy sold him to the Temple of Apollo in the city centre. He was now in his mid-teens and was an attractive and sought-after young man. He had worked ever since as a sex slave at the Temple servicing the gratifications of devotees of Apollo. His life had been brutal as all manner of sexual activity was required of him.

"What is your name, my son?" asked Paul.

"They call me Apelles at the Temple, but I think my birth name was something else. I can hear my father calling me Vincto or something like that. It's all I can remember really. My father and mother were killed by the Romans long ago and far away. I really don't know who I am now."

A tear welled up and rolled down his cheek as he spoke, and Paul put his hand on his shoulder, guiding him to a bench near the Fountain of Peirene in the Forum.

Fear clouded the boy's eyes as he looked at Paul. Paul looked at him and realised what was going on inside the boy's mind and took his hand off his shoulder. "There is no need to be afraid of me, Apelles. I want nothing of you. You are safe with me. So, you became a follower of Jesus?"

"Yes, some weeks ago, a woman at the place where I live told me about Jesus. She used to be one of Aphrodite's girls up on the Acrocorinth. She started going to gatherings at the house of a woman called Chloe who is helping her get away from her life as a prostitute. She's now working as a servant in Chloe's house. I went with her to one of those meetings when you were speaking. That's how I knew who you were. I became a follower of Jesus about a month ago and was baptised not long after."

"What are you doing now? asked Paul.

Again, tears welled up in Apelles' eyes as he struggled to speak. "It's so difficult. I have to pay for my room in a stinking brothel from my earnings. I can't stop working. I am a slave; my owner takes most of everything I earn. I'm trapped. Every time a man comes to me and demands my services my heart breaks. It never used to before. I just did what I had to do. I had convinced myself this was my lot in life and I have to make the best of it. But now…Sometimes men are kind to me and I cope somehow. Other times…" Tears flowed freely and he tried to dry his face on his sleeve.

"Some men can be brutal. I don't know how long I can survive like this. I know a number of boys who have killed themselves. The problem is the prettier you are, the more you are in demand. One day I decided to burn my face but I couldn't do it." Paul put his arm around him, and he buried his face into Paul's shoulder and sobbed.

People in the Forum stopped to look at what was happening, and Paul suggested they go to Chloe's house to continue their talk. On arriving, Chloe's steward welcomed them and showed them to a quiet room. Paul asked if they could have some food and in a few minutes Chloe herself arrived with a tray.

"Paul, what a lovely surprise! And Apelles? What are you doing here?" she asked as she looked at Apelles' grubby tear stained face. Paul explained and asked Chloe to sit with them while Apelles continued his story. It all poured out. Apelles said he felt dirty and defiled. He wanted to break away but could see no way forward in this. After some time, Paul spoke.

"You know, Apelles, you are God's temple and God's Spirit lives in you. Your body is a temple of the Holy Spirit. You are not your own; you were bought with a price. You may have been sold as a sex slave at the Temple of Apollo. But you have been redeemed by Jesus. He washed you clean. You are now sanctified, you are justified in the name of the Lord Jesus Christ and by the Spirit of our God. This is who you are now. Your true identity is now in Christ. This is why your physical body reacts to what is happening to you when you work at the Temple of Apollo."

"I think we need to find a way of getting you out of there," continued Paul.

"But how? If I run away they will come after me. I will be caught and I will end up as food for the lions in the arena or practice material for the gladiators after they have had their way with me. That would be worse than now." Again, he sobbed deeply.

"I have an idea," said Chloe. "I have a girl working for me who used to be a prostitute in the city. I can't take on any more staff here, but I have a relative in Rome who is a believer. He may have room in his household. We could find out how much it would cost to get him released from the temple and then I could send him to Rome to start a new life in that city.

"Wouldn't it look like you bought him because he was pretty? What if he just disappeared?" asked Paul. "People go missing all the time."

"I don't know, we need to think about this. I don't care what people think about me. I'd rather pay than have some slave hunter track him down in Rome one day," said Chloe.

A day later Chloe accompanied by Apelles arrived at Priscilla and Aquila's workshop looking for Paul. They all went upstairs to hear what had happened.

"This is a very expensive young man!" said Chloe. Apelles blushed deeply.

"Effectively, he is my slave now. Of course, it is not how I see it, but I have all the paperwork done. He never has to go back to that abominable Temple again. Apparently, he is a highly sought-after commodity on account of his good looks." Chloe said with a smile. "But I still think he needs to leave Corinth as he is easily recognised in the city, and I think he needs a fresh start. So, I am willing to send him to my relatives in Rome."

"Who do you know in Rome?" asked Priscilla, "We may know them."

"Narcissus," said Chloe, "he is my brother."

"Oh yes. We know him well. I had no idea! Then of course there is Andronicus and Junia who are Paul's relatives too. Oh, Apelles! There is a whole new family waiting for you!"

"And you can take letters from me to my relatives," said Paul. "I want them to have copies of the two letters I have written to Thessalonica and also the one I wrote a few years ago to the Galatians. They might find them helpful."

Apelles was overwhelmed with the news and the events of the last twenty-four hours. His life was about to take on a very different path.[53]

Not long after Apelles left for Rome, Paul gathered Timothy, Titus, Aquila and Priscilla together one evening to talk to them about a plan which was forming in his heart.

"For some time now," began Paul, "I have been thinking about returning to Jerusalem and Antioch to report back on all that has happened in Asia Minor, Macedonia and here in Achaia. It's been four years since I was in Jerusalem and not much less since Silas and I left Antioch. I'm eager to hear how things are in the East. In particular, I have a longing to go to Jerusalem and stand in the temple again."

"What do you have in mind, Paul?" asked Titus. "Why Jerusalem, after the way you have been treated by your own countrymen?"

"It is exactly because they are my countrymen. I long for them to know the truth about Jesus the Messiah, the hope of Israel. I long for Israel to be saved and know God almighty as their true Father as we do. I often think of the words Jeremiah the prophet spoke long ago,

"I myself said, 'How gladly would I treat you like sons and give you a pleasant land, the most beautiful inheritance of any nation. I thought you would call me 'Father' and not turn away from following me.'"(54)

"It has been on my mind so much of late. In fact I have vowed to God I will have my head shaved and by the time it has grown again I will be standing in the temple precincts in Jerusalem." Paul folded his arms which was his way of saying, 'No discussion.'

Titus started to speak and then stopped. A look from Aquila said, "Don't go there." Titus shrugged his shoulders and looked at Timothy who was also looking mystified. They knew with Paul there were times when he was going to do what he was going to do and there was no point in arguing.

"I want to talk also about you four," said Paul after some moments of silence.

"The work here in Corinth is growing and is spreading to other cities and towns across Achaia. It is very encouraging. We are seeing a wonderful group of gifted and anointed men and women emerging who are leading these communities. People like Crispus, Chloe, Gaius and Sosthenes really carry the revelation in their hearts. We need them to stay and continue to encourage the brothers and sisters here. Erastus is another key man. I have my eye on him. I am wondering if he will stay on as City treasurer much longer."

"I don't plan to stay away from Corinth forever, there are other places on my heart I want to see filled with the good news about Jesus. When I look at some of the key cities in the East, it is from these places the gospel has spread into their provinces. Look at Antioch in Syria, Thessalonica in Macedonia and here in Corinth in Achaia. There is one major city in the East as yet untouched."

"Ephesus!" said Priscilla. "It is the key city in the whole of Asia Minor."

"Exactly, said Paul. "I have been thinking we could go to Ephesus from here."

"I thought you planned to go to Jerusalem?" said Timothy.

"I do, but I think we should go via Ephesus. The spring is almost here and sea travel will be starting again soon. My idea is we five go to Ephesus first. Then perhaps Aquila and Priscilla, you stay there and establish your business and break ground in the city in the way you did here in Corinth. How do you feel about that?" Paul asked.

"It makes sense to me." Aquila replied. "We have business contacts in Ephesus already. I have been thinking about expanding the business lately as it is such a helpful way of raising resources to fund the bigger mission we share. You know me well, Paul. I am a businessman and love to release funds to help you and the others." The couple looked at each other and nodded.

"Priscilla is gifted in other ways," added Aquila looking at his wife. "She has a heart to see the believers established and grow. She is like a mother to so many, particularly the young slaves in our community. You have heard her speak many times. Her words carry great weight and anointing." He smiled proudly at his wife who looked slightly embarrassed.

"It seems good to me and the Holy Spirit that you two come with us as far as Ephesus. You can also keep in touch with how things are here in Corinth as it is just across the sea," said Paul

"We agree with this plan, Paul," said Priscilla. "And you, Aquila! You are a sweetie!" She started to giggle at Aquila.

"Oh please, you two! Enough already," said Titus as they all laughed. "What about me and Timo? Can we come with you to Jerusalem?"

"I have been thinking you two boys might like to accompany me to Jerusalem. My sister and her family are in the city, and I would like to see them. We might see Cephas, I mean Peter, and probably James."

Paul paused and his face clouded slightly.

"Who knows, I might even bump into Barnabas somewhere along the way? Then we could go up to Antioch and see everyone there before heading back through Galatia to Ephesus. More to the point, you can see your families and friends on the way. How does that sound?"

"I have longed to visit Jerusalem all my life," said Timothy, "and now since my 'operation', I will be allowed to even go into the Temple. If we take the overland route through Galatia, we will be able to visit my mother and grandmother. I think it is a good plan. Count me in."

"Me too, just as long as I'm not required to have the operation. I don't need to go into the Temple," grinned Titus. "When do we leave, Paul?"

"I think we should wait a few more weeks until the worst of the winter weather is over. I would also like to send a message to Silas

CORINTH FIRST VISIT AD 51 - 53

and Lucas up in Macedonia, so they know what we are thinking and where we are."

Six weeks later, many of the believers in Corinth gathered in Gaius' house to pray for the five friends before they set out on their journey eastwards. They had collected money together to help on the journey, to get passages by ship and for them to stay in inns along the way when needed.

Erastus spoke on behalf of them all. "We will miss you dreadfully and long for your return. All of us here owe you so much. Our hearts are knitted together with your hearts." There was murmurs of agreement from all.

"When you arrived here, Paul, you were so weak and physically broken after all your troubles up in Macedonia. But in your weakness the power of God was revealed to us. We owe you our very lives. Thank you."

Murmurs of approval came from everyone. "God's speed and may you travel safely. Be careful too. We know there are people out there who want to destroy the good work our Father is doing. But he is with you. You are in our prayers. If you ever need any of us to help you, just say the word and we will come." There was loud applause at Erastus' words and they gathered around to hug and kiss them.

The next day, they left Corinth and went down to the port of Cenchreae. Priscilla went to the house of Phoebe, one of the leaders in the community to arrange last minute food supplies to take with them. Paul sent Aquila and the two young men to the harbour to secure passage on a ship, and he went off into town on his own. They gathered in Phoebe's home to spend a night before sailing. Paul sat down and he took off his traveling scarf from around his head. To their surprise they saw he had indeed had his head shaved because of his vow. Titus looked as if he was going to say something but Priscilla's look said, "Don't say a word."[55]

EPHESUS AD 52

CHAPTER XIV

Four days later the ship entered the Gulf of Ephesus and slowly approached the quayside. The port was protected by a massive artificial breakwater shielding it from the worst of the winter weather. It was crowded with ships of all sizes from all parts of the Mediterranean Sea. The city sprawled over the surrounding hills built from local limestone. Many of the buildings were faced with white marble which made the whole city dazzle in the sunlight. In the distance Paul spotted a huge temple complex which he guessed was the fabled Temple of Artemis. In the city itself, cut into the side of a hill was a huge amphitheatre. The biggest he had ever seen.

As soon as they disembarked, Priscilla and Aquila went ahead and sought out their business contacts in the city. Paul along with Titus and Timothy walked from the harbour along the column lined magnificent Arcadian Way which led into the city centre. Passing the huge amphitheatre to their right, they wandered around the city and found a synagogue. They had agreed to meet Aquila and Priscilla later in the day by the entrance of the amphitheatre.

Aquila and Priscilla were welcomed warmly by their business contacts and they secured a shop and workshop with rooms attached where they could base themselves. They met up as agreed, and Aquila took the three men to the lodgings he had secured for them. The Sabbath was two days away, so they decided to stay a few days.

EPHESUS AD 52

On the Sabbath, Paul went into the synagogue and debated with the Jews as he had done in every city where there was a synagogue. When they asked him to spend more time with them, he declined. But as he left, he promised,

"I will come back if it is God's will. In the meantime, my friends here will be staying in the city and they can speak on my behalf if you will let them."[56]

Three days later, he set sail again with Timothy and Titus. The spring winds were kind and within a few days they were sailing past the southern coast of the island of Cyprus. Within a few hours and with a strong easterly wind behind them they sighted the coast of Phoenicia. The ship turned south and made a speedy run down the coast to the large port of Caesarea.

Within days of Paul having left Ephesus, a Jewish man named Apollos, from Alexandria in Egypt arrived in the city. Alexandria had a large Jewish community, the biggest outside of Judea. There were many connections between the Alexandrian Jews and those in Judaea and Jerusalem. They were more Greek in their cultural outlook than most Jews within Israel but had a strong tradition of study and learning. Several hundred years earlier, a group of seventy Jewish scholars in Alexandria started work on a translation of the Jewish Scriptures into Greek which became the widely used Greek version of their Scriptures. This was Apollos' background as he was highly educated with a thorough knowledge of the Jewish Scriptures in both Greek and Hebrew. There had been a number of Alexandrian Jews in Jerusalem at the time of the death and resurrection of Jesus who became his followers. Apollos was one of them and he had become a follower of the way of the Lord as he put it. Whenever he got an opportunity, he spoke passionately and taught about Jesus' life and ministry. He had left Jerusalem before the day of Pentecost.[57]

As a result, he only knew of the baptism of John. There were big gaps in his understanding, but he was extremely enthusiastic. He found a synagogue in Ephesus made up of Alexandrian Jews. He eagerly attended the Sabbath meetings and was invited to speak. A number in this synagogue were open to what he was teaching and he met with them for some weeks. Eventually they asked Apollos to baptise them which he readily did. But he baptised them in the way John the Baptist had done as a sign of their repentance. He did not have any knowledge of the work of the Holy Spirit having left Jerusalem before the coming of the Holy Spirit on the day of Pentecost.

One Sabbath Apollos' enthusiasm took him to another of the synagogues in the city. His impressive presence inevitably led him to be invited to speak. Sitting in the congregation were Priscilla and Aquila and they listened intently to his teaching. From time to time they looked at each other with slightly raised eyebrows. Afterwards they whispered together at the back of the meeting room. It was clear to them he had some significant gaps in his knowledge and understanding of what they knew to be the message of Jesus. At the end of the meeting they approached him and introduced themselves. He was delighted to meet them as he realised they were also believers in Jesus the Messiah. They invited him to their home to share a meal. Over the meal he eagerly listened as they explained how they experienced the power of the Holy Spirit in their lives. They told him about Paul and filled in many of the gaps in his understanding. Over several days he spent as much time with them as he could, stitching tents in their workshop. After a few days he asked them to baptise him in the name of Jesus which they readily agreed to do.

EPHESUS AD 52

Apollos was an eager and enthusiastic student and very quickly grew in his faith and understanding. His particular gift was the ability to see how the coming of the Messiah was predicted in the Jewish Scriptures.

He had not intended to stay in Ephesus long as his original plan had always been to travel to Achaia in particular where he had relatives. When he told Aquila and the others he wanted to go to Achaia, they encouraged him. In order to ease his introduction, they wrote to the believers in Corinth to welcome him.

Within a very short time news filtered back to Ephesus that Apollos was a great help to the believers in Corinth. The reports said he was vigorously engaging in public debate with the Jews in the city, proving from the Scriptures that Jesus was the Messiah. He had an eager following of supporters and adherents among the believers in Corinth. Week after week, he spoke in the synagogue and argued persuasively. Many of the Jews and Greek God-fearers were convinced by his explanations. He was an engaging and likeable person, and people were attracted to his warm personality and outgoing nature. He was extremely handsome and many began to describe him as a 'super apostle', something he actively tried to discourage.[58]

JERUSALEM AND ANTIOCH
AD 52

CHAPTER XV

Meanwhile Paul and his two young companions landed at Caesarea. After they disembarked they went straight to Jerusalem without lingering in Caesarea. It was a hard three day walk uphill all the way, and they arrived at dusk on the third day feeling exhausted. However, Paul was elated to be back in the City of David where he had spent so much of his youth. He was glad it was dark when they arrived because he did not want to draw attention to himself. He looked very different to the young Pharisee who had studied in the School of Gamaliel. Now he was thirty-five years older. His body was more bent on account of the numerous beatings he received and the hardships he experienced. His hair, which was growing back, was grey and thinning. Hardly anyone would have recognised him. His sister was surprised at his arrival and welcomed them into her home. The next morning Paul asked his young nephew to take a message to where he thought the leaders of the local community of believers might be living.[59]

The boy returned an hour later saying James was at home and would receive him. Paul thought this was an odd way of putting it but he got ready to go. He asked Timothy and Titus to stay behind or take a look around the city and to not get into trouble. Paul wound his scarf around his head and shoulders and went off to see James.

James received him politely. Paul was surprised at the modest home in which James lived. It was so different to the spacious homes he was used to in Corinth and other cities. They broke bread together and started to share each other's news. James informed Paul the community in Jerusalem was struggling in many ways. Most of the original group of apostles had left in order to take the gospel across the empire and beyond its borders to distant lands and rarely came back to the city. James said,

"Simon, who calls himself Cephas or Peter these days, left some time ago to visit Rome. He is being seen as an important figure in Rome apparently."

When Paul excitedly recounted the beginnings of the community of believers in Corinth, James looked surprised.

"The last I heard Simon was planning to go to Corinth on his way to Rome."

When James talked about the believers in Jerusalem it became apparent the group was much smaller than it had been in the early days. It included a large number of dependant elderly widows and orphans. Paul remembered the awful persecution he had inflicted on them twenty years before.

"I don't think the people have ever recovered after what you did, Saul, sorry I mean Paul." James' words hung in the air. His face was hard and the conversation pierced Paul's heart.

"Most of the Hellenistic Jews who became Followers of the Way have all gone back to their own lands, and we are left with a group of very poor and needy people. Then as you know there has been a series of famines in Judea. Plus, the Zealots are making life very difficult for the occupying Romans. All in all, life is hard for us here. We have to provide regular food handouts, otherwise some would have nothing and would starve."

"When do you meet? Can I come and bring some word of encouragement to the people? I have two young men with me who I would like to introduce to you."

"Are they Gentiles?"

"One is, the other is half Gentile and half Jew, you will—"

"I think not!" interrupted James. "It would be too complicated. We have many members who were originally from the sect of the Pharisees who would have difficulty with them being present. They can be quite vocal at times. I do not want you to offend them any more than you have already."

"Do you know a man called Matthias, a former Pharisee?"

"Yes, why do you ask?"

"I keep coming across him on my travels. He often opposes me and stirs up trouble wherever he can. He claims to have the support and backing of the elders here."

"He is a law unto himself and does not speak for us. He is one of the most outspoken of the former Pharisees among us. All I would say is…" James hesitated and looked awkward, "be careful; he does not like you." With that James made it clear the meeting was over.

Paul was very saddened by the tone of the conversation with James and he agreed to come on his own and meet a handful of the believers who James would gather together. Later the same day, Paul met them and was astonished at the poverty exhibited by their clothes and appearance. He was saddened as he walked back to his sister's house but he felt a prompting in his heart, which he recognised was the Holy Spirit. By the time he got to the house he had decided to start a collection among the new communities in Achaia, Macedonia and Galatia to support and bless the believers in Jerusalem.

After a few days they left Jerusalem heading north for Antioch. They took the coast road and after two weeks arrived in Antioch. Three and a half years had passed since Paul left Antioch. His heart beat with excitement as they approached the walls on the south side of the city. This was Titus' home where he had grown up, and he was eager to find members of his family and friends. He told Timothy he had so many things to show him. The two young men headed off into the labyrinth of streets and alleys which made up the huge city. They agreed to meet at the home of Manaen, Paul's close friend and one of the leaders of the community in Antioch.[60]

Paul walked to Manaen's house and knocked on the door of the large domus. A doorkeeper appeared asking who he was as he did not recognise him. Paul was ushered into the vestibule and told to wait while the doorkeeper went off to call his master. In moments, Manaen came running through the atrium.

"Paul? Paul? Is it really you?" The two men embraced each other warmly and stood back looking at each other.

"It is so good to see you again, my friend," said Paul.

"I can't say you are looking well, Paul. Look at you. You look exhausted. Where have you come from? Is Silas with you?"

"I have been briefly in Jerusalem but before that I was in Corinth. It's been a long journey and I have much to tell you. But how are you and how is everything here in Antioch?

JERUSALEM AND ANTIOCH AD 52

"All is well here, my friend." Then Manaen paused and looked as if he was not sure how to continue.

"What is it, Manaen? Is something wrong?"

"No! Nothing is wrong at all. I am thrilled to see you here." He paused then looked intently at Paul. "There is someone here in my house who I know will be pleased to see you too."

Paul looked at Manaen, and then past him into the Atrium. He saw a figure in the shadows at the back of the atrium. Paul strained to see the figure who was slowly walking towards him.

"Hello, Paul," said a familiar voice.

"Barnabas? Barnabas, is that you?"

"Yes! It's me."

The two men stood looking at each other for a few moments, embraced each other, then both burst into tears. They walked into the garden of the house and sat down to talk. About two hours later, Timothy and Titus arrived at the house and Manaen brought them through to the garden. Titus had found Tychicus and brought him along to Manaen's house also to greet Paul who was very happy to see him again. Titus was delighted to see Barnabas and quickly realised he and Paul had been discussing some painful issues between them. Timothy remembered meeting Barnabas the first time he and Paul came to Lystra five years earlier. Very quickly they were all chatting together sharing stories and hearing about the way the message of Jesus was spreading.

As the afternoon became evening, Manaen announced dinner was ready and they went into the triclinium where Manaen's wife was waiting to greet them. Servants stood with foot basins for each guest and hand bowls also for each of them. Soon they were all reclining around the table as servants brought platters of food. Manaen was a wealthy man who had grown up in the Herodian royal family in Judea. The meal was served on beautiful glazed Samian-ware pottery and some of the platters were silver. Flickering oil lamps hung from candelabras in the corners of the room.

The meal was a wonderful reunion for them all. There was laughter at times and also moments of silence when Paul and Barnabas just looked at each other. Timothy commented on the particularly fine wine being served, which broke the silence. Towards the end of the meal, Paul who had been looking thoughtful spoke.

"I am sensing the Spirit wants to say something to us…" Everyone looked at Paul intently. "Now we are united with Christ, we have become a new creation. The old has gone, the new is here! All this is from God, who reconciled us to himself through Christ and has given us the ministry of reconciliation. God was reconciling the world to himself in Christ, not counting our sins against us."

They all listened closely to Paul's words and there were murmurs of agreement.

Paul took a mouthful of wine. "Timothy is right, this is excellent wine, Manaen. Is it Cypriot?" Manaen nodded and smiled, and they all drank together and agreed it was very good wine indeed. Then Paul continued,

"God our Father has committed to us this message of reconciliation. It is as if we are Christ's ambassadors, as though God himself is making his appeal through us. We are indeed God's co-workers."

Paul then looked straight at Barnabas. "My dear friend, I am so glad we have had a chance to talk and for us to be reconciled.

We are indeed God's co workers. I feel I have learned something through this about the nature of our ministry. I confess to you all, I felt sometimes my words were just words. But now I see how Father has been doing a work in my heart. I have longed for this day."

Barnabas looked at Paul and reached out across the table with his hand. Paul grasped it and they both smiled at each other. The others around the table murmured their approval and support for what happened.

"A new day," said Manaen, "a new day indeed."

Then they all raised their silver goblets and drank again.

After a few days Paul told Timothy he felt it was time to move on and head back to the west. He was eager to get back to Ephesus but wanted to visit as many of the groups of believers along the way as they could. He wanted to let them know about the needs of the believers in Jerusalem and start gathering an offering for these poor brothers and sisters. His plan was to take to the overland route from Antioch via Tarsus and then on through Galatia and Phrygia.

"Of course, we will go to Lystra so you can see your family, Timothy."

"Will Barnabas be coming with us?" asked Timothy.

"No, we have talked, and we both agree he is needed here in Antioch. The believers love him and he has a heart for them like a shepherd who looks after his sheep. He is able to get across to Cyprus easily from here. He has family on the island and knows the believers. We both feel it is right for him to stay here in Antioch. But I have asked Tychicus to join us in Ephesus. He thinks he will be able to come in a few months."

Many of the believers gathered together before they left Antioch, prayed for them and gave them a purse with money to help them on their journey. They set out from Antioch taking the Via Sebaste westward and travelled from place to place throughout the region of Cilicia visiting the groups of believers, then visited Iconium and Lystra. Timothy was particularly glad to spend time with his mother and grandmother. Titus was eager to stay behind to continue his visits to the outlying communities in the area while Paul and Timothy pressed on and went north into Phrygia. Paul asked Titus to join them in due course in Ephesus. Meanwhile they went on strengthening all the believers wherever they encountered them.[61]

The road through southern Phrygia turned due west into Asia. It passed through Colossae, Laodicea and Hierapolis. They stopped first in Colossae where they met a man named Epaphras. He was a Greek who had an interest in the Jewish faith and heard Paul speak at the synagogue. At the end of Paul's address, he approached Paul and Timothy and began to ply them with questions. The three of them walked to the forum in the city and found a shop selling food. They bought bread, olives, some dried fish, a jug of wine and sat on a bench to eat and enjoy the autumn sunshine. They talked all afternoon. As the sun began to set below the hills to the west of the city, Paul stood and said he and Timothy needed to go back to the Tavern of the Three Cockerels where they were staying. Epaphras wrinkled his nose and stood.

"My brother owns a hostelry on the main road into the city. You probably walked past it on your way into the city. You are welcome to stay with us there as long as you like. It is better than the tavern you are in, much cleaner and my sister-in-law's food is excellent," explained Epaphras.

JERUSALEM AND ANTIOCH AD 52

They went back to the tavern, collected their belongings and followed Epaphras to the hostelry. Paul looked up at the two storey domus occupying the corner of the insula. It was a large and impressive structure. Epaphras knocked and a slave opened the door.

"Ah, Onesimus, is my brother home?"

"Yes, sir," said the slave bowing, "he is in the bath house bathing. Shall I call him?"

"No, but I want you to take these two visitors to one of the guest rooms upstairs," said Epaphras. "Then inform your mistress they will be joining us for dinner." He turned to Paul and Timothy. "You are most welcome to stay as long as you need on one condition. Please tell my brother and his family what you have told me today. We are all God-fearers and long to know the truth. I hear hope in your words and I want to know this hope too."

An hour later the slave Onesimus knocked on their door and invited Paul and Timothy to join the family in the triclinium. He led them down the stairs and along a decorated corridor paved with a geometric mosaic. They entered the atrium where Epaphras was standing talking with three people. They all turned as Paul and Timothy entered.

"Paul, Timothy, you are both welcome! I would like to introduce you to my brother Philemon and Apphia, my sister-in-law. This is their son Archippus."

The family looked curiously at Paul and Timothy. Archippus was about the same age as Timothy. Philemon stepped forward and bowed. "You are most welcome in our home as our guests. Epaphras has been telling me some very interesting things. We want to hear all about it."

"But first we eat!" interrupted Apphia. She graciously waved towards the triclinium and led the way into the ornate dining room. The walls were decorated with the latest fashionable colours with panels depicting animal hunting scenes. The guests all reclined on couches around the central table which was laid out with several dishes of fine foods. Paul reclined between Philemon and Apphia as the guest of honour.[62]

A week later a small gathering of people met in Philemon and Apphia's house. Among them was their son Archippus, Epaphras and their slave Onesimus and a woman named Nympha who was Apphia's sister from Laodicea. Paul and Timothy had spent the week sharing with them the message about Jesus being the son of God and how God was their Father. As the week unfolded they had eagerly accepted his words, and on this night, they gathered together in order to be baptised as believers in Philemon's private bath house. After he baptised Archippus, Paul prayed for him.

"While I was praying for you, Archippus, I sensed the Father is calling you to be a soldier for him and he is going to give you a commission to take this message to many. He does not demand this of you but invites you to take this up. He will put the desire in your heart and he will instruct you where to go and when if you are willing. You are in Christ and he is in the Father and they will go before you, showing you the way leading you by the Holy Spirit."

Archippus looked wide eyed at Paul and blinked a few times. "How will I know when?" he asked.

"Don't worry, the Father will show you. He will not rush you; he will teach you how to be a son in your heart first. It was a long time between the day he called me and the day I began to speak. I was very eager and in a great rush. But he needed to get the Pharisee out of my heart and his love in first. There is still a lot of Pharisee in me, which he is working on."

Timothy smirked and winked at Archippus.

"And your point is, Timothy?" asked Paul.

Timothy shook his head. "Nothing, nothing at all, Paul!"

All the diners in the room broke into laughter as the two men teased each other. Paul turned to Epaphras. "Before the onset of winter I would like to get to Ephesus as soon as possible to meet up with our friends Aquila and Priscilla. Would you be willing to come with us? I'd like to introduce you to the believers in the city." Then he said,

"I sense you and I are bound together in some way in this mission. Are you willing to come and work with us?"

"But I hardly know anything. I have so much to learn."

"It is not about what you learn, Epaphras, it is about what God has put in your heart. You have a great heart. Will you come with us?"

"Absolutely!" replied Epaphras.

They left the following morning for the short journey to Laodicea accompanied by Nympha. They followed the road on the southern bank of the Lycus river and could see a city in the distance on the left bank.

"What city is that?" asked Timothy.

"Hierapolis," answered Epaphras. "It is a smaller city but the road north from there goes to Philadelphia, Sardis then on to Pergamum and eventually it goes to the coast to Troas."

"You know this area well, my young friend," said Paul. "Perhaps you and your nephew Archippus can travel there and spread the message in those cities one day."

They arrived in the early afternoon, and Nympha took them to her home. It was also a domus which she used as a hostelry but on a much smaller scale than the house of Philemon and Apphia.

"My father established a number of hostelries in the province of Asia, and before he died he gave one to each of his daughters. My older brother retains control of a number of other hostelries in the bigger cities on the coast including Ephesus and Pergamum."

"Epaphras, why don't you introduce Paul to my brother when they arrive in Ephesus? Perhaps they could stay at his establishment."

The following day they set off again for Ephesus following the Lycus River until it joined the Meander River which flowed down to the coast at Ephesus. The journey was wet and cold and it rained every day. The days were shortening and travel difficult. The three men entered Ephesus through the Magnesian Gate, tired and cold. Timothy had picked up a fever and was weak and sick.[63]

EPHESUS FIRST VISIT AD 53

CHAPTER XVI

The journey since Paul and Timothy had left in the spring had taken them many months and they arrived back in Ephesus after the winter had begun. Epaphras took them to Nympha and Apphia's brother's domus where they were warmly welcomed by Apollonius himself.

The large establishment had a private wing and an extensive guest wing. The House of Apollonius as it was known was run by an army of slaves overseen by his head steward, Hymenaeus a freedmen. According to Epaphras, Apollonius was a man of high standing in the city and a personal friend of Marcus Junius Silanus, the Proconsular Governor of the Province of Asia. The Proconsul Silanus was a member of the imperial family being a cousin of Agrippina, wife of the Emperor Claudius. As a direct descendant of the Emperor Augustus he could style himself as part of Caesar's household and was entitled to a detachment of the Imperial Praetorian Guard as his personal bodyguard. If any of the imperial family ever visited Ephesus, they would stay in his palace and less senior senators or aristocrats would often stay at the House of Apollonius. Apollonius was one of a class of wealthy Asian aristocrats referred to in the province as Asiachs.

The next day Paul went to find Aquila and Priscilla to share news of his travels and to introduce Epaphras to them.

The main news they wanted to share with Paul was about their encounter with Apollos and his journey to Corinth. Paul was very interested in their report about Apollos, and he asked about the character of the man. Hearing Timothy was sick Priscilla immediately went to arranged for his care and to pray for his fever to break.

The next day, Timothy was sufficiently better to be up and about again. The slaves at the House of Apollonius were amazed at how quickly he had recovered. This gave him the chance to share with them how he believed Jesus had healed him through Priscilla's prayers. He showed them a handkerchief Paul had sent with her to mop his fever and as a sign of the Holy Spirit's presence with him. The slaves were very impressed with this.[64]

A few days later Timothy noticed the handkerchief had disappeared from his room. He asked one of the slave girls if she had seen it. She looked terrified and said she had not stolen it but simply borrowed it.

"What are you talking about, girl?" asked Timothy.

"Well, we heard how Paul prayed for you and sent his handkerchief. Then you recovered straight away. So, we thought if we could borrow the handkerchief perhaps others might get cured too," said the girl. "Well, sir, they have! Two of the slaves in this house had the pox and they are now completely cured. Oh, sir! Please do not tell my master I stole it or he will whip me and maybe even sell me."

"You did not need to take it, I could have come and prayed for the others," said Timothy. "However, let me have it back now, please."

"But that's just it, the other slaves took it and won't give it back 'cos they say it is magic. They are going to use it to make money. I am so sorry, master, please don't punish me. I meant no harm."

Timothy smiled kindly at the sobbing girl and was wondering what to do when Paul arrived and came into the room. On seeing him, the girl looked even more terrified.

"Please, sir, don't curse me! I didn't mean to steal it. Please don't put a demon on me," she spluttered through her tears. Paul waited for her to settle before asking Timothy to explain the reason for her distress. Then Paul said to her, "Why don't you take us to the ones who stole it from you and let us talk to them?"

She agreed and led Paul and Timothy down the stairs and along dark corridors into the slave quarters. They were very different from the luxurious apartments and rooms in the main house. The rooms were dark and cramped. Two or three slaves occupied each room and there was a common eating area with utensils and jars made from rough clay, nothing like the elegant tableware in the guest wing. The slaves working in that part of the house all stopped and looked alarmed when Paul walked in.

A man stepped forward, "What do you want?" he asked.

"I'm looking for my handkerchief," said Paul. "I left it with Timothy and it seems to have disappeared. I wondered if someone had kindly taken it and washed it for me?"

The man who was obviously one of the overseers turned and scowled at the cowering slaves. "What is going on here? Which one of you has stolen it? If you don't get it now and bring it to me, I will have you all whipped. Come on, own up." A slave girl fell on her knees before him and pulled it out from inside her shift.

"Please, Epenetus, I didn't steal it. I just used it because it's magic." As soon as she uttered the word magic, all the slaves stepped back in fear, staring wide eyed at the cloth on the floor in front of Epenetus.

EPHESUS FIRST VISIT AD 53

A slave boy spoke up. "It's true, sir. It is magic. I had a terrible rash from the pox. When she put it on me, it disappeared immediately. Look, sir!" To everyone's horror he started to lift up his tunic.

"That will do!" said Paul. "There is no need for that! It's not magic. But God has used this simple handkerchief not only to heal you but also to get your attention. With your permission, Epenetus, may I explain?"

"Please do, sir," he said.

Paul and Timothy sat down and began to talk with them. That morning a number of the slaves became believers in Jesus, and Paul prayed for them all to be filled with the Holy Spirit. The first one who professed his newfound faith was Epenetus the overseer. He was the first fruit of Paul's ministry in the city.[65]

This caused a great deal of joy and excitement so much so the head steward Hymenaeus came into the slave quarters demanding to know what was happening. Paul tried to explain and reassure him he would have a much happier household with so many professing faith in Jesus as the Son of God.

"I see," said Hymenaeus, though he did not look convinced at all. "Well, thank you, gentlemen. Now, if you don't mind, please leave this part of the house. And in the future, if you want access the slave quarters, do ask my permission before you come down here." He extended his hand, "This way."

Hymenaeus haughtily escorted Paul and Timothy back towards their rooms in the guest wing. Over his shoulder, he boomed, "Epenetus, I'll talk to you later."

Paul and Timothy went and found Epaphras. As they walked together to Aquila and Pricilla's workshop, Paul reflected on their experience.

"We have been given such a great treasure, yet it is like the treasure is held in clay pots. I think the simple and humble ones receive this easier than the wealthy and noble."

On arriving at the workshop, they shared the news about what happened to the slaves at the House of Apollonius. There was other news to share. Priscilla said,

"I was on my way through the Forum early this morning when I heard some men talking about Jesus in one of the colonnades. I stopped to listen and asked them who they were referring to. You can imagine my surprise when they told me a man named Apollos had spoken to them about Jesus some time ago." The men told her their story. She realised Apollos had met them some months previously before he had known the full truth.

"I asked if they would like to find out more about Jesus and if I could bring Paul to meet them. They are very eager to meet you."

Paul was delighted by this news and wanted to set off immediately, however Priscilla said she had arranged to meet them the next day. The following day Paul and Timothy went to the Forum with Priscilla. Awaiting them in the shade of the colonnade were about a dozen men. Paul asked them to tell him how they had become believers in Jesus. After they explained, Paul asked another question.

"Did you receive the Holy Spirit when you believed?"

"No, we have not even heard there is a Holy Spirit."

Paul asked, "Into whose name were you baptized?"

"John, the prophet who announced the coming of Jesus," they explained.

Paul realised they had only part of the message, so he explained about the difference between John's baptism and baptism into Christ.

"John baptized as a sign of repentance, he told the people to believe in the one who was to come after him, Jesus." Paul explained the good news to them and on hearing it, they asked to be baptized in the name of the Lord Jesus. There was a large fountain in the Forum where children often splashed and played. Paul suggested this would be the perfect place to get baptised. And without any further ado, he climbed into the fountain and one by one baptised them.

When Paul laid his hands on them, the Holy Spirit came on them, and they began speaking in tongues and prophesying. This caused a large amount of interest and quickly a crowd gathered to stare and point at the dripping wet people. This was an opportunity Paul could not miss![66]

In the following weeks, Paul continued his usual practice of visiting the local synagogues. He and his friends formed quite a group of people each week in the congregation. Initially, he was well received by the local Jewish community and a large number became followers of Jesus. Each week he became bolder and bolder. He reasoned with them constantly referring to the Jewish Scriptures. He explained to them the kingdom of God was the real kingdom in which they lived not the Roman one. This raised more than a few eyebrows.

After a while some of the more outspoken members of the synagogue started to challenge Paul and interrupted him while he was speaking. They were spreading rumours about Paul and his friends. They accused him of trying to extort money from people, especially after he began talking about organising a collection to send relief to the believers in Jerusalem. They took every opportunity to speak

EPHESUS FIRST VISIT AD 53

evil of Paul and the followers of Jesus. Finally, he withdrew from them and took the growing group of believers with him.

Apollonius had extended the hospitality of his guest mansion to Paul. The attitude of the household slaves had markedly changed in the last few months. Even the rather grumpy steward Hymenaeus had to admit they were happier and more diligent in their work. Apollonius had listened to Paul and Timothy many times. He was not in the least bit hostile, but he could not take a step into becoming a believer. On hearing about Paul having to leave the synagogue, he was sympathetic and approached him with a suggestion.

"Paul, my friend, I hear you need somewhere where you can teach without interruption. I have a friend called Tyrannus who owns a lot of property across the city. He is an Asiach like me. He has a warehouse he sometimes used as a hall for political meetings. These meetings were banned some years ago, and I know it is empty. If you like, I can approach him and ask if you can use it."

Paul was delighted at this news and readily agreed.[67]

The next day, Hymenaeus took Paul and Epaphras to the building owned by Tyrannus. It was in a district of the city where there were many warehouses and workshops. It was not in very good repair but it would provide them with the ideal place to gather and teach people without attracting too much unwanted attention. For the next two years Paul based himself in the hall of Tyrannus to teach and explain the message of Jesus.

As the number of believers grew, he started to send small teams out into the surrounding countryside and cities. Epaphras led one of the first of these bands back up to his home town of Colossae. Archippus his nephew joined him in this and together they went to

EPHESUS FIRST VISIT AD 53

Hierapolis and then further inland to Sardis and Philadelphia. They worked closely with the believers in Laodicea who met in Nympha's house and the newly established gathering of believers in Hierapolis.

Throughout the provinces of Asia, Macedonia, and Achaia, Jews in such large numbers had become followers of Jesus it was affecting the annual collection of the temple tax, which was regularly sent to Jerusalem for the upkeep of the temple dropped two years running.

This did not go unnoticed in Jerusalem and the priests became alarmed. They sent some men to Asia to investigate. On their return, they reported back to the Sanhedrin, "The whole Jewish Community in Asia has been seduced by the teachings of a former Pharisee called Saul of Tarsus who is a member of the sect of the Nazarenes. They are followers of Jesus of Nazareth who you recall was crucified over twenty years ago in this city."

As the Sanhedrin met to discuss the lack of funds, they were approached by a Pharisee who wanted to offer a solution. Matthias bowed to the high priest and the leaders of the Sanhedrin and presented a plan. His plan involved dispatching a number of trusted Pharisees to some of the key cities where there were large Jewish communities. Their task was to do whatever they could to undermine the credibility of Saul of Tarsus. Matthias pointed out that he was known as Paul in these Greek speaking provinces. He offered to select the best people for the job. The Sanhedrin were relieved someone was willing to do something and gave Matthias their full backing and considerable funding.

This time Matthias was determined to succeed. He handpicked a group of five friends who were willing to work with him. They all claimed to be believers in Jesus but were opposed to Paul's activities among the Gentiles. The plan involved splitting into two groups.

EPHESUS FIRST VISIT AD 53

One group of three would go to Corinth, and the other led by Matthias would go to Ephesus. He recommended they accuse Paul of financial irregularities, which would get the attention of the local authorities. He also encouraged them to question Paul's credentials as an apostle in an attempt to undermine his authority in the eyes of the believers in Jesus. Matthias' personal hatred of Paul had become all consuming. With the plan in place, the two groups set off. One went by sea to Corinth; the other led by Matthias took the slower overland route to Ephesus.

Meanwhile, visitors from the growing groups of believers across the Provinces of Asia and Macedonia came to Ephesus and reported news of what was happening. Lucas visited regularly. Tychicus arrived in Ephesus bringing news from Antioch and Barnabas. He brought with him an unexpected visitor, John Mark who was carrying a very important scroll. It was an almost complete first draft of his account of the life of Jesus.

"John Mark, my dear boy, how good to see you again," said Paul as soon as he met him. "It has been a long time since Cyprus and Antioch. How are you and how is Barnabas?"

"He is well and sends you his warmest greetings. The believers in Antioch are thriving," said Mark.

"What brings you here?" asked Paul.

"I am trying to find Simon Peter," he replied. "He left Jerusalem some time ago and was apparently going to Rome again. I wondered if he had passed through Ephesus at all on his way?"

"No, he did not come here as far as I know. The last news we heard of him was that he visited Corinth a while back and spent some time with them. I think he went on to Rome after that. My relatives Andronicus and Junia are in Rome, and they say he visits from time to time. Why do you need him?" asked Paul.

"Well, you may remember I was writing down the things Peter said about Jesus," said Mark rather sheepishly.

"Yes, I do" said Paul. "I remember I was not very enthusiastic about it, but I was so wrong. I am sorry I did not encourage you at the time. I realise there would be great value in having such a document, especially as there are so many people who never saw or met Jesus. For them to have something to read about the life and ministry of Jesus would be immensely valuable. Have you finished it?"

"No, not yet. That is why I want to find Peter. I want him to read it and correct any errors or things I have not written accurately and there are a few gaps I need to fill in."

"May I read it?"

"Of course!" answered Mark. He could not hide the surprise from his voice. This was not the reception he was expecting.

"Perhaps you can read it to me. My eyes are not very good with small writing these days. In fact, I have a better idea. It would be wonderful to gather everyone together and then you read it to all of us. It would be such a great encouragement." Paul looked thoughtful, then continued,

"I have another thought. There is someone else whom I would like you to meet. He is also very interested in this sort of thing. His name is Lucas. He is from Philippi and has shown great interest in writing down the events taking place among us. He would be very eager to read your account. He often comes to visit here. If you are not in a hurry to get to Rome, we could send a message to Lucas

EPHESUS FIRST VISIT AD 53

and ask him to come while you are here."

Others crossed the Aegean Sea to Ephesus bringing news from Corinth. Apollos made a return visit to Ephesus, which gave Paul an opportunity to meet him and get to know him and hear what was in his heart. Like so many, Paul warmed to him and could see why he was well loved. He stayed for many weeks in Ephesus and was able to spend considerable time with Paul and learn from him.

"You are a good man, Apollos!" said Paul one day. "Your heart is so open. I can see Father has deeply touched you and is transforming you. You also have a great mind. Your knowledge of the Jewish Scriptures is profound. I would urge you to consider writing down things Father reveals to you."

"I have wondered this too, Paul. I thought of maybe writing to our countrymen, the children of Abraham, the Hebrew people scattered across the world," mused Apollos.

"Hmm, a letter to the Hebrews, perhaps," said Paul. "Why not ask Father? He may have brought you here at this time to enable you to do this. There are people here who could help you with this. Priscilla is a gifted woman who also carries an anointing in her words when she teaches. Maybe she would be willing to help you." A seed was planted in Apollos' heart that day.

Mostly the news from Corinth was good. However, news arrived that some new converts from a promiscuous background wanted to continue their activities whilst professing to be believers. They maintained their freedom in Christ meant they could act as they pleased because they were forgiven by Jesus. They were drawing other new believers into their point of view. Gaius and Crispus sent a message to Paul asking for advice as to how to handle this situation.

EPHESUS FIRST VISIT AD 53

Paul decided to write to encourage them to confront these people about their behaviour and try to win them over with a loving and gracious but firm response.

Paul dictated a letter to Timothy in his usual way. First, he reminded them of the things he said to the Galatian believers. He encouraged them to restore a person gently if they were caught in sin. He also urged them to live by the Spirit and watch themselves lest they be tempted.

Paul's approach was to encourage them to carry each other's burdens, and in this way, fulfil the law of Christ and to not sit in judgement on those who stumble and fall. As leaders in the community, he urged them to not think they were something when they were not. Each one needed to test their own actions. He was equally straightforward with those who were promoting sexual promiscuity. He told them to not to be deceived, to not mock God's kindness and grace. A man would reap what he sowed. When someone sowed to please their natural lusts, they would reap destruction in their bodies. Instead, he urged them to sow to please the Spirit because from the Spirit they would reap eternal life.

Finally, if all this failed and these people did not respond, then he advised the believers to not associate with these sexually immoral persons. He emphasised he was not meaning the immoral of this world. These people needed to hear the good news about the real freedom there is in Christ. He took a firm line with the persistently sexually immoral among the believers in Corinth.[68]

Paul urged them to not be yoked together with unbelievers asking what did righteousness and wickedness have in common? Or what fellowship could light have with darkness? What harmony was there between Christ and Belial, the personification of all that was evil?

He spelt it out very simply. What did a believer have in common with an unbeliever? What agreement was there between the temple of God and idols?

He passionately described their bodies as the temple of the living God, quoting the Jewish Scriptures, 'I will live with them and walk among them, and I will be their God, and they will be my people. Therefore, come out from them and be separate, says the Lord. Touch no unclean thing, and I will receive you. And, I will be a Father to you, and you will be my sons and daughters, says the Lord Almighty.' He urged them because of these promises to purify themselves from everything that contaminated the body and the spirit out of reverence for God.[69]

Finally, Paul introduced a plan he had for raising money for the relief of the poor believers in Jerusalem that he had shared with all the groups of believers he was connected with.[70]

When he had finished writing, Timothy gathered up several sheets of papyrus, which had been discarded because he had made mistakes. He looked at them and wondered what to do with them since they contained sections of the letter. He did not want to throw them away and decided to collect them, thinking they might be useful one day.

When all was finished, Paul sent off the letter and waited to hear how things were in Corinth. He did not have to wait too long to hear how it was received. Visitors from Chloe's household arrived in Ephesus from Corinth bringing further bad news. They informed Paul there were quarrels among the believers in Corinth over who they looked to for leadership. It seemed there was a growing tendency among the believers to group together around whom they considered the most important apostles. Some looked to Paul, who they considered the founding father of the community. Others looked to Apollos, who had made a big impression on them during his recent visit. Some even had grouped around Peter, who had visited the city, because of his personal connection to Jesus.

Three men coming recently from Judea had joined the community. They claimed to have been Followers of the Way since the very beginning and had heard Jesus speak on a number of occasions. They said their true allegiance was to Jesus. They announced they were considered super apostles because of the length of time they had been believers. They didn't follow any man but Jesus only. This had really impressed many of the Corinthians.[71]

Another group of visitors, Stephanas, Fortunatus and Erastus' freedman Archaicus arrived. Paul was very happy to see them and got a chance to hear first-hand what was happening. They had an objective assessment of the situation. They also brought a letter from the leaders in Corinth to give him as full a picture as they could of the nature of the various issues which had arisen in the community since Paul's departure two years earlier.[72]

"Just to see you again, my dear friends, and spend time with you brings such refreshment to my spirit," said Paul as they sat together in the House of Apollonius.

"We have missed seeing you these last two years, Paul," said Stephanas.

"It has been wonderful having help from Apollos, and Peter's visit was a great encouragement to us all. But there have been so many challenges as well. Is there any way you could come back to visit us and speak to everyone yourself? We think it would really help. Even if you came for only a short time."

EPHESUS FIRST VISIT AD 53

Paul considered their request carefully, then said, "Let me think and pray about it for a while. We don't want to get out of step with what Father is doing. In the meantime, come, friends. I want you to meet everyone here. They will be encouraged to know what is happening in Achaia. But first, let's have the letter you brought."

Paul met with Apollos, Priscilla, Aquila and Timothy who read the letter to them all. They listened carefully with a sense of sadness as the letter spelt out the issues and challenges they were facing in Corinth. As they talked together, a plan emerged. They agreed Paul would write another letter in reply to address the issues the believers in Corinth had written to him about in the first place and the things that Stephanas and the others had reported on.

Paul felt one of them needed to carry his letter to Corinth and to explain things, which might need extra teaching where necessary. They felt this needed to be someone who knew Paul's heart for them. It was agreed Timothy would be the best person to do this as he perhaps knew Paul best and also the believers in Corinth. It was also agreed Paul would try to make a personal visit to Corinth going overland via Macedonia aiming to spend a longer time with the community in Corinth rather than a quick hurried visit. He felt he was to stay in Ephesus at least until after Pentecost and depart in the spring.

Paul also thought Apollos should go with Timothy to Corinth. Apollos, however, disagreed and said he wanted to stay in Ephesus. Paul became annoyed with Apollos for disagreeing with him, and the conversation grew tense as the two strong characters stood up to one another. Paul was used to getting his own way and did not like it when someone resisted him.

Finally, Priscilla spoke. "May I say something? I don't like what

I am seeing here. May I to speak candidly to both of you?"

"But I have not finished what I am saying yet," interjected Paul loudly.

"That is exactly what I want to speak about," replied Priscilla. "You have a habit of speaking over people and using the sheer power of your personality to dominate. It feels very manipulative and controlling."

Paul looked shocked as she confronted him.

"If you continue like this, there will be a rift between the two of you and it will end up with regret on both sides. And we know how damaging this is both personally and to the wider work we have been called to. We don't want another situation like the one in Antioch all those years ago between you and Barnabas, do we?"

At the mention of Barnabas' name, Paul visibly winced and put his head in his hands. There was a heavy silence between them all. Finally rubbing his eyes, he looked up at the four of them. "I am so sorry, dear friends. Priscilla is right. I know I do this. Please, Apollos, all of you, forgive me."

Apollos spoke next. "I am sorry too. I have been so stubborn. All my life I have been like this. I want to learn how to submit my heart to you as my fellow brothers and sisters."

Paul was silent for a while with his eyes closed. When he opened them again, he spoke softly. "The Spirit is talking to me about being submitted to one another in the same way Jesus submitted to the will of the Father. I guess this is what this looks like in practice."

Apollos looked directly at Paul and said,

"Paul, I will go to Corinth, but as you know I am writing a

letter to my Hebrew countrymen in Alexandria. Priscilla and I are working on it together. I would like to try to finish it first, then I will go over to Corinth as soon as I get the opportunity. How do you feel about that?"

"Yes, that would be good!" said Paul. "I will write to them in Corinth, and at the end of the letter I will share these plans so they know what is in our minds and hearts." Paul stood and stretched, "And I think we need to commend Stephanas, Fortunatus and Archaicus to them. I trust these men, along with Gaius, Crispus and Sosthenes. I want the believers to know these men carry an authority and our support."[73]

Paul set aside time to dictate another longer and more detailed letter to the Corinthian believers as his main priority.

CORINTH SECOND VISIT
AD 53

CHAPTER XVII

Barely two weeks later Sosthenes arrived from Corinth bringing the money collected by the Corinthian believers for the relief of the poor in Jerusalem. Sosthenes told Paul more was promised and would come in due course. He went on to tell Paul alarming news of a deteriorating situation among the believers in Corinth. Sexual immorality had reared its ugly head again as one of the young believers was discovered to be sleeping with his stepmother behind his father's back. This was considered shocking by even the unbelieving citizens in the city. The man had justified his behaviour by saying since as he was in Christ he had the right to do anything he wished. He had interpreted Paul's words about grace to mean he had licence to please himself.

Paul gathered all the key people involved in the situation: Aquila and Priscilla, Timothy and Apollos and the four leaders from Corinth. Between them, they tried to decide what were the main issues needing to be addressed in Paul's forthcoming letter. They also had in front of them the letter sent from Corinth.

The problems were numerous and pastorally complex. Most of it boiled down to people believing their newfound freedom in Christ meant any sort of behaviour was permissible. Given that many of them came from a background of paganism and had been sex slaves or sex workers in a city renowned for its promiscuity, it really was no surprise.

As they discussed the situation, Paul made it clear he wanted to emphasise who they really were in Christ. He turned to Timothy and said, "Write this down while I think of it."

Timothy quickly started to write as Paul said, "I do not want you to be deceived, neither the sexually immoral, nor idolaters, nor adulterers, nor men who have sex with men, nor thieves, nor the greedy, nor drunkards, nor slanderers, nor swindlers will inherit the kingdom of God. That is what some of you were before you became believers. But you were washed, you were sanctified, you were justified in the name of the Lord Jesus Christ and by the Spirit of our God." He paused and then said, "I want to include this in the letter."[74]

"I do not want to sit in judgement on them but somehow I need to be clear how destructive this behaviour can be," Paul continued.

As they discussed the situation, it became apparent this would be a very long letter and quite different in tone from the letters Paul had written to the believers in Thessalonica or Galatia and the shorter letter to Corinth he had recently sent. It was decided Sosthenes would help Paul and Timothy would be the amanuensis while Paul dictated. A large quantity of papyrus was acquired for the purpose of writing the letter, and Timothy supervised the supplies. They set up a room at the Hall of Tyrannus where they could work undisturbed. Paul was also able to continue his teaching in the Hall at certain times during the day.

The letter writing began in earnest. Paul walked up and down the room as Timothy scratched away with his stylus often asking Paul

CORINTH SECOND VISIT AD 53

to slow down or repeat things. Paul would pause at times and ask Timothy to read back what he had just said. Corrections were made, amendments inserted and the pile of discarded papyrus sheets grew on the floor. Timothy also produced the sheets of papyrus he had saved from the previous letter. Paul reviewed what he had written and decided to restate some of it in the current letter.

The sense of the presence of God filled the room as Paul's heart was suffused with revelation. There were moments of great weight as the words tumbled out of Paul's mouth onto the page.

"Brothers and sisters, think of what you were when you were called. Not many of you were wise by human standards; not many were influential; not many were of noble birth. But God chose the foolish things of the world to shame the wise; God chose the weak things of the world to shame the strong. God chose the lowly things of this world and the despised things and the things that are not, to nullify the things that are, so that no one may boast before him. It is because of him that you are in Christ Jesus, who has become for us wisdom from God—that is, our righteousness, holiness and redemption. Therefore, as it is written: 'Let the one who boasts boast in the Lord.'[75]

"When I came to you, I did not come with eloquence or human wisdom as I proclaimed to you the testimony about God. For I resolved to know nothing while I was with you except Jesus Christ and him crucified. I came to you in weakness with great fear and trembling. My message and my preaching were not with wise and persuasive words, but with a demonstration of the Spirit's power, so that your faith might not rest on human wisdom, but on God's power."[76]

Paul stopped and suggested they all have a rest and drink some

CORINTH SECOND VISIT AD 53

wine to refresh themselves.

"It sounds to me you are writing like you are a father speaking to your children," said Timothy as he sipped his wine. When they started again, Paul took up this theme.

"I am writing this not to shame you but to warn you as my dear children. Even if you had ten thousand guardians in Christ, you do not have many fathers, for in Christ Jesus I became your father through the gospel. Therefore, I urge you to imitate me. For this reason, I have sent to you Timothy, my son whom I love, who is faithful in the Lord. He will remind you of my way of life in Christ Jesus, which agrees with what I teach everywhere in every assembly."[77]

Timothy looked at Paul, "Am I going to Corinth then? It sounds like it!"

After some days, Paul felt he had addressed most of the difficult pastoral situations they had written to him about. He shared this with Stephanas, Fortunatus and Archaicus. All three agreed his letter would be helpful.

Paul started to address some of the questions concerned with worship and the love feasts being held when the believers remembered the death of Jesus and celebrated by breaking bread and drinking wine together. He sent a message to John Mark to join him as he had some questions to ask him.

"How can I help?" asked Mark when he arrived.

"I remember you telling me your mother had an upstairs room in her house in Jerusalem. If I remember correctly it was where Jesus met with his disciples to celebrate the Passover on the last evening he was with them before he was arrested."

CORINTH SECOND VISIT AD 53

"Yes, that's right. I was there too. I served at the meal and took food up to them as they ate together," said Mark.

"Tell me what happened," said Paul.

"I've written it down in my story of Jesus' life," Mark answered. "While they were eating, Jesus took some bread lifted it up to give thanks. Then he broke it and gave a piece to each of his disciples. As he did so he said, 'Take it, this is my body.' Then he took a cup of wine, and in the same way when he had given thanks to God for it, he gave it to them, and they all drank from it. Then he said to them, 'This is my blood of the covenant, which is poured out for many. I tell you the truth, I will not drink again from the fruit of the vine until that day when I drink it new in the kingdom of God.'"[78]

"I want to include what you have just told me in my letter," said Paul. "I sense this is something the Lord wants us to receive, Mark, and I want to pass it on to them too. It is so important because whenever we eat the bread and drink the cup in this way, we are proclaiming the death of Jesus. We will keep doing it until he comes back to us. Thank you for sharing this with me, Mark."[79]

The next day Paul arrived unexpectedly late at the Hall of Tyrannus. Sosthenes and Timothy were chatting as he walked in. "Hello, Paul! You are late this morning," said Timothy. They both looked at him. "Are you all right? What is the matter?"

"Nothing! Nothing at all! In fact, the opposite, I have been deeply touched as Father has been speaking to me. He has shown me something which makes sense of everything. It is the foundation stone of all we do and say and are," said Paul. "Come quickly! I want you to write it down in the letter."

Timothy took a new sheet of papyrus and readied his ink and

stylus. Sosthenes pulled up a chair for Paul to sit on. He sat back in the chair, closed his eyes and quietly spoke the words the Spirit placed in his heart.

"If I speak in the languages of men or of angels, but do not have love, I am only a resounding gong or a clanging cymbal. If I have the gift of prophecy and can understand all mysteries and all knowledge, and if I have a faith that can move mountains, but do not have love, I am nothing. If I give all I possess to the poor and give over my body to be burnt that I may boast, but do not have love, I gain nothing."

He paused as he waited for Timothy to write the words, then continued.

"Love is patient, love is kind. It does not envy, it does not boast, it is not proud. It does not dishonour others, it is not self-seeking, it is not easily angered, it keeps no record of wrongs. Love does not delight in evil but rejoices with the truth. It always protects, always trusts, always hopes, always perseveres. Love never fails."

Paul stopped while Timothy finished. After a few minutes he opened his eyes and spoke again.

"But where there are prophecies, they will cease. Where there are inspired languages, they will be stilled. Where there is knowledge, it will pass away. For now, we know in part and we prophesy in part, but when completeness comes, what is in part disappears. When I was a child, I talked like a child, I thought like a child, I reasoned like a child. When I became a man, I put the ways of childhood behind me. For now, we see only a reflection as in a mirror; then we shall see face to face. Now I know in part; then I shall know fully, even as I am fully known."

Again, Paul stopped, closed his eyes and continued, "And now these three remain, faith, hope and love. But the greatest of these is love."(80)

The words hung heavily in the room. Timothy put down the stylus and wiped his eyes, and then blew his nose on the sleeve of his tunic. Sosthenes stood looking out of the window into the street at the people passing by, getting on with their busy lives. A muleteer was passing with a line of heavily laden mules taking them from the docks to a warehouse. Two slave girls, whispering to each other and carrying bundles, were walking behind an elegantly dressed lady who had obviously been shopping. A young boy was skipping from stone to stone on the pavement. A group of young men came along together joking and making rude gestures at the slave girls. An old man leaning heavily on a stick hobbled along the street stopping from time to time to rub his back.

"This is the answer for them all," said Sosthenes. "It is what the whole world needs. This is truly a revelation from our Father."

Paul rubbed his hands up and down his arms. "I'm cold. I think that is enough for today."

They gathered again in the morning and Paul talked animatedly about the resurrection of Jesus and the implications it had for all believers. He listed as many appearances of the risen Jesus he could remember. Timothy wrote as fast as he could.

"And last of all he appeared to me as one abnormally born." Paul stood and walked to the window looking far into the distance remembering. Finally, he came to the issue of the collection he was organising to help the impoverished believers in Jerusalem.

"Now about the collection for the Lord's people, do what I told the Galatian believers to do. On the first day of every week, each one of you should set aside a sum of money in keeping with your income, saving it up, so that when I come no collections will have to be made. Then, when I arrive, I will give letters of introduction to the men you approve and send them with your gift to Jerusalem. If it seems advisable for me to go also, they will accompany me."[81]

Finally, Paul wrote about the plans they had all agreed to earlier. He expressed his hope to visit them after going through Macedonia and perhaps to stay with them for a while, or even spend the winter. He told them he did not want to make only a passing visit. His plan was to stay on in Ephesus until Pentecost on account of the great door for effective work open to him in spite of the opposition.

He went on to write about Timothy's visit. He wanted to be sure Timothy had nothing to fear while he was with them, for he would be carrying on 'the work of the Lord' as he put it, so that no one would treat him with contempt.

"Do I really have to write this?" asked Timothy half grinning.

"Yes, you do!" said Paul. "Come on, I've not finished yet. Write this. 'Send him on his way in peace so that he may return to me. I am expecting him along with the brothers.' Now read it back to me to make sure you have put it all in." Paul stood at Timothy's shoulder while he read it back to him. When he finished, Paul ruffled his hair and said, "Well done, my son."

Aquila and Priscilla and the others joined Paul as they all knew the letter was almost finished.

"Please send our warmest greetings to them," said Priscilla. "In fact, we all do."

"Now, Timothy, let me have the stylus so I can write a few words,"

CORINTH SECOND VISIT AD 53

said Paul. Timothy stood from the desk so Paul could sit. He picked up the stylus as Timothy pointed to the place where he could write.

"I, Paul, write this greeting in my own hand," speaking out loud as he wrote.[82]

Having finished the letter, a second copy was made so it could be kept in Ephesus. They decided the quickest way to return to Corinth was by sea. Timothy, accompanied by Stephanas, Fortunatus and Archaicus, set sail and with fair winds, arrived safely in Corinth within three days.

Soon after arriving, Timothy and the others met with Gaius and Crispus who were particularly encouraged to receive Paul's letter. Timothy asked how best to communicate its contents to the wider group of believers. It was decided to read the letter in small groups in people's homes. They started with the group meeting in Gaius' house where it was well received.

However, within a few days Timothy discovered several groups who would not even read the letter because they insisted Paul was not truly apostolic. They claimed true apostles were only those who had been with Jesus throughout his earthly ministry. Clearly, Paul did not qualify. Their contention turned on the validity of Paul's apostolic credentials. Another group claimed Apollos was a 'super' apostle and they questioned why he had not written to them instead of Paul. Timothy found the believers fragmented and at odds with one another. He was shocked to hear talk among them suggesting Paul's money raising was for his own benefit. He encountered one man who was a former Pharisee from Jerusalem who had been sent by Matthias to bring people back to the true apostolic faith which had originated in Judea rather than Antioch. This was news Timothy felt he needed to relay to Paul as quickly as possible.

CORINTH SECOND VISIT AD 53

Timothy spent just a few days in the city and found himself opposed on every side. He finally decided he needed to return to Ephesus to report the situation back to Paul. Sosthenes and the others encouraged him to stay and help them explain the letter. However, Timothy became paralysed by anxiety and felt he lacked the wisdom needed to help. Early one morning he left the city and took a ship bound for Ephesus from the port of Cenchreae.

A week later, a fragile Timothy arrived in Ephesus. Aquila and Priscilla were away with Epaphras visiting his family in Colossae. Apollos was sick with a fever, so it was to Paul alone that Timothy blurted out his report. As he spoke, his emotions overwhelmed him and he started to weep.

"I'm so sorry, Paul," sobbed Timothy. "I failed you completely."

Paul was alarmed by Timothy's reaction and the news he brought. He concluded it was a mistake to have sent Timothy on his own. He should have gone himself. He decided there was no time to lose; he needed to go straight to Corinth himself to confront them before they influenced more people and did more damage.

Without waiting for Aquila or Priscilla to return, Paul left for Corinth. This was a change of the plan which he had told the Corinthians about at the end of the letter he had just sent. His unannounced arrival would surprise them, but Paul felt the urgency of the situation required immediate action.

On arriving in Cenchreae, Paul hurried up the road from the port to Corinth and made his way straight to Gaius' house. Gaius was surprised to see him. Paul was agitated and tired and wanted to meet with all the key people immediately. Gaius prevailed on him to rest first and sent messages to the various groups around the city. In the evening, Chloe came to the house and told Gaius her group had reacted badly to Paul's letter and had no confidence any longer in her as she was a supporter of Paul.

Erastus also came with Archaicus and cautioned about getting everyone together as there were a number of strongly opinionated people they felt had infiltrated the community. They doubted they were true believers. An emerging thread was the influence of newcomers from Judea. Erastus told them he had picked up rumours at the city treasury office about Paul's collection for the poor in Jerusalem. It was being questioned as being for his own personal benefit. He said the report came anonymously, but his investigations had identified the newcomers from Judea as its source. The Proconsul become involved and instructed him to investigate the matter and have Paul arrested if he found any truth in the accusation.

The situation was clearly serious.

The following day Paul decided he still wanted to gather the whole community together in order to address the issues among them. Several of the leaders strongly disagreed with this and advised against this approach. Gaius and Fortunatus told Paul they thought this was too heavy handed and they could not support him in this. Paul became angry with them and said he still would meet with the people.

"Not in my house!" said Gaius, "It's too small." Paul misunderstood Gaius and assumed he was refusing to host the meeting so he stood, ending the discussion and left the room.

Later the same day, a large number of the community gathered to hear Paul speak. They met outside the city in an amphitheatre in the side of a hill. A number of the local leaders were not present and those who had come represented people who were not sympathetic to Paul. He stood to speak. After a few minutes someone shouted out, "What makes you think you have the right to speak to us. You are not a true apostle. Why should we listen to you?" There were murmurings of agreement from many.

Another young man called out, "You have no right to tell me what to do. I'm saved and forgiven. It's not for you to say who I can sleep with. It is between me and the Lord."

"And the woman you are sleeping with," shouted another. Laughter broke out and people started to get up to leave. The whole meeting broke up with most people returning to the city.

Paul walked back to Gaius' house deeply dejected and depressed. Gaius sat him down and said, "Well, don't say we didn't warn you!" Crispus and the others were there and tried to reassure Paul. But it did no good. Paul went to bed and the pain of the visit swept over him. He decided there was no point in staying. He thought he could sort out the whole situation himself but realised he was concerned as much about his own reputation as an apostle as anything else, and now he felt like a failure. He blamed himself for the whole fiasco, struggling to do it in his own strength again. Had he learnt nothing over the last few years?[83]

The next morning Paul told the leaders his visit had been ill timed and he needed to come back for a more extended visit in order to confront the situation. He said next time he would come via Macedonia as had been his original plan. Paul went on to say on his return he would not spare those who sinned earlier or any of the others. He would not respond to those who were demanding proof of Christ speaking through him. Instead, he would come in weakness in the same way Jesus was crucified in weakness and let

God's power deal with them.

Barely a week after his arrival in Corinth, Paul boarded a ship to take the crossing of the Aegean Sea to Ephesus. One day into the crossing, the ship foundered in a storm. After having drifted for a night and a day in the open sea Paul was rescued by a Roman naval vessel, along with a young fellow passenger named Onesiphorus.[84]

After the storm the sea had returned to an almost flat calm. The sails flapped listlessly. The captain ordered the slaves to row and the drum master began his slow beat. And Paul told Onesiphorus his story.

EPHESUS SECOND VISIT
AD 53

CHAPTER XVII

The bireme rowed slowly into the harbour at Ephesus. Paul was lost deep in thought as he leant against the gunwales of the ship. Recounting his story to Onesiphorus had left him feeling pensive. The last week had been exhausting and painful. He felt he had acted in haste in his own strength outside the plan of God. In his concern for the situation among the Corinthian believers he had acted impulsively, and it had been disastrous. He felt his credibility as an apostle was in shreds and his confidence at rock bottom. He had not felt so low for many years.

Onesiphorus came and stood beside him looking at the city stretched out on either side of the harbour. Paul looked at the boy. Even in this disastrous week, God had brought at least one good thing out of his fruitless and painful visit to Corinth.

"Look! Paul, look over there," Onesiphorus pointed to a group of large houses built along the hill to the north of the harbour.

"You can see my father's house on the hillside. It's over there, to the left of the Proconsul's palace, that's it. I want you to come home with me and meet my father and mother. He will want to reward you for saving my life." Paul followed Onesiphorus' arm pointing towards the hillside. He saw the Proconsul's palace and to its left he saw another large palatial house.

"My father is Cassander Maximus Alba, he is one of the Asiach's of Ephesus." Paul assumed his host Apollonius would know Cassander.

After they landed Paul said goodbye to Onesiphorus who was eager to get home, and Paul made his way to the House of Apollonius. He was met by Timothy who quickly judged Paul's mood. He left him to go and rest, then went and sought out Aquila and Priscilla. They had just returned to Ephesus after several weeks in Colossae and Laodicea having spent time encouraging the new believers in the two towns. Timothy brought them to Paul so they could hear what had transpired during Paul's visit to Corinth.

After reporting the news of Epaphras and his nephew Archippus' trip north to Sardis, Priscilla looked intently at Paul. "So, tell us about your visit. Timothy tells us your ship foundered and you were nearly drowned!"

"Not quite, but almost." he said softly. "Thankfully, Father saved me and another young man from here, Onesiphorus the son of Cassander one of the Asiachs. However, we were adrift all night in the sea until we were rescued." Paul slowly and painfully explained the full details of his disastrous visit to Corinth. When he finished, they all sat in silence. After a while, Priscilla spoke.

"I think before we do anything else we all need to rest and let Father comfort and restore us. It may be true you acted rashly but you are not disqualified Paul. It may be true you panicked and were overwhelmed by fear, Timothy, but Father understands and knows your heart. I think we all need to let Father minister his love to us. We all need this. Remember the words you wrote in your letter to the Corinthian believers? Love is patient, love is kind. Let Father show his love and kindness to you, Paul, and you, Timothy."

EPHESUS SECOND VISIT AD 53

While they were talking Hymenaeus knocked on the door and entered.

"The master requests your presence in the atrium. You have visitors. Come quickly, they are important people," he said in his usual haughty manner. After indicating they should follow him, they stood. Hymenaeus shook his head, "Not all of you, just Paul." With that, he turned on his heels.

Paul followed Hymenaeus down the stairs and the others went along the corridor to the gallery above the central atrium where they could see the guests below. A group of elegantly dressed people were waiting in the atrium. Apollonius and his wife were talking with another couple. Between them stood Onesiphorus. Seeing Paul enter, he walked straight up to him with his arms outstretched.

"Paul, I want you to meet my father and mother. This is my father Cassander Maximus Alba and my mother Julia Lavinia Alba." He turned to his parents. "This is the man who saved my life in more than one way."

Paul bowed deeply to them.

"We owe you our son's life," said Cassander to Paul. "We can never repay you but if ever we are able to help you in any way, we will. I would like to reward you," said Cassander. He took a leather pouch from his belt.

Julia was a beautiful Roman matron with curled hair piled up in the latest fashion and was dressed in expensive silks. She smiled as she approached Paul.

"Thank you, sir. He is our only son. You have done our family a great service. He tells us you were aided by your god. We would like to know who this god is. May we offer sacrifice in gratitude? Is there a temple here in the city we can endow with a gift for our son's life?"

"You owe me nothing," said Paul shaking his head. "But I would very much like to introduce you to the God who helped me. This is all the reward I ask for."

Apollonius was grinning at this point and winked at Paul. "Friends, all this talk of gods in my atrium is exhausting. My triclinium is a far more congenial place for religious discussion. Let's all meet again for dinner tonight, and we will let Paul introduce you to his God. Will that work for you all? And also, you three up there!" he said smiling and looking up to the gallery above where Aquila, Priscilla and Timothy leaned over watching the interaction below.

The meal raised Paul's spirits as he spoke openly to the group of aristocratic Asiachs. Still unwilling to commit, Apollonius had become what the Jewish people called a God-fearer. Onesiphorus had already become a believer and was eager for his parents to embrace his new faith. His mother Julia was a Roman patrician who had married into Cassander's family which had raised his status among the local nobility. When Silanus was appointed the Proconsul of Asia and took up residence in the Proconsular Palace in Ephesus, Cassander and Julia became regular guests. Their association with Silanus who was related to the Empress Agrippina brought them even greater prestige.

In the following days, Julia invited Priscilla to her huge domus many times. Eventually, to the delight of her son, Julia also embraced his faith. Both mother and son were baptised by Priscilla at their mansion. One of those who attended was a close friend of Julia's, Antonia Domitilla, the wife of the Proconsul.

Soon after this, Titus arrived from Galatia with news of the

EPHESUS SECOND VISIT AD 53

believers in the province. Paul and Timothy were delighted to see him again. He had grown both physically and in his relationship with God. His arrival was a great encouragement to Paul. Following his return to Ephesus, Paul talked with Apollos and the other leaders about the situation in Corinth, purposefully including Timothy and Titus in the discussions. Paul decided another letter to express his sorrow at the outcome of his painful visit was needed. He did not intend to make another visit like the last one. Instead, he wanted the Corinthians to know his love for them.[85]

So Paul began to write yet another letter. He asked Tychicus to be his amanuensis. Even as Paul wrote he found himself often reduced to tears as he struggled to dictate. He completed the short letter and it was dispatched to Corinth with Titus. He hoped Titus would return with a good report. He desperately wanted to hear good news from across the Aegean Sea.

While all this was going on the collection for the relief of the poor in Jerusalem was continuing a pace. Also, the numbers of believers in the city were increasing. Messengers arrived from Colossae and Laodicea who not only brought good reports of the health of the believers but also more donations. Soon there was a substantial amount of money to be sent to Jerusalem.

Aristarchus arrived from Macedonia. Erastus and Gaius came bringing better news from Corinth. Erastus told Paul how Titus' presence had done much to calm things down and he planned to stay in the city a while longer. Erastus told Paul his visit to Ephesus involved official business as he brought letters from Gallio to Silanus. He intimated he would probably stay in the city quite some time as part of his brief was to review the finances of the city. Paul asked Erastus to oversee the gathering of the money for the poor in Jerusalem while he was about it. He readily agreed to do so. Ephesus was developing into a major hub of Paul's apostolic ministry as people came and went.

Unknown to Paul, others had also arrived in Ephesus, Matthias and two colleagues from Jerusalem. He contacted the leaders of the synagogues and instructed them to keep his presence a secret for the time being while he assessed the situation.

Many in the Jewish community had embraced Paul's message and this was seriously impacting the synagogues, both in attendance and in the gathering of the Temple Tax. This ancient tax was paid by all Jewish men over the age of twenty and went to the upkeep of the Temple and Levites in Jerusalem. Jews all over the Roman world sent money to Jerusalem for this. Ephesus as major city in the Province of Asia was a gathering centre for this tax. Since the time of Augustus laws had been enacted, which allowed Jews protection to worship as they chose. In order to get around Roman laws banning secret societies synagogues had been classified as colleges because they were used as places of learning. As a result, they were allowed to collect the annual Temple Tax. The local synagogue leaders were well aware of the drop in income as a result of the spread of Paul's teaching in the province. Matthias had come to the province with the backing of the Sanhedrin supposedly to investigate this decrease in revenue.

A number of incidents happened around the same time, which significantly assisted Matthias in his plans. A family of Jewish exorcists who had been operating in the Province started to use the name of Jesus to cast out demons. One day they were overwhelmed by one of the spirits who had said through the voice of the helplessly possessed man, "Jesus I know, and Paul I know about, but who are you?" Then the man who had the evil spirit attacked them and gave them such a beating they ran out of the house naked and bleeding. Word of this incident rapidly spread among not only the Jewish community but the general populous as well. Superstition was rife in the city and as a result many were seized with fear, and it seemed everyone was talking about Jesus.[86]

Many claimed to believe in Jesus, but it was difficult to ascertain how real their faith was. There was talk about judgement and fear. Even though they were professing faith in Jesus it was deeply mixed with superstition and fear of the forces of darkness and the underworld. People routinely consulted soothsayers and practitioners of the dark arts. They wore amulets to ward off evil spirits and bought spells and curses from these people, wrote them on scraps of papyrus and hid them in the houses of their enemies. Every area of life was touched by these things. New-borns would have amulets hung around their necks. Anyone who was sick would go to a priest or sorcerer to buy something to protect them or help in their cure. The papyrus these 'abracadabras' were written on was strapped to their bodies like a bandage. Fear gripped the city and the superstitious use of the name of Jesus by these Jewish exorcists precipitated a desire to rid themselves of their involvement in sorcery and pagan practices.

In the Palestra, alongside the Arcadian Way, new converts started piling up their scrolls and paraphernalia associated with their pagan practices, publicly renouncing their old beliefs. They set fire to the scrolls and soon a large crowd gathered around the bonfire. Then crowds started to attack the booths of traders who sold artefacts and images of the goddess Artemis and also of some Jewish merchants. What started as religious zeal became a full-scale riot. News spread widely in the city and many people began to call

EPHESUS SECOND VISIT AD 53

themselves believers.[87]

Matthias met with some of the local Jewish leaders and raised his concerns.

"Unless something is done to stop Paul and his gang of followers this will result in more attacks on the Jews in the city. And, we need to bring people back to the true worship of Adonai and get the flow of funds restored for the Temple in Jerusalem," he urged them. One of their number, a man called Alexander spoke up.

"We have to find a way to stop him. What do you suggest, Matthias?"

"When I was in Corinth we tried to get Governor Gallio to condemn them for propagating an unlawful cult but it didn't work. He dismissed it as a theological issue for us Jews to sort out. We need to find something more effective. We need to find people of influence in the city whose businesses and livelihoods are being damaged by these people. If we can get the city to turn on Paul, then the Proconsul and city authorities will have to act. We can add our own concerns about all the money he is taking. Who knows what he is doing with it all. We can make a formal accusation of how he is robbing the temple and misappropriating the funds. With luck we can get him thrown into prison and maybe even executed for embezzlement." They all nodded their agreement. "But we need to plan carefully and not be seen to be the ones behind this," added Matthias.

"I know just the man we need to talk to," said Alexander. "Demetrius, the silversmith who makes silver images of Artemis. He is a loud mouth, and he leads a guild of silversmiths and craftsmen. He is our man. Leave it to me."

EPHESUS SECOND VISIT AD 53

Meanwhile, Paul and the leaders of the Christian community gathered together to consider how best to encourage and integrate the new believers. Paul was still feeling agitated and was prone to act too quickly. His concern was also to get the money sent to Jerusalem as soon as possible. He wanted to take the money to Jerusalem himself via Macedonia and Achaia.

"After I have been there," he said, "I must visit Rome also."

"But, Paul, you can't do it all! What is the most important? What is Father saying to us?" asked Priscilla.

They agreed to wait, pray and see how they felt God was leading. Two days later there was a much more peaceful atmosphere and a plan had emerged. They all agreed Paul would stay a little longer in the province along with Aquila, Priscilla and Apollos to ensure the community was grounded deeply in the love of God. Timothy and Erastus were to travel to Macedonia to share with the believers in Philippi and Thessalonica and to collect the offering for Jerusalem. Then they would return and the gift would be sent to Jerusalem. Erastus set off for Thessalonica accompanied by Archaicus. Timothy planned to go to Philippi in a week or so.[88]

The talk and rumours about the 'Way' as some were calling it continued in the city. Wherever Paul or the others went, people would approach them and ask them to pray for them. But not all were so eager. Demetrius the silversmith, who made images of the goddess Artemis urged on by Alexander the Jew noticed how badly impacted his takings were in his trade. People were abandoning their interest in the goddess and turning to Jesus.

Demetrius became very vocal in his opposition to Paul and called together other silversmiths and workers in related trades. Lucas, who was visiting Ephesus, witnessed the events unfold and later included a full account in his writing. As people gathered in the Agora, Demetrius addressed the angry crowd.

"You know, my friends, we receive a good income from this business. And you see and hear how this fellow Paul has convinced and led astray large numbers of people here in Ephesus and practically the whole province of Asia. He says gods made by human hands are no gods at all. There is danger not only that our trade will lose its good name, but also the temple of the great goddess Artemis will be discredited and the goddess herself, who is worshiped throughout the province of Asia and the world, will be robbed of her divine majesty."[89]

The tradesmen became extremely angry at this and began shouting, "Great is Artemis of the Ephesians!" Soon, the whole city was in an uproar. As the mood in the city deteriorated, someone recognised Gaius and Aristarchus as associates of Paul. They seized them and dragged them into the amphitheatre which was right next to the Agora.

The local riffraff and layabouts who had nothing better to do joined in the uproar. Someone shouted they should go and find Paul himself. Groups of men spread out across the city looking for him. He was with Epaphras at the House of Apollonius and they could hear the chanting coming from the amphitheatre. Onesiphorus arrived and reported what was happening.

"I should go immediately to the theatre to speak to the crowd," said Paul.

"Absolutely not, Paul, they will lynch you," said Epaphras. As they waited at the house, a messenger arrived from Cassander and

Apollonius who seeing what was happening begged him not to venture out of the house and certainly not go to the amphitheatre. Onesiphorus left in order to find out what was happening.

The assembly in the amphitheatre was in confusion. Some were shouting one thing, some another. Most of the people did not even know why they were there. There were a number of Jewish traders in the crowd and they pushed their spokesman Alexander to the front to speak as they shouted instructions to him. He called for silence in order to make a defence before the people because he did not want the Jews to become the focus of the anger; he wanted to direct it at Paul.

When the crowd realised he was a Jew, they all shouted in unison "Great is Artemis of the Ephesians!" This went on for hours. Things went badly for Alexander as he was set upon and beaten up by a group of louts who could not miss the chance of a fight. Finally, one of the most senior city officials sent by the Proconsul arrived to disperse the crowd. Surrounded by armed guards, he addressed the crowd.

"Fellow Ephesians, the whole world knows the city of Ephesus is the guardian of the temple of the great Artemis and of her image, which fell from heaven. Therefore, since these facts are undeniable, you ought to calm down and not do anything rash. You have brought these men here, though they have neither robbed temples nor blasphemed our goddess. If, then, Demetrius and his fellow craftsmen have a grievance against anybody, the courts are open and there is the Proconsul. They can press charges. If there is anything further you want to bring up, it must be settled in a legal assembly. As it is, you are in danger of being charged with rioting because of what happened today. In that case, we would not be able to account for this commotion, since there is no reason for it."

As soon as he said this, he dismissed the assembly and to everyone's surprise the drama evaporated almost as quickly as it had begun. The crowds who had been shouting their heads off were exhausted by the chanting and quickly dispersed and the city's taverns did a roaring trade.[90]

Gaius and Aristarchus had been beaten and shaken up but were not arrested. Instead, Gaius went back to Aquila and Priscilla's house and Aristarchus went to Paul at the House of Apollonius to tell him what had transpired. Demetrius and the other ring leaders did as was suggested and went to the Proconsular Palace to present their accusations about Paul. A rather bruised and bloodied Alexander also went to represent the Jewish community. Finally, they were admitted to the Proconsul's office where they laid their accusations against Paul. The accusation from Demetrius was about the loss of business. For the Jews, it was about misappropriation of funds. After he listened to the charges, Silanus summoned an officer of the guard to go and arrest Paul and anyone with him. He told them to have him brought to the Palace for his safety and to give the city time to settle down. Then in due time a proper investigation would be mounted.

At the House of Apollonius, Paul, Epaphras and Aristarchus were resting in the garden when soldiers arrived from the Palace demanding to know the whereabouts of Paul. Hymenaeus escorted them to the garden.

"More visitors for you, Paul," he said with a superior look.

The officer in charge arrested the three of them and the soldiers escorted them to the Proconsul's residence. As they passed through the streets, some people, staggering drunk out of the taverns, hurled insults at them. Others, recognising them, fled to their homes fearing a pogrom against the believers.

When they arrived at the palace, they were thrown unceremoniously into an underground windowless cell to await their fate. The next day a delegation of Paul's friends including Apollonius arrived to petition Silanus for their release. The Proconsul was not willing to release them even when Apollonius explained Epaphras was a relative.

"They will be kept in protective custody for their own safety pending investigation of the charges of misappropriation of funds," announced the Proconsul. Silanus, always with an eye to his reputation and career, was firm in his decision as he did not want to be accused of favouritism in the case of Apollonius' relative.

Paul's arrest and imprisonment however, coincided with Silanus' departure from Ephesus a day later. The Proconsul began a major tour around the Province of Asia. His first visit was to be to Aphrodisias where he wanted to pay homage at the newly completed temple of Aphrodite and also to commission a number of statues of himself made from the white and blue grey Carian marble which was quarried there. He planned also to visit other major cities in the north of the province, Sardis, Smyrna, Pergamum and even Troas. He would be away from Ephesus for weeks if not months. So there was no possibility of any investigation beginning for some considerable time.

One concession Silanus made was to have the three of them moved from the underground cell to two rooms in the rear of the Palace where they could be confined. Their conditions were easier but they were still effectively in prison. They were chained to a guard who was one of the more junior members of the Praetorians assigned to Silanus' household.

Visitors were allowed, so Priscilla, Aquila and Timothy regularly came bringing food, clothing and news. Apollonius sent furnishings. One of Apollonius' slaves, Epenetus who had been one of the first converts in the Province was assigned to ensure they had all they needed. A desk was set up in one of the rooms where Paul could read and write. He would read everything aloud as was the custom, so the guards were continually exposed to Paul's heart and teaching. In time, a number of them even became believers.[91]

CHAPTER XIX

Soon after Paul's arrest, Gaius returned to Corinth but deliberately travelled overland through Asia taking the news of Paul's arrest to the believers in Colossae, Laodicea, and Troas. He crossed over to Philippi by boat then travelled to Thessalonica and took the road south to Corinth. Wherever he stopped he encouraged the believers to pray for Paul and his companions. Within a couple weeks Lucas arrived with Demas one of the other leaders from Troas. Lucas was anxious about Paul's physical condition and was ready to provide whatever care he could give.

Some weeks after this, Epaphroditus arrived from Philippi with news and a substantial gift sent by the believers in the city. They were anxious and eager to know how Paul was. Epaphroditus was feeling weary and unwell when he arrived and within a couple of days he was in bed with a raging fever and a very dry cough. He was having trouble breathing and became increasingly weak. Priscilla had arranged for him to stay with them. Lucas, who was also at their home, was able to care for Epaphroditus. After a few days he felt a bit better, then suddenly the fever returned with a vengeance. His breathing came in fits and starts and he was semi-conscious.

Timothy reported Epaphroditus' condition to Paul. "You remember when we first arrived here in Ephesus I was sick with a fever?"

Paul nodded. "Yes, what are you thinking?"

"Well, you recall you mopped my fevered brow with a cloth and I was healed almost immediately? I still have the cloth. I got it back from the slaves who had taken it. I was thinking I could go to him with it now. What do you think?"

"Do you believe that it will bring healing to him also?"

"I do and I will also pray for him and anoint him with oil. I believe Father wants me to do this. I believe Father is going before me. I remember you telling us as sons we have authority, in the same way Jesus had the Father's authority, to heal the sick."

"Go then and God go with you."

Timothy left and went straight to Priscilla and Aquila's house. Opening the door to him their faces were very grave.

"How is he?"

"Not good," whispered Priscilla. "Lucas is upstairs with him. I do not think Epaphroditus will be with us for much longer."

Timothy went up to the dark room where Epaphroditus lay on a bed. His breathing was shallow and laboured, and he was barely conscious. Lucas was sitting beside him and looked up at Timothy. He shook his head.

"I have brought something from Paul it was used to heal me." Timothy took the cloth out of his belt and showed Lucas. "And I want to pray for him and anoint him with oil as well."

Lucas stood and made room for him to sit on the edge of the bed. Timothy placed the folded handkerchief on Epaphroditus' head and then opened a small vial of oil. He looked up and prayed,

"Father, I ask you to heal our dear brother Epaphroditus. I pray this oil will bring healing and wholeness to him. Dear Father, may this cloth which brought healing to me, bring healing to my brother also." He anointed Epaphroditus' forehead with the oil and placed his hand on his head. "In the name of Jesus, I command this fever to leave immediately."

Epaphroditus lay very still on the bed. Slowly, he opened his eyes. As his breathing changed, he looked at Timothy.

"Hello, Timo! What are you doing here? Lucas? You too? Is someone sick?" He pushed himself up on his elbow and took the cloth off his forehead.

"What's this? It's all sticky and oily. What have you two been up to?" he asked with a grin. Timothy and Lucas looked in amazement and delight at Epaphroditus. He threw off the covers and began to get out of bed. "Don't just stand there staring at me. Pass me my clothes," he said as he realised he was naked. "I've got things to do."

The news of the healing rapidly spread through the community who were overjoyed, none more so than Paul. Epaphroditus went to visit Paul and the others at the prison the same afternoon. There was great rejoicing as they greeted one another. The guard looked scared when Epaphroditus came in, fearing he would catch the fever from him. As the soldier listened to the story, his eyes opened wider and wider.

Epaphroditus passed on the news from Philippi which really encouraged Paul and the others. After he left, Paul shared with Epaphras and Aristarchus he wanted to write a letter to the believers in Philippi. He wanted to thank them for their encouraging gift.

He also wanted to make sure they knew Epaphroditus was well and had recovered from his sickness.

In the next few days Epenetus, with the help of Timothy, organised everything needed to write a letter. They obtained permission from the captain of the Praetorian guard in the palace to have the supplies of papyrus and ink brought to the cell so he could write the letter.

Paul was very happy in spite of his confinement and it would spill out into the letter he was about to write. There were some issues he wanted to address with them. In particular, he wanted to write to Euodia and Syntyche who had some sort of disagreement. He wanted to encourage them to sort it out so there would be no hindrance to the spread of the good news among them. More than anything else Paul wanted to be able to express his deep gratitude and joy he felt towards them at their partnership in the work he was doing.

Epenetus arrived with sheets of papyrus, styluses and freshly made ink, and Timothy agreed to be his amanuensis as usual. He sat stylus in hand ready to write.

Paul began with his usual introduction, "Paul and Timothy, servants of Christ Jesus, to all God's holy people in Christ Jesus at Philippi, together with the overseers and servants."[92]

He then launched straight into his plan to encourage them.

"Now I want you to know, brothers and sisters, that what has happened to me has actually served to advance the gospel. As a result, it has become clear throughout the whole palace guard and to everyone else that I am in chains for Christ. And because of my chains, most of the brothers and sisters have become confident in the Lord and dare all the more to proclaim the gospel without fear."[93]

EPHESUS SECOND VISIT AD 53

Paul sensed the flow of the Holy Spirit stirring him, revealing truth as he was speaking. He said as sons of God they were united with Christ. They were comforted by his love and united and likeminded with the Spirit. He encouraged them to have the same mindset as Jesus himself.

"Jesus, who being in very nature God, did not consider his equality with God something to be used to his own advantage. Rather, he made himself nothing by taking the very nature of a servant. Being made in human likeness and being found in appearance as a man, he humbled himself by becoming obedient to death, even death on a cross!

"Therefore, God exalted him to the highest place and gave him the name that is above every name, that at the name of Jesus every knee should bow, in heaven and on earth and under the earth, and every tongue acknowledge that Jesus Christ is Lord, to the glory of God the Father."[94]

As he reflected on these words dripping with revelation from the very heart of God, he could not help but reflect on his own situation and wondered if he was not about to be poured out as a sacrifice also.

As Paul dictated, Timothy scratched away with the stylus on the papyrus. Paul looked at Timothy working away at the letter. His heart was full of gratitude for this young man who was like a son to him. The son he never had. As much as it grieved him to be parted from him, he knew he would ask Timothy to be the carrier of the letter. But he knew Timothy would return with up to date news from them.

"I hope in the Lord Jesus to send Timothy to you soon, that I also may be cheered when I receive news about you. I have no one else like him who will show genuine concern for your welfare. For everyone looks out for their own interests, not those of Jesus Christ. But you know that Timothy has proved himself. As a son with his father, he has served with me in the work of the gospel." Timothy paused and looked at Paul with a look that said, "Do I really have to write this?"

"Yes, you do. Come on just write what I say, dear boy!" said Paul. "Where was I? Oh yes! And I am confident in the Lord that I myself will come soon."[95]

Next, Paul turned his thoughts to Epaphroditus and his situation.

"But I think it is necessary to send back to you Epaphroditus, my brother, co-worker and fellow soldier, who is also your messenger, whom you sent to take care of my needs. For he longs for all of you and is distressed because you heard he was ill. Indeed, he was ill and almost died. But God had mercy on him, and not on him only but also on me, to spare me sorrow upon sorrow. Therefore, I am all the more eager to send him, so that when you see him again you may be glad and I may have less anxiety. So then, welcome him in the Lord with great joy, and honour people like him, because he almost died for the work of Christ. He risked his life to make up for the help you yourselves could not give me."[96]

Paul paced the small room thinking about his dear friends who had fallen out with each other.

"Therefore, my brothers and sisters, you whom I love and long for, my joy and crown, stand firm in the Lord in this way, dear friends! I plead with Euodia and I plead with Syntyche to be of the same mind in the Lord. Yes, and I ask you, my true companion, help these women since they have contended at my side in the cause

EPHESUS SECOND VISIT AD 53

of the gospel, along with Clement and the rest of my co-workers, whose names are in the book of life."(97)

Towards the end of the letter Paul gave an honest answer to describe his current situation. He was grateful they had shared in his troubles and reminded them how they above all the other groups of believers had supported him financially. Even when he was in Thessalonica, they had sent aid more than once when he was in need. He told them how he felt amply supplied, especially after Epaphroditus had arrived with the gifts they sent. Paul described them as a fragrant offering, an acceptable sacrifice, pleasing to God. He reassured them God would meet all their needs according to the riches of his glory in Christ Jesus.(98)

Late in the afternoon on the second day of his writing the captain of the guard himself came down to the cell. Everyone stood when he walked into the cell. The guard who had been dozing on the floor jumped to attention when Epaphras jerked him awake by pulling on his chain.

"You have important visitors. Get up all of you and don't speak unless you are spoken to. Do you understand?" he growled. He stood to one side as two extremely well-dressed ladies walked into the cell.

"Thank you, officer. You can go. We will be quite safe here." Julia Lavinia the wife of Cassander waved the officer out with an elegant hand gesture. She was accompanied by none other than the wife of the proconsul Silanus, Antonia Domitilla. Paul and the others bowed to the ladies.

"Enough of that, Paul, we are fellow sisters in Christ. We are here to see if there is anything we can do to help you," said Julia.

Paul held up his chain and smiled at them. "Apart from the

obvious, we have all we need. Thank you for asking, my Lady."

"I am so sorry," said Antonia Domitilla. "If my dear husband had not decided to spend longer at Pergamum, I would ask him to have you released. But he has asked me to join him there for the winter as he has decided to refurbish the old Imperial residence in the city and wants my eye for detail."

"Do not be concerned, my Lady. I am convinced I am in these chains for the sake of the gospel and Christ is being glorified through this."

Reassured of his welfare, the ladies chatted with them. Julia smiled as the proconsul's wife shared how she became a believer. After telling Paul of her conversion, she asked what he was writing. Paul told her about the believers in Philippi and asked Timothy to read part of the letter to her. As he finished she asked him to send their greetings to these fellow believers in Philippi.

"We who live here in Caesar's household greet them also," she said.[99]

CHAPTER XX

When he finished the letter Paul asked Timothy to make a copy to remain with the Ephesian believers. Epaphras also requested a copy for the believers in Colossae and Laodicea.

"And while you are about it how about one for Thessalonica too. Oh! And then there is Corinth," added Aristarchus.

"At this rate we will need a whole group of scribes, one person dictating and the scribes making copies," said Timothy.

"Now that is a wonderful idea," said Paul.

The papyrus scroll was rolled up and sealed, ready for dispatch. Timothy and Epaphroditus set off for Philippi with it. As per Paul's instructions, after delivery of the letter, Timothy was to return to Ephesus. In the meantime, Paul had started to think about copying some of the other papyrus manuscripts they were collecting. Paul enlisted Tychicus, a skilled amanuensis who had helped when he wrote to the Galatians, to start organising the process. He asked Mark and Lucas to assist. They used a room at the Hall of Tyrannus for this purpose.

Assisted by Priscilla, Apollos' detailed and thorough explanation of the Jewish Scriptures was nearly finished. He explained how the Scriptures always pointed to something new and better to come. He saw this as Jesus the Messiah. Apollos' deep knowledge of Jewish practice, customs and history along with their interpretation of their Scriptures enabled him to write to his beloved people, the Hebrews with clarity and insight. He regularly visited Paul and talked through what he was writing.

Epenetus came every morning with fresh food for the three prisoners. As was his way, he chatted away keeping them up to date with all the coming and goings. He told Paul how the copying of manuscripts was going.

"I meant to tell you, a young man turned up yesterday. He said he knew you, Paul. He was very nervous, almost shifty. He is a slave but to be honest I think he may be a runaway. He claims he is a believer. But I'm sure he is in some sort of trouble."

"What's his name and where's he from? Why was he asking after me?" asked Paul.

"He said he was from the 'interior'. He didn't seem to want to say where exactly, which added to my opinion of him as a runaway. He said his name was Onesimus," answered Epenetus.

Epaphras and Paul exchanged glances. "Is he young, dark haired, a Greek perhaps?" asked Epaphras.

"That sounds about right. Do you think you might know him, Epaphras?"

"I know an Onesimus who is one of my brother Philemon's slaves back home in Colossae. Do you remember him, Paul? He became a believer the first time you visited us. But I didn't have him down as a runaway. If it is him and he has run away, he must be in serious trouble.

"Why don't you bring him here tomorrow, Epenetus?" said Paul. If it is the same Onesimus and he hears Epaphras is here he might run again, so don't mention him. Just tell him I would like to see him. When he comes we will have to keep you out of sight somehow, Epaphras. Maybe you can hide under the bed!"

"Well, that will certainly liven up my day!" Epaphras laughed.

The next day, Epenetus came with a nervous looking Onesimus.

"Onesimus! It is you. Welcome, my boy! Have you come with a message from your master Philemon?" asked Paul.

The young man looked awkward and shifted from foot to foot. "Err, no, not exactly."

"Is he well?"

"Umm, he was when I last saw him," replied Onesimus, but he could not look Paul in the eye.

"When was that, my boy?"

He looked at the floor, and then up at Paul with fear in his eyes.

"I, umm, haven't seen him for a while," he said trying to control his voice.

"Why don't you tell me all about it? Come on sit down here."

Instead of sitting on the stool which Paul had pointed to, he sat down heavily on the bed. There was a grunt and cry from under the bed, and Onesimus jumped up with terror in his eyes as Epaphras' hauled himself out from under the bed.

"You nearly crushed me under there. Hello, Onesimus! Fancy seeing you here!" said an amused Epaphras.

Onesimus fell on his knees in front of Epaphras and grabbed his feet. "Please, sir! I didn't mean to run away. I didn't take the money either. Please, sir! Don't beat me," he pleaded.

Paul could barely hold back his laughter. Leaning down and taking Onesimus by the arm, he lifted him up. "Come on. No one is going to beat you. Let's hear the story from the beginning, the truth, mind you, no lies or excuses."

"Then we will decide whether to throw him to the lions or not," said Epaphras grinning.

The whole story came tumbling out. There was a mixture of misunderstanding, youthful stupidity and a genuine mistake. Onesimus felt the only solution was to run away, taking some money he found in the house of his master Philemon.

The reality was he had taken money and this was sufficient to have him executed if Philemon wished. Paul wanted mercy for the boy, for him to be spared but to learn and grow through this incident. In the meantime, they decided to put him to work and then contact Philemon. They agreed Onesimus would go with Epenetus to the Hall of Tyrannus where Tychicus and the others were busy copying Paul's letters. Since he knew how to write he would be set to work as a scribe under Tychicus' supervision.

The coming of Onesimus prompted Paul and Epaphras to discuss the developments over the last few years in the towns in the Lycus valley. Timothy came to visit them one day as they discussed things. Epaphras had worked hard in the area along with his nephew Archippus. They had travelled inland to Sardis and beyond and had established communities in the area also. Paul longed to visit them and wondered when and if it would ever happen given their current situation in prison.

EPHESUS SECOND VISIT AD 53

"One thing is for sure, my brother Philemon will always have a guest room ready for you," said Epaphras. "Something troubles me however about these new believers, it is the mixture of cultures they come from."

"What do you mean?" asked Paul.

"There are Jewish believers and Gentile believers who have very superstitious backgrounds. Sometimes they want to attribute all sorts of mystical and mythical stories to Jesus. It becomes a muddle at times. One minute they are saying we should celebrate all sorts of festivals to do with angels or the moon or something. Then next they are almost advocating circumcision again," explained Epaphras.

"It sounds to me it would be a good idea to send someone like John Mark to visit them," said Timothy. "He can tell them stories about Jesus, some of which he was an eyewitness of himself. It would be really helpful for them. I wonder if he would go for a visit on your behalf, Paul?"

"You know what, Paul? A letter from you would be a real help. You have the time and the people to help you do it at the moment," said Epaphras. "Timothy here could write as you dictate. Couldn't you, Timo?"

"I was thinking this too," said Paul. "I could also send a personal letter to Philemon about Onesimus. What's more I could get Onesimus to write it for me so he knows exactly what I am saying to Philemon. Then we could send it off to Colossae with the general letter for the community at the same time. We could ask Tychicus to go as our messenger and representative with Onesimus acting as the courier. That way we would make sure he gets there and doesn't run off somewhere. What do you think, lads?"

EPHESUS SECOND VISIT AD 53

Timothy and Epaphras looked at each other and nodded.

"Sounds like a plan," they said almost simultaneously.

Epenetus was commissioned again to bring papyrus, ink and a stylus so Paul and Timothy could write. Paul started off with a general letter addressed to the believers in Colossae.

Whenever Paul embarked on these letters he found himself caught up in a wave of the Holy Spirit's presence. His natural mind would often be overtaken by his heart as he sensed revelation flowing through him and out of his mouth. Sometimes it would be things he had been thinking about in the long hours in the prison, which suddenly made sense as he spoke them out. Other times he would almost gasp with surprise at the words themselves. Occasionally, he would say, "I didn't know I knew that!"

The letters would also reflect things he had been praying about for the people he was writing to. This was the case in one to the believers in Colossae.

"We continually ask God to fill you with the knowledge of his will through all the wisdom and understanding that the Spirit gives. In order that you may live a life worthy of the Lord and please him in every way. Bearing fruit in every good work, growing in the knowledge of God, being strengthened with all power according to his glorious might. So that you may have great endurance and patience, and giving joyful thanks to the Father, who has qualified you to share in the inheritance of his holy people in the kingdom of light."

Paul paused, reflecting on exactly what Jesus had done.

"For he has rescued us from the dominion of darkness and brought us into the kingdom of the Son he loves, in whom we have redemption, the forgiveness of sins."

As Paul spoke the words and Timothy wrote them, there was a synergy between the two of them as if the Spirit was making them one. Often, they would lose track of time and only the setting of the sun through the small window would halt their work. Paul continued,

"The Son is the image of the invisible God, the firstborn over all creation. For in him all things were created, things in heaven and on earth, visible and invisible, whether thrones or powers or rulers or authorities. All things have been created through him and for him. He is before all things, and in him all things are held together. And he is the head of the body, the assembly of believers. He is the beginning and the firstborn from among the dead, so that in everything he might have the supremacy. For God was pleased to have all his fullness dwell in him, and through him to reconcile to himself all things, whether things on earth or things in heaven, by making peace through his blood, shed on the cross."

In these profound moments of revelation Paul was caught up in the Spirit and at times would weep for joy at the incredible nature of the truth he was seeing.

"In the past you were alienated from God and were enemies in your minds because of your evil behaviour. But now he has reconciled you by Christ's physical body through death to present you holy in his sight, without blemish and free from accusation. Continue in your faith, established and firm, and do not move from the hope held out in the good news. This is the good news that you heard and that has been proclaimed to every creature under heaven, and of which I, Paul, have become a servant."[100]

EPHESUS SECOND VISIT AD 53

Paul continually related what he was seeing and hearing from God to their personal situations. He wanted them to not only receive revelation but also for it to impact their lives.

"So then, just as you received Christ Jesus as Lord, continue to walk in him, rooted and built up in him, strengthened in the faith as you were taught, and overflowing with thankfulness."

"See to it that no one takes you captive through hollow and deceptive philosophy, which depends on human tradition and the elemental spiritual forces of this world rather than on Christ."

"For in Christ all the fullness of the Deity lives in bodily form, and in Christ you have been brought to fullness. He is the head over every power and authority. In him you were also circumcised with a circumcision not performed by human hands. Your whole self ruled by the flesh was put off when you were circumcised by Christ, having been buried with him in baptism, in which you were also raised with him through your faith in the working of God, who raised him from the dead."

As Paul spoke he remembered his own experience of meeting the risen Jesus on his journey to Damascus. Prior to this he had been so convinced Jesus was dead. He knew Jesus had died on the cross. He had seen many a crucifixion back in his days in Jerusalem. His words reflected the language of crucifixion. He had seen how nails held the victim to the cross. He had seen the public spectacle of the death of the victim, and he received revelation of what the death of Jesus had done for them as sons of God.

"When you were dead in your sins and in the uncircumcision of your flesh, God made you alive with Christ. He forgave us all our sins, having cancelled the charge of our legal indebtedness, which stood against us and condemned us; he has taken it away, nailing it to the cross. And having disarmed the powers and authorities, he made a public spectacle of them, triumphing over them by the cross." Paul saw how this truth set them free from the restrictions of man-made rules and religious practices.

"Therefore, do not let anyone judge you by what you eat or drink, or with regard to a religious festival, a New Moon celebration or a Sabbath day. These are a shadow of the things that were to come; the reality, however, is found in Christ."[101]

With many other practical instructions and advice, Paul spoke about how to live in Christ, including their family relationships with each other, how they worshipped together, and how they treated their slaves as believing masters. He encouraged believing slaves to serve their masters as if they were serving the Lord. This was a radical statement to make in a world where there were vast numbers of slaves. Finally, as was his custom, he turned to personal messages and news of those he loved and worked with.

"Tychicus will tell you all the news about me. He is a dear brother, a faithful minister and fellow servant in the Lord. I am sending him to you for the express purpose that you may know about our circumstances and that he may encourage your hearts." Then Paul addressed the issue of Onesimus the runaway slave.

"Tychicus is coming with Onesimus, our faithful and dear brother, who is one of you. They will tell you everything that is happening here. My fellow prisoner Aristarchus sends you his greetings, as does Mark, the cousin of Barnabas. (You have received instructions about him; if he comes to you, welcome him.) Jesus, who is called Justus, also sends greetings. These are the only Jews among my co-workers for the kingdom of God, and they have proved a comfort to me.

EPHESUS SECOND VISIT AD 53

Epaphras, who is one of you and a servant of Christ Jesus, sends greetings. He is always wrestling in prayer for you, that you may stand firm in all the will of God, mature and fully assured. I vouch for him that he is working hard for you and for those at Laodicea and Hierapolis. Our dear friend Lucas, the doctor, and Demas send greetings. Give my greetings to the brothers and sisters at Laodicea, and to Nympha and the assembly that meets in her house."

At the very end of the letter he wrote,

"After this letter has been read to you, see that it is also read to the Laodiceans believers and that you in turn read the letter from Laodicea."

"What letter to the Laodiceans?" asked Timothy.

"One I am thinking about writing next." Paul replied. "Let's finish this one. I have something I want to say to Archippus.

"Tell Archippus: 'See to it that you complete the ministry you have received in the Lord.'"

Taking the stylus from Timothy, he said out loud as he wrote, "I, Paul, write this greeting in my own hand. Remember my chains. Grace be with you."[102]

The next day Paul sent a message asking Onesimus to come and visit him in the prison. As usual, the small room was crowded with Paul's fellow prisoners Aristarchus and Epaphras. Tychicus was there and of course the guard. Before Onesimus arrived more of Paul's group of friends turned up. This time it was John Mark with Lucas and his friend Demas.

There was talk about the copying of the manuscripts and letters. Lucas and Mark had become good friends and Mark had given

EPHESUS SECOND VISIT AD 53

Lucas a copy of his unfinished account of the life of Jesus. Lucas told them he was thinking of visiting Judea and Galilee at some point to meet people who had known Jesus and write an account of Jesus' life ministry.

"I have a patron back in Philippi whom I have served as his physician for many years. His name is Theophilus, a Greek. I want to write it with people like him in mind who do not know the ways of the Jews. So Paul if you ever travel back to Jerusalem, I would like to accompany you," said Lucas.

"If you do go, it would be good to try to meet my cousin Barnabas, he can introduce you to all sorts of people. He knows everyone!" said Mark.

"The person I would really like to meet is Mary, not your mother, Mark, but Jesus' mother. I hear she is still alive and living in Galilee. I imagine she has some wonderful memories to share. Anyway, that is for the future," said Lucas.

Talk moved to the letter Paul had written for Colossae and the personal one he was about to write to Philemon. Timothy arrived accompanied by Onesimus who also brought several baskets of food sent by Priscilla. Onesimus was a little surprised to see so many crammed into the small room used for writing.

"So how are you, Onesimus?" asked Paul. "I hear you have been invaluable to Tychicus in the copying of manuscripts."

"I am well, Paul." Onesimus bowed. "I have greatly enjoyed working with the brothers at the Hall of Tyrannus."

"Good, good," said Paul. "Now I have another letter to write and I have asked you here to be the amanuensis, Onesimus."

EPHESUS SECOND VISIT AD 53

Onesimus looked around the room, somewhat awed by the presence of all the men there. They were gifted and skilled scribes in their own right so he was surprised at Paul's request.

"If you are sure," Onesimus said, somewhat nervously. "Who is it to?"

"Your master Philemon in Colossae," said Paul.

The words hung in the atmosphere. No one spoke. Instead, all eyes were on Onesimus. He looked at Paul as fear gripped his stomach. He tried to speak, but words would not come out as his mouth was dry as dust.

"I want you to return to him, Onesimus," said Paul. "Timothy and I have discussed this, and the brothers here all agree with us. We all feel you are to return and I want to commend you to your master and ask him to show mercy to you and forgive you. I also will repay anything you owe him so there will no longer be an issue between you and him."

As Paul spoke, Onesimus visibly began to shake and weep. Epaphras stood up and embraced him. He held him in his arms while he sobbed. After a few minutes, the boy stopped and looked at his master's brother.

"Will your brother treat me as you have, sir?" asked Onesimus.

"If I know my brother, I believe he will," replied Epaphras. "To me, you are not a slave but a fellow brother in Christ."

Before Paul started the letter they all ate the food Priscilla had sent. Even the guard was included. He liked being there when the food for the prisoners was delivered because it was much nicer than his usual meals the soldiers were given.

EPHESUS SECOND VISIT AD 53

Timothy said, "I'm sorry, boys, we seem to have eaten all your lunch and your supper! I'll get Epenetus to send more." They all laughed and settled down to listen to Paul dictate the letter to Philemon. Onesimus nervously took up the stylus and wrote as Paul spoke.

"Paul, a prisoner of Christ Jesus, and Timothy our brother, to Philemon, our dear friend and fellow worker, also to Apphia our sister and Archippus our fellow soldier, and to the community of believers that meets in your home.

"Grace and peace to you from God our Father and the Lord Jesus Christ. I always thank my God as I remember you in my prayers, because I hear about your love for all his holy people and your faith in the Lord Jesus. I pray that your partnership with us in the faith may be effective in deepening your understanding of every good thing we share for the sake of Christ. Your love has given me great joy and encouragement, because you, brother, have refreshed the hearts of the Lord's people.

"Therefore, although in Christ I could be bold and order you to do what you ought to do, yet I prefer to appeal to you on the basis of love. It is as none other than Paul, an old man and now also a prisoner of Christ Jesus, that I appeal to you for my son Onesimus, who became my son while I was in chains. Formerly he was useless to you, but now he has become useful both to you and to me. I am sending him, who is my very heart, back to you."

Paul let these words sink into Onesimus' heart as much as onto the papyrus sheet.

"I would have liked to keep him with me so that he could take your place in helping me while I am in chains for the gospel. But

EPHESUS SECOND VISIT AD 53

I did not want to do anything without your consent, so that any favour you do would not seem forced but would be voluntary. Perhaps the reason he was separated from you for a little while was that you might have him back forever, no longer as a slave, but better than a slave, as a dear brother. He is very dear to me but even dearer to you, both as a fellow man and as a brother in the Lord. So if you consider me a partner, welcome him as you would welcome me. If he has done you any wrong or owes you anything, charge it to me."

At this point Paul took the stylus out of Onesimus' hand. He squinted at the papyrus sheet and said, "I, Paul, am writing this with my own hand. I will pay it back, not to mention that you owe me your very self. I do wish, brother, that I may have some benefit from you in the Lord; refresh my heart in Christ. Confident of your obedience, I write to you, knowing that you will do even more than I ask."

Paul gave the stylus back to Onesimus then, as if an idea had suddenly come to him, indicated for him to continue.

"And one thing more, prepare a guest room for me, because I hope to be restored to you in answer to your prayers. Epaphras, my fellow prisoner in Christ Jesus, sends you greetings. And so do Mark, Aristarchus, Demas and Luke, my fellow workers. The grace of the Lord Jesus Christ be with your spirit."[103]

During the next few days the letters were copied and Tychicus and Onesimus set off for Colossae. Onesimus was still anxious as to how he would be received when he got back. He hoped Paul's plea to Philemon would not fall on deaf ears.

John Mark prepared to go to Colossae a few weeks later, and Erastus had returned. Upon hearing about the accusations of misappropriation of funds levied at Paul, he set about producing records so that when Silanus returned he would be able to speak on Paul's behalf.

When the Proconsul Silanus finally returned to Ephesus, Paul hoped his case would be opened and finally he and the others would be released from prison. Apollonius advised them to wait a week or so, and then he and Cassander and Erastus would make representation on Paul's behalf to the Governor.

EPHESUS SECOND VISIT AD 53

CHAPTER XXI

Late one afternoon a few days later, Timothy, along with Onesiphorus, Erastus and Archaicus sat outside a tavern at the dock in the city, drinking wine and enjoying the warm sunshine. Together, they snacked on a bowl of olives and some roasted almonds. As they chatted, Erastus spotted a large naval ship entering the harbour. He watched as it came around the mole into the inner harbour.

"Look at that, lads, a trireme. You don't often see many of them," he said. They all turned and watched the huge three-tiered galley slowly make its way to the quayside. The whole dock area became a frenzy of activity. Flying from the mast head was an imperial flag.

"See the pendant at the mast head?" said Erastus. "There is someone important on this galley. I wonder who it is? I've seen a flag like that before back in Corinth. We had a visit from one of the imperial household. I wouldn't be surprised if it's not someone from Rome."

Its arrival had been noticed by lookouts at the Palace. A detachment of the Praetorian guard came down from the Proconsular Palace and marched onto the quayside. In the middle of the Praetorians was a group of local dignitaries led by Silanus. Onesiphorus spotted his father Cassander among them and several other Asiachs.

"Quite a welcoming committee," commented Erastus. "It must be someone very important to have dug Silanus out of his palace and get him down here."

The trireme's oars were all raised in a perfectly synchronised move as ropes were thrown and quay workers catching them tied the great ship to bollards on the dock. A gangplank was lowered over the side and an honour guard appeared on deck. Silanus and the official dignitaries stood in a group as the Praetorians formed around them. A man appeared on deck in full military uniform denoting a high-ranking officer, his helmet crested by red feathers.

Erastus looked closely. "He's a real high up official. By the look of his uniform, he is a member of the Order of Equestrians. I've seen one of them before. I dare say he is bringing important news from Rome for Silanus."

As they watched, the officer walked down the gangplank followed by another man in civilian clothes. They stopped and saluted Silanus who as a Proconsul and member of the imperial family outranked the officer. They talked together, and then Silanus called over the Asiachs with him. He was obviously telling them the news. There seemed to be great consternation among them. Silanus, accompanied by his squad of Praetorian guards, hurried back to his palace with the two visitors from Rome. Onesiphorus walked over to the group of Asiachs who were talking anxiously together and approached his father.

"What's going on, Pater?"

"It's news from Rome. The emperor is dead. He died in his palace on the Palatine Hill in Rome. His wife Agrippina was apparently at his side as he died. The senate in Rome has recognised Agrippina's

EPHESUS SECOND VISIT AD 53

son as the new emperor, Nero Claudius Caesar Augustus Germanicus. He's announced he will be known as the Emperor Nero. This man who has brought this news is Publius Celerius. He is a close associate of Agrippina, and she has sent him to inform her cousin Silanus of these events."

"Wow, that is news indeed. This will impact Silanus. Surely, he is a closer relative to Claudius than Nero? Wouldn't he have had a claim to the purple?"

"Shh! Be careful; don't speak too loud. You might think so, son. I can't possibly comment!" answered Cassander with a knowing look. "I must go. We have all been summoned to a banquet tonight at the Proconsular Palace to celebrate the accession of the divine Nero. They will want you their too, Erastus."

Cassander hurried off and Erastus turned to the others. "I'm going to see Paul and tell him the news. Timothy, I think you should go and tell Apollonius. No doubt he will be at the banquet tonight."

During the day, various other passengers and dignitaries disembarked the ship. One group was taken to the House of Apollonius as he had a number of guest rooms. One of them was a man called Helius who was Publius Celerius' freedman. He was not important enough to be hosted in the Proconsular Palace and was very annoyed to be downgraded to the House of Apollonius.

Timothy decided to stay around at the house and listen to the gossip and rumours which were beginning to proliferate. As far as he could make out, the talk coming from Rome was that Claudius had not died of natural causes but may have been murdered or rather assisted to cross the River Styx. The main candidate was his wife Agrippina. Timothy thought if this were true the visit of Publius

EPHESUS SECOND VISIT AD 53

Celerius to Ephesus had more significance than could be imagined. He found Apollonius in his private quarters talking quietly with his wife. They had heard the rumours too and were clearly anxious.

"What do you make of all this?" asked Timothy.

Before Apollonius could answer loud voices could be heard coming from downstairs. Apollonius' wife went down to find out what was happening. She returned with Hymenaeus who was very agitated.

"Publius' freedman Helius is causing chaos among the kitchen slaves," explained Hymenaeus. "He has demanded access to the kitchens and insists he be allowed to prepare a special dish of mushrooms to be served at the banquet at the Palace tonight. Then he has insisted in having a slave carry the dish with him to the banquet, it is supposed to be presented to Silanus as a gift from Agrippina. And he wants it served in one of our best silver dishes."

After sunset, the guests had all assembled at the Palace. All the Asiachs were present with their wives. Apollonius and his wife reclined close to Cassander and Julia. Erastus was also present. Silanus and Antonia Domitilla were the hosts and Publius Celerius the guest of honour. The tension in the banqueting hall was palpable as the rumours arriving with the passengers had reached everyone's ears. Halfway through the meal, Publius rose to propose a toast to the new Emperor Nero. Then he turned and addressed Silanus.

"As a token of affection for you, Silanus, the Empress Mother Agrippina the Younger has sent a gift to you, her dear cousin. Like you, she is a great grandchild of the Divine Augustus. Therefore, she bids you receive the gift I bring on her behalf."

With that he clapped his hands and Helius, his freedman, entered the banqueting hall carrying the dish of cooked mushrooms in a beautiful silver bowl. The whole room fell silent as he placed the dish in front of Silanus whose face had drained of all colour. No one dared to breathe.

"Come, Silanus," said Publius, "do not dishonour the empress by refusing her gift. Come eat."

Silanus turned to his wife and looked deeply into her eyes. "I love you," his eyes said. Then taking a spoonful of mushrooms, he put them in his mouth. Everyone in the room watched with anxious eyes except Publius who was smirking at him.

Silanus quickly ate the whole dish of mushrooms as all those present watched in horror. Within moments, he gripped his stomach and began to choke and gag. He slumped sideways on his couch and his wife, sobbing, cradled him in her arms. The end was mercifully swift.

Publius called for the Praetorian guard who entered the room. They blocked the exits, and Publius addressed all the Asiachs.

"In the absence of a Proconsul in Asia, I will fulfil the role until another is appointed by the emperor. News will be sent back to Rome of the sad demise of Marcus Junius Silanus. The Empress Agrippina will no doubt be heartbroken."

Cassander stood from the couch where he had been reclining with clenched fists. "You, murdering bastard! You will not get away with this." He grabbed a knife from the table and made towards Publius. Publius nodded to the captain of the guard who quickly stepped forward with a drawn sword, which he thrust through Cassander's ribs. Held down by Apollonius, Julia Lavinia screamed as Cassander fell to the floor, his blood spreading in a pool on the mosaic.

EPHESUS SECOND VISIT AD 53

"If anyone else has anything to say, I suggest you say it now. Otherwise get out of my sight and await my instructions," said Publius. Everyone left silently. Julia and Antonia were helped out by Apollonius and his wife. Slaves came and removed the two bodies.

The shock waves of the events at the Palace rocked the city.

The next day the news was worse. Timothy came to the House of Apollonius and told them he had been to the Palace to visit Paul and Epaphras only to discover they had been taken along with some other prisoners to cells attached to the stadium. He found them along with others who had been rounded up overnight by order of Publius. This included most of Silanus and Cassander's freedmen. Paul was very distressed and feared for his life. The guards had told them Publius would soon be holding games in honour of the new emperor and they would be part of the show. They would be used at the climax of the games as sport for the gladiators or food for wild beasts as they were all under sentence of death.

Publius had taken control of the city and was rounding up the friends and supporters of Silanus. They wondered how long it would be before they came for Apollonius.

Aquila and Priscilla were the next ones to come to the house. They brought more bad news. Silanus' widow, Antonia had been arrested and confined by Publius.

"Erastus told us Antonia is being sent to Rome to join her son Lucius who was arrested before Publius even arrived in Ephesus. Onesiphorus and his mother have also been arrested and their house confiscated. Julia has been ordered to accompany Antonia to Rome," said Aquila.

As the week went by Apollonius and his wife waited, expecting to be arrested at any moment, but no one came. Apollonius talked with his wife and decided to send their slave to accompany the two ladies. But first he wrote a letter of manumission, which he gave to Epenetus.

"With this I am giving you your freedom," he said handing Epenetus a sealed scroll. "You will be my freedman from this day forward, but I am asking you first to go to Rome with the Lady Julia and the Lady Antonia. I know you are a believer as are they and I ask you to ensure they are connected with other believers in the city. The Lady Priscilla will give you names of people she knows there who will help you when you arrive."

Apollonius then handed a small leather pouch containing silver coins to Epenetus. "Take this! Keep it safe, you will need it when you arrive in Rome."

After the ship left, the mood among the general populous of Ephesus grew ugly. Even the promise of gladiatorial games to honour the Emperor Nero did not cool the mood. Onesiphorus had been freed but commanded to stay in Ephesus and await the arrival of the next proconsul who would decide his fate. The Asiachs had been meeting secretly and were furious at the treatment of Cassander and his family. Plans were afoot to try to have Publius Celerius and his freedman Helius seized and held for the murders of Silanus and Cassander. However, it was a very high stakes plan.

This did not help the prisoners held in the cells at the stadium. Conditions were appalling. Visitors were not permitted. A basket of food was sent in each day for Paul, Epaphras and Aristarchus who were chained together. Their confinement for the last few months at the palace was luxury in comparison. They were crammed in with a number of other newly arrested prisoners who had been caught up

EPHESUS SECOND VISIT AD 53

in Publius' sweep of the city. Everyone was traumatised and fearful. They could barely lay down to sleep. There were no latrines and they were forced to sit in their own waste.

Over several days one or other of the prisoners would be called out by the guards and not return. Eventually the prisoners realised someone from outside had come and bribed the guards to get them released. After ten days Paul, Epaphras and Aristarchus' names were called. They were unchained and stood stiffly as they waited for what was going to happen to them. Paul could hardly walk through the door of the cell. They were roughly pushed along a corridor and suddenly were out in the open air. There stood Aquila, Priscilla, Timothy and Erastus.

Leaving the stadium prison, they hurried back to Aquila and Priscilla's house.

"Why aren't we going to Apollonius' place," asked Epaphras.

"It's no longer safe," said Erastus. "Apollonius and his wife are under house arrest and Hymenaeus has taken over the establishment having informed on his master. Helius, Publius' freedman has moved to the Palace thankfully. I'm still lodging in the residence but it's best you are not there. No one trusts Hymenaeus."

In light of the dangerous situation, it was agreed they go inland to Colossae as soon as possible. Aquila and Priscilla had decided to leave Ephesus and return to Rome. They heard the new Emperor had overturned the restriction on Jews living in Rome and decided to return. Apollos had decided to leave also but was going to Alexandria in Egypt. Erastus and Archaicus planned to return to Corinth taking a collection of papyrus scrolls and more importantly the money raised for the believers in Jerusalem. As the city treasurer of Corinth,

Erastus would not raise suspicion carrying a large amount of money.

Epaphras decided to stay in Ephesus for the time being to support Onesiphorus but would leave if things got too difficult. They were seen as key leaders among the community of believers and wanted to stay to serve and encourage them as long as possible. Paul, Timothy, Aristarchus, Luke and Demas quickly packed up their things and headed inland to Colossae. The long three years in Ephesus had come to an end for Paul.

MACEDONIA AD 56

CHAPTER XXII

The five of them hurried out of the city through the Magnesian Gate. Epaphras came with them as far as the gate and wished them well as they left.

"Don't leave it too long before you come back, Paul. Our hearts are knit to your heart. Things will settle down here eventually," said Epaphras as he embraced them one by one. "Give my love to my brother and his wife and tell them I will do all I can to look after Apollonius."

They carried with them a large bag of precious manuscripts, copies of the letters Paul had written. The paved road went up a slow incline past mausolea and cemeteries. At the top of the hill they turned and looked back at Ephesus spread out below them, the blue Aegean Sea sparkling in the distance. A tiny figure could still be seen down by the ornate gate in the city walls. They waved and the tiny figure returned the wave. Finally turning their backs on Ephesus, they took the road inland to Colossae. Paul did not know this would be the last time he would set eyes on the city. He had invested three years of his life in the people of the city and loved them deeply. At the same time, he was anxious and exhausted having been confined for many months in prison. His legs had already started to ache. The last few weeks had taken a huge toll on them. Paul and Aristarchus were both physically and emotionally exhausted and traumatised.

They were glad Lucas and Demas were with them. Lucas set the pace and had advised short journeys each day rather than rushing to get to Colossae.

As they trudged along, they were overtaken by a line of wagons loaded with expensive household articles. In the middle was an ornately decorated carriage drawn by magnificent horses surrounded by a small group of armed household slaves. Paul recognised the lead rider on a horse, and then caught a glimpse through the drapes around the carriage of a wealthy lady passenger cradling small children. The rider saw Paul, acknowledged him with a wave but did not pause to speak.

"We are not the only ones fleeing the city," Paul said to Lucas. "I recognise him, he is one of the Asiachs."

"He knew you, Paul, we must be careful. Less friendly people might report our whereabouts," said Timothy.

For several days they followed the road alongside the Meander River. They came to its confluence with the Lycos River which flowed from the uplands in the interior close to where Laodicea and Colossae were situated. Arriving in Laodicea they rested for two nights at Nympha's house. She sent a messenger on to Philemon to alert him of their arrival. She was delighted to see them and relieved they had left Ephesus safely. She told them she would accompany them to Colossae and arranged a carriage to carry Paul as he was struggling from the journey.

Two days later, the company approached the city gates of Colossae. A small group of people were waiting, ready to help and to welcome them. In the centre stood Philemon and next to him was Onesimus. There was Archippus, Philemon's son, John Mark and Tychicus all eager to greet the travellers. A wonderful reunion ensued. As they gathered together, spontaneous shouts of thanksgiving and praise to God broke out. Paul felt happier than he had in months. There were many stories to tell and much news to share. Paul was particularly delighted to see Onesimus standing obviously at ease alongside Philemon.

"Have you met my new freedman, Paul?" asked Philemon grinning widely. "I think you may know him." Onesimus smiled at Paul and then turned to Philemon, "I'll run ahead and let Apphia know we are all on our way." He turned and bounded off through the gate of the city.

Paul and his companions stayed for several weeks in Colossae, which gave them time to recover from the ordeal of the last months in Ephesus. Apphia's house was noted for its good food and the group ate well. Assisted by Lucas' constant monitoring of his health, Paul was physically on the mend. However, his spirits were low. He found himself staring out of the window looking at the hills beyond Colossae and sometimes inexplicably breaking down in tears. He was concerned about the communities of believers across Asia Minor, Macedonia and Achaia and he longed for news of them. In particular, he wanted to know how things were in Corinth. Having left Ephesus he realised it would make it difficult for Titus to send him news. Every passing week his longing for news grew stronger. He began to talk with Timothy about moving on and heading north to Troas then crossing over to Philippi and Macedonia.

Before he left Colossae, Paul started to write another letter to the believers in Corinth about the collection. Then he decided not to send it as he worried it would be misunderstood. Tychicus, who had been the amanuensis, could hear the hesitation and anxiety in

Paul's words.

"Why don't you wait until we get up to Macedonia? We are sure to hear news from Titus at some point. Then if the letter is still relevant you can send it from there. You may even want to write a more detailed letter and include this in whatever you write."

The sense in Tychicus' words calmed Paul's fears, and he agreed to postpone sending it. "Keep it with us though, you never know I may send it later."

Finally they felt it was time to move on. Archippus wanted to take Paul up into the cities to the north where he and Epaphras had established communities of believers. The main road to Troas would be through these cities and they decided to take this route. John Mark however, wanted to stay longer in Colossae to encourage the believers in the city and Laodicea and Hierapolis. The group set off after saying their farewells again. Tychicus joined them along with Archippus, and the group was now seven. They also carried with them a contribution of money for the poor believers in Jerusalem. Paul's plan for the collection was progressing.

The road took them north west from Colossae to Hierapolis then down into the Meander valley where they crossed the river. They continued over the hills and eventually arrived in the city of Philadelphia where Archippus introduced them to the believers in the city. People were delighted to meet Paul and Timothy as they had heard about them from Epaphras and Archippus. After staying some days, they moved on to Sardis where they received exactly the same reception. The welcome of these believers was a great encouragement to Paul and it was clear they had not been visited by any of Matthias' group. It was a relief to not to have to spend all their time trying to correct erroneous teaching but could simply impart life and encouragement into them. Instead of going down to the coast to Smyrna and taking the coast road north via Pergamum to Troas they continued inland to Thyatira. Paul had expressed an interest in visiting the city which was Lydia's hometown in the hope she might be there.

On arrival in the city, Archippus took them to the home of one of the believers. They were welcomed and heard that Lydia was in Philippi. This was as far north as Archippus had travelled sharing the good news about Jesus. Paul suggested he remain in the area while the rest went on to Pergamum.

"Do you remember what I wrote to you when I was in prison in Ephesus, Archippus?" asked Paul. "What I said was something like 'make sure you complete the ministry you have received in the Lord.' Having watched you and walked with you this last few weeks, I can see your heart and the love you have for the believers in these cities. I have met these dear people in these communities. They are rooted in the same love you are rooted in. I can see how they love you and how you love them. They look to you even though you are young. You are being a father to them. I want to bless you to stay and continue in what Father has prepared for you."

Archippus, whilst sad not to be continuing with Paul on his journey, knew this was the way forward for him. He added,

"When Epaphras comes, we can do this together. I have been thinking we could also go south from Colossae to Aphrodisias and Halicarnassus. There are the Islands just of the coast, Cos and Rhodes too. Then there is Crete to think about. My heart gets very excited when I think about these places."

"You have the heart of an evangelist, Archippus. I understand this. It is how I think too, said Paul.

"I wonder where I get it from," Archippus laughed.

They said their farewells and headed over the hills to Pergamum. After a brief visit they continued around the coast seeing the island of Lesbos across the water until the road swung north.

The band of travellers finally arrived in Troas. Paul had been hoping he would find Titus there. He had sent a message to him with Erastus when they all left Ephesus about his plan to go to Macedonia via Troas. His overriding concern was to get news from Corinth. He was becoming increasingly anxious and his friends were at a loss to know how to help him. He kept saying, "I'm trusting Father to comfort me in this time. My heavenly Father knows." Though he admitted privately to Timothy one day. "It is one thing to say it and another thing to live it!"

They made their way to Carpus' house. Paul's pace increased and his hopes rose as they turned the corner into the street. He hammered on the door in his excitement at being back on familiar territory. A young man answered the door and broke into a huge smile.

"Paul! Is it really you? Lucas, Demas and you, Timothy," said the very excited young man.

"Eutychus! Is it really you?" said Paul mimicking the young man's excitement. "My goodness, you are a man now and a very handsome one too. It must be five years since I saw you. You were still a young boy then. Now look at you."

Eutychus grinned and hugged Paul.

"Now tell me," said Paul. "Is Titus here?"

"No," said Eutychus, "were you expecting him?"

Paul was visibly disappointed. "Is there any message from him at all, perhaps your father knows?"

They all went inside and met Carpus. Food was organised and beds for them all to sleep. Lucas was particularly glad to be back in his home territory. Carpus shared the news and asked Paul if he would speak at a gathering for the people who had never met him. He also said the door was wide open in the city as people were very interested in the message the believers were spreading. It became apparent Paul could have stayed many days and be very busy there. But his mind was not at rest because he had not found Titus or heard from him. After a few days, Paul said,

"I want to move on and head into Macedonia to continue my search for Titus."

"It's winter already, Paul. It would be more sensible to stay here until the spring. Besides it will be virtually impossible and dangerous to attempt a sea crossing. I know the dangers a journey like that would bring," said Demas.

But nothing he said could dissuade Paul. Lucas joined Demas in his advice and there were a few days of tension between them all. It became apparent Paul was in no mood for discussion and he resorted to a pattern of behaviour which often afflicted him. He made up his mind and refused to listen to anyone else. Demas was equally adamant and firmly told Paul he was stupid to attempt to travel. But Paul refused any further discussion.

"I am staying in Troas anyway. If you insist on going on your head be it. Don't say I didn't warn you," said Demas. So, Lucas, Tychicus, Aristarchus and Timothy crossed over with Paul into

Macedonia. They said their goodbyes, and Paul promised he would return as soon as he could.[104]

They left town and as a concession instead of going to the harbour to find a boat, they walked north up to the shore of the Sea of Marmara where the Hellespont channel entered the sea. It was a much shorter crossing on one of the many smaller boats that crisscrossed the water at this point. Taking this route would add many more days on foot but even Paul agreed it would be better to cross here. As soon as they landed on the Macedonian side of the Hellespont, they took the main road, the Via Egnatia, which went west towards Philippi and Thessalonica. It was late winter and the weather was atrocious. They hurried as fast as they could but even the usually good straight paved road was impassable at some places because of floods. It seemed everything was conspiring against them to make the journey difficult. They felt harassed at every turn.

Finally, after more than ten days on the road in the pouring rain, they saw Philippi appear in the distance shrouded in low clouds. They made their way into the city and went straight to Lydia's house where they were received with great joy by Lydia and her family. The house was warm with braziers burning in the main rooms, and Lydia quickly organised food and wine which comforted and nourished them. Lucas went off to his home and they all agreed to meet the following day.

The next morning, Clement and Epaphroditus came with exciting news for Paul. They greeted Timothy, Paul and Tychicus warmly and told them they had news about Titus. He was in Thessalonica. Paul was all for leaving immediately and rushing there to find him but Lydia put her foot down.

"Oh no you don't," said Lydia strongly. "You are not rushing off tired and sick. Just look at you. You are staying here. Wait until Lucas comes, I am sure he will agree. You need rest, and we can look after you and feed you here. You are all skin and bones."

"Yes, but—" began Paul.

"Don't you 'Yes but' me. Do as you are told and stay put. I can organise a messenger to go to Thessalonica and get Titus to come here. He is half your age and will be here in no time at all."

"But," Paul began again, and then he stopped. He knew when he had met his match.

Timothy was smiling at this whole exchange. Paul would not have taken it from one of the boys he thought. But Lydia? It was obvious why she was a successful business woman.

Within a week Titus arrived. Paul was much recovered and eagerly awaiting him. He was delighted when Titus walked into Lydia's house and jumped up from his chair and ran to embrace him. He and Timothy sat with Titus, hearing all the news from Corinth. Just having him there was a great comfort to Paul. He realised his description of God being the Father of compassion and a God of all comfort was very personal to him. He experienced Father expressing his loving comfort for his sons and daughters many times through each other. To Paul, Titus was an expression of the Father's love and comfort to him.

Titus told Paul how his visit to Corinth had been worthwhile. He said the Corinthians were in a very different place than they had been a year before. They had been a real blessing and comfort to him personally.

"They are longing for you both to come and visit them. They are deeply sorry for the way some of their behaviour wounded you, Paul.

The last thing they wanted was to cause you such grief," said Titus.

Paul was relieved and overjoyed by this news. Over the next few days, as they enjoyed the warmth and comfort of Lydia's home, Paul framed another letter to the Corinthians in response to the new situation. He wanted to tell them about how the Father comforts his sons and daughters. He wanted to also write about the weakness he experienced and how in his weakness it enabled the power and strength of the Lord Jesus to shine through. There was also the offering and various other things he wanted to raise with them. So again, with Tychicus and Timothy's help, he began yet another letter to the Corinthians.[104]

CHAPTER XXIII

Paul began to dictate in his usual fashion. "Paul, an apostle of Christ Jesus by the will of God, and Timothy our brother, to the gathered assembly of God in Corinth, together with all his holy people throughout Achaia. Grace and peace to you from God our Father and the Lord Jesus Christ."

As he thought about how to begin he decided to begin the letter with a very honest account of how things had been for him. He reflected on the recent challenges of hardships and trials he had experienced and saw how the Father had held him all the way through. He could not help but express his thanksgiving and praise to God.

"Praise be to the God and Father of our Lord Jesus Christ, the Father of compassion and the God of all comfort, who comforts us in all our troubles, so that we can comfort those in any trouble with the comfort we ourselves receive from God. For just as we share abundantly in the sufferings of Christ, so also our comfort abounds through Christ. If we are distressed, it is for your comfort and salvation; if we are comforted, it is for your comfort, which produces in you patient endurance of the same sufferings we suffer. And our hope for you is firm, because we know that just as you share in our sufferings, so also you share in our comfort."[105]

Paul wondered how much they knew of his recent circumstances

MACEDONIA AD 56

and decided to be very straight with them.

"We do not want you to be uninformed, brothers and sisters, about the troubles we experienced in the province of Asia. We were under great pressure, far beyond our ability to endure, so that we despaired of life itself. Indeed, we felt we had received the death sentence in our bodies. But this happened that we might not rely on ourselves but on God, who raises the dead. He has delivered us from such a deadly peril, and he will deliver us again. On him we have set our hope that he will continue to deliver us, as you help us by your prayers. Then many will give thanks on our behalf for the gracious favour granted us in answer to the prayers of many."[106]

Paul felt he needed to give them an explanation to why his plans had changed from what he had originally told them he was going to do. "I was confident of this, I wanted to visit you first so that you might benefit twice. I wanted to visit you on my way to Macedonia and to come back to you from Macedonia, and then to have you send me on my way to Judea. Was I fickle when I intended to do this? Or do I make my plans in a worldly manner so that in the same breath I say both "Yes, yes" and "No, no"?[107]

As he dictated these words, he was mindful of the painful visit he had made some time before to Corinth. He also thought about the letter he had written to them which was full of distress and written through tears. However, he wanted them to see his intention was not to grieve them but for them see the reality of the depth of his love for them.[108]

Paul thought about one man in particular who had caused so much of the trouble in Corinth because of his promiscuous behaviour. He had learnt from Titus how the community had resolved the issue. He wrote in a similar way to the one who had failed and

MACEDONIA AD 56

fallen in Galatia, and he wanted the Corinthians to so the same.

"If anyone has caused grief, he has not so much grieved me as he has grieved all of you to some extent, not to put it too severely. The punishment inflicted on him by the majority is sufficient. Now instead, you ought to forgive and comfort him, so that he will not be overwhelmed by excessive sorrow. I urge you, therefore, to reaffirm your love for him. Another reason I wrote you was to see if you would stand the test and be obedient in everything. Anyone you forgive, I also forgive. And what I have forgiven, if there was anything to forgive, I have forgiven in the sight of Christ for your sake, in order that Satan might not outwit us. For we are not unaware of his schemes."[109]

Paul wanted to tell them how he had been eager to hear news of them and how he longed to see Titus to hear first-hand how they were.

"Now when I went to Troas to preach the gospel of Christ and found that the Lord had opened a door for me, I still had no peace of mind, because I did not find my brother Titus there. So I said goodbye to them and went on to Macedonia."[110]

The letter was not written in haste. Paul and Timothy worked on it together and discussed what they wanted to say to their friends in Corinth. As a boy, Paul had once seen a military parade in Tarsus when a Roman general rode in triumph through the city following a campaign in the East leading captive prisoners in his vanguard. He remembered how the procession was surrounded by girls with baskets of flower petals, which they liberally scattered around creating a fragrant aroma. As he thought about this event, he compared it to his own experience.

"But thanks be to God, who always leads us as captives in Christ's triumphal procession and uses us to spread the aroma of the knowledge of him everywhere. For we are to God the pleasing aroma of Christ among those who are being saved and those who are perishing. To the one we are an aroma that brings death; to the other, an aroma that brings life."[111]

Paul was conscious as he wrote how some had accused him of preaching to enrich himself and he wanted to make it clear this was not the case. Nor did he need letters of introduction as some claimed he lacked.

"Unlike so many, we do not peddle the word of God for profit. On the contrary, in Christ we speak before God with sincerity, as those sent from God. Are we beginning to commend ourselves again? Or do we need, like some people, letters of recommendation to you or from you? You yourselves are our letter, written on our hearts, known and read by everyone. You show that you are a letter from Christ, the result of our ministry, written not with ink but with the Spirit of the living God, not on tablets of stone but on tablets of human hearts. Such confidence we have through Christ before God. Not that we are competent in ourselves to claim anything for ourselves, but our competence comes from God. He has made us competent as ministers of a new covenant, not of the letter but of the Spirit; for the letter kills, but the Spirit gives life."[112]

Having addressed a number of the contentious issues he knew had caused pain in Corinth, Paul's heart was also stirred with more noble themes. As he spoke about the Spirit giving life, it was as if the Holy Spirit surged through his whole being as he considered the glory of the new covenant made between God and mankind. In the midst of dictating he was taken up by the Spirit of God and experienced great revelation. It was as much as Tychicus could do to keep up writing. The stylus seemed to fly across the sheet of papyrus.

"Now if the ministry that brought death, which was engraved in letters on stone, came with glory, so that the Israelites could not look steadily at the face of Moses because of its glory, transitory though it was, will not the ministry of the Spirit be even more glorious? If the ministry that brought condemnation was glorious, how much more glorious is the ministry that brings righteousness! For what was glorious has no glory now in comparison with the surpassing glory. And if what was transitory came with glory, how much greater is the glory of that which lasts!

"Therefore, since we have such a hope, we are very bold. We are not like Moses, who would put a veil over his face to prevent the Israelites from seeing the end of what was passing away. But their minds were made dull, for to this day the same veil remains when the old covenant is read. It has not been removed, because only in Christ is it taken away. Even to this day when Moses is read, a veil covers their hearts. But whenever anyone turns to the Lord, the veil is taken away. Now the Lord is the Spirit, and where the Spirit of the Lord is, there is freedom. And we all, who with unveiled faces contemplate the Lord's glory, are being transformed into his image with ever-increasing glory, which comes from the Lord, who is the Spirit." (113)

The room was silent as the full weight of these truths flowed from Paul's heart and voice then was transferred in writing through the hand and stylus of Tychicus onto the sheets of papyri. Paul saw this was a treasure indeed not of their own strength and power but God's power at work within them and through them.

Timothy spoke up. "Paul, do you remember the time in Ephesus when you and I were talking with the slaves in the House of Apollonius? It was the day Epenetus became a believer."

"Yes, I remember it well, Timo. What about it?" asked Paul.

"Well, I remember you commenting about the food bowls and jars in the slave's quarters and comparing them to the fancy tableware in the guest rooms. You said at the time we were like those clay pots carrying this treasure," said Timothy.

Paul immediately stated dictating again.

"Yes! Of course! That's it! Come, Tychicus, write this down. We have this treasure in jars of clay to show that this all surpassing power is from God and not from us. We are hard pressed on every side, but not crushed; perplexed, but not in despair; persecuted, but not abandoned; struck down, but not destroyed. We always carry around in our body the death of Jesus, so that the life of Jesus may also be revealed in our body. For we who are alive are always being given over to death for Jesus' sake, so that his life may also be revealed in our mortal body. So then, death is at work in us, but life is at work in you."[114]

Paul continued in this vein for quite some time explaining to the Corinthians how the ministry he had received reflected the suffering of Jesus. He talked about how there was a new body prepared for him and how he longed to be with the Lord. He told them the compelling motivation of his ministry to them was the love of Christ.

Again, he returned to his favourite description of their position as believers,

"If anyone is in Christ, the new creation has come. The old has gone, the new is here! All this is from God, who reconciled us to himself through Christ and gave us the ministry of reconciliation, that God was reconciling the world to himself in Christ, not counting people's sins against them. And he has committed to us the message of reconciliation. We are therefore Christ's ambassadors, as though God were making his appeal through us. We implore you on Christ's behalf. Be reconciled to God. God made him who had no sin to be sin for us, so that in him we might become the righteousness of God. As God's co-workers, we urge you not to receive God's grace in vain. For he says, 'In the time of my favour I heard you, and in the day of salvation I helped you.'"

With passion Paul concluded this section of the letter with a great declaration. "I tell you, now is the time of God's favour, now is the day of salvation."[115]

"I think that will do for today," Paul stretched and rubbed his eyes after some minutes of silence. "Let's start again tomorrow. Thank you, boys. I couldn't do this without you." He embraced each of them in turn. Then he slowly walked out into the garden in Lydia's house. He knelt on the grass and buried his head in his hands. Timothy and Tychicus quietly walked away as they left him there soaking up the sunshine and enjoying the Father's comforting presence.

Paul rested for a few days and when he was ready gathered Timothy, Tychicus and Titus together again to continue the letter.

"We have spoken freely to you, Corinthians, and opened wide our hearts to you. We are not withholding our affection from you, but you are withholding yours from us. As a fair exchange, I speak as to my children, open wide your hearts also." He encouraged them to be clear where their true allegiance was, not with the forces of darkness or idols. He quoted from the Jewish Scriptures and as was often his practice would translate them into Greek from memory adding insights and truth as he spoke them out. He culminated this section of the letter with an astonishing revelation.

"I will be a Father to you, and you will be my sons and daughters, says the Lord Almighty."[116]

This letter was intensely personal. As Paul opened his heart to them, he asked them to reciprocate by opening their hearts to him.

"Make room for us in your hearts. We have wronged no one, we have corrupted no one, we have exploited no one. I do not say this to condemn you. I have said before that you have such a place in our hearts that we would live or die with you. I have spoken to you with great frankness. I take great pride in you. I am greatly encouraged. In all our troubles, my joy knows no bounds.

"For when we came into Macedonia, we had no rest, but we were harassed at every turn, conflicts on the outside, fears within. But God, who comforts the downcast, comforted us by the coming of Titus, and not only by his coming but also by the comfort you had given him. He told us about your longing for me, your deep sorrow, your ardent concern for me, so that my joy was greater than ever.

"In addition to our own encouragement, we were especially delighted to see how happy Titus was, because his spirit has been refreshed by all of you. I had boasted to him about you, and you have not embarrassed me. But just as everything we said to you was true, so our boasting about you to Titus has proved to be true as well. And his affection for you is all the greater when he remembers that you were all obedient, receiving him with fear and trembling. I am glad I can have complete confidence in you." [117]

"Have we finished do you think?" asked Timothy.

"No. Not yet," said Paul. "There are still a number of things on my heart I want to say. I want to remind them about the offering I am collecting for the poor believers in Jerusalem. I really want to take this as soon as I can to Judea."

"I kept a copy of the letter you were thinking of sending when we were in Colossae," said Tychicus. "Would this be a good place to include it now?"

"Thank you for reminding me. Read it to me and let's think about it. I want more than anything to be in the flow of what Father is saying."

Tychicus rummaged through the sheets of papyri he brought with him and found the letter. Stained from the rain on the journey, it would need to be rewritten but it was still legible. They all sat down as he read it aloud to them. When he had finished reading it, Paul felt he wanted to amend a few things to reflect their changed circumstances. So they began again. After a while, they began to talk about the practicalities of not only the collection but the delivery of the letter to Corinth. Paul wanted to stay longer in Macedonia and continue to preach the message of Jesus in the province and even further west along the Via Egnatia into Illyricum before going himself to Corinth.[118]

"I would really like to carry the letter to Corinth for you," said Titus.

"Yes, that is a good idea, but I would like two others to accompany you." As they considered this, Paul looked at Timothy and Tychicus in a knowing way and then continued dictating.

"Thanks be to God, who put into the heart of Titus the same concern I have for you. For Titus not only welcomed our appeal, but he is coming to you with much enthusiasm and on his own initiative. And we are sending along with him the brother who is praised by all the assemblies of believers for his service to the gospel. What is more, he was chosen by the assemblies to accompany us as we carry the offering, which we administer in order to honour the Lord himself and to show our eagerness to help. We want to avoid any criticism of the way we administer this liberal gift. For we are taking pains to do what is right, not only in the eyes of the Lord but also in the eyes of man.

"In addition, we are sending with them our brother who has often proved to us in many ways that he is zealous, and now even more so because of his great confidence in you. As for Titus, he is my partner and co-worker among you; as for our brothers, they are representatives of the assemblies and an honour to Christ. Therefore, show these men the proof of your love and the reason for our pride in you, so that the assemblies of believers can see it."[119]

Tychicus put down the stylus and rubbed his hands which were stiff after writing. "Do I presume from what I have just written Timo and I are to accompany Titus to Corinth? If this is so won't it leave you with a smaller team to continue as far as Illyricum?"

"I understand what you are saying. I thought I would go to Thessalonica and team up with Silas again. But let's think about it after we have finished the letter. I want to add something else before we go any further." Paul concluded this section of the letter about the collection with an encouraging blessing on them.

"This service that you perform is not only supplying the needs of the Lord's people but is also overflowing in many expressions of thanks to God. Because of the service by which you have proved yourselves, others will praise God for the obedience that accompanies your confession of the gospel of Christ, and for your generosity in sharing with them and with everyone else. And in their prayers for you their hearts will go out to you, because of the surpassing grace God has given you. Thanks be to God for his indescribable gift!"[120]

They all needed a break from the writing and in the last hour or so, delicious aromas were wafting from the kitchen arousing their hunger.

Lydia came into their writing room. "It's time for rest," she said. "It's not good to be writing all day. I've had my servants prepare a meal to refresh us all. Come on, you boys lead the way and, Paul, make sure you get enough to eat too. Don't let them eat it all."

Lydia had laid on a feast. Lucas, Epaphroditus, Clement and Aristarchus joined them along with Euodia and her sister Syntyche. Soon the triclinium was filled with chatter and laughter as the group of friends shared a meal together. As was their custom they passed the bread around the table and gave thanks as they remembered the broken body of Jesus. Then as they all paused and reflected, Paul poured out wine from a silver jug into individual goblets. "This represents the blood of Jesus that was poured out for us." They all drank with thanksgiving and appreciation.

As the meal drew to a close, Titus and Paul talked about the situation in Corinth. "Are you thinking you will write something about these so-called super apostles in Corinth?" asked Titus.

"What is your concern about them and who do you have in mind?" asked Paul.

"Well," began Titus. "What I would say is it is an attitude as much as a group of people. When Apollos first arrived in Corinth, many were amazed at his oratory and grasp of rhetoric and began to say you were untrained as a speaker with no credentials. They viewed him a super apostle in the sense of being superior to you in his gifting. Also, when those Judaisers turned up and started to say they came with the full backing of the leaders and apostles in Jerusalem, they alleged you didn't have it. Some people were saying you are very bold and impressive in writing but timid and unimpressive face to face. It feels like it is a personal attack on you, Paul. They boasted about their achievements and credentials, continually pointing out how effective their ministry was, listing their achievements. It seems they got their sense of significance out of wanting to be seen all the time. It's quite hard to pin it down."

"It can be a real pitfall in our ministry, Titus. Human nature wants to claim something for itself rather than recognising the true source of our success. When it comes down to titles, boasting about successes and drawing the attention to us rather than the Lord, they are all symptomatic of not a true apostle but a false apostle."

"It reminds me of the Greek story of Narcissus falling in love with his own refection," said Titus.

"Let's get back to this tomorrow. I think we can write some more about this." Paul reclined back on his couch at the table, ate another of Lydia's delicious honey cakes and took another mouthful of wine. Within a few minutes, he began to snore and one by one the guests quietly got up and left. Lydia came back with a warm blanket and carefully covered the sleeping man.

The next morning Paul and the three T's as he was calling them gathered again in the tablinum, the writing room, which was just off the atrium.

"I want to finish the letter with looking at where real ministry is found. It is in our weakness and not in our own strength. These so-called super apostles even if they have no name represent a real danger to us all. I think I have addressed some of their concerns already. So where do we begin? Tychicus, please read me the last thing we wrote." After hearing the last few lines, Paul began again.

"By the humility and gentleness of Christ, I appeal to you. I, Paul, who am "timid" when face to face with you, but "bold" toward you when away, I beg you that when I come I may not have to be as bold as I expect to be toward some people who think that we live by the standards of this world. For though we live in the world, we do not wage war as the world does. The weapons we fight with are not the weapons of the world. On the contrary, they have divine power to demolish strongholds. We demolish arguments and every pretension that sets itself up against the knowledge of God, and we take captive every thought to make it obedient to Christ.

"You are judging by appearances. If anyone is confident that they belong to Christ, they should consider again that we belong to Christ just as much as they do. So even if I boast somewhat freely about the authority the Lord gave us for building you up rather than tearing you down, I will not be ashamed of it. I do not want to seem to be trying to frighten you with my letters. For some say, 'His letters are weighty and forceful, but in person he is unimpressive and his speaking amounts to nothing.' Such people should realise that what we are in our letters when we are absent, we will be in our actions when we are present."[121]

Paul addressed the issue of boasting about personal ministry, concluding by saying, "Let the one who boasts boast in the Lord." Then, he went on to address the super apostles specifically. "I do not think I am in the least inferior to those 'super-apostles.' I may indeed be untrained as a speaker, but I do have knowledge." He warned them to recognise what was really going on. "For such people are false apostles, deceitful workers, masquerading as apostles of Christ. And no wonder, for Satan himself masquerades as an angel of light. It is not surprising, then, if his servants also masquerade as servants of righteousness. Their end will be what their actions deserve."(122)

Paul's following 'argument' was in the style of rhetoric the Corinthians would immediately have recognised but he turned it on its head. Instead of listing his achievements or boasts in the way the Romans did on carved marble inscriptions on their public monuments, he listed his weaknesses and struggles. He used irony and then began what was a truly shocking catalogue of suffering and hardship.

"Whatever anyone else dares to boast about. I am speaking as a fool. I also dare to boast about. Are they Hebrews? So am I. Are they Israelites? So am I. Are they Abraham's descendants? So am I. Are they servants of Christ? (I am out of my mind to talk like this.) I am more. I have worked much harder, been in prison more frequently, been flogged more severely, and been exposed to death again and again. Five times I received from the Jews the forty lashes minus one. Three times I was beaten with rods, once I was pelted with stones, three times I was shipwrecked, I spent a night and a day in the open sea, I have been constantly on the move. I have been in danger from rivers, in danger from bandits, in danger from my fellow Jews, in danger from Gentiles; in danger in the city, in danger in the country, in danger at sea, and in danger from false believers. I have laboured and toiled and have often gone without sleep; I have known hunger and thirst and have often gone without food; I have been cold and naked. Besides everything else, I face daily the pressure of my concern for all the assemblies of believers. Who is weak, and I do not feel weak? Who is led into sin, and I do not inwardly burn? If I must boast, I will boast of the things that show my weakness. The God and Father of the Lord Jesus, who is to be praised forever, knows that I am not lying."[123]

Paul recounted an experience his companions knew was his own. Even in this rhetorically masterful section of the letter he could not attribute it to himself but modestly depersonalised it.

"I must go on boasting. Although there is nothing to be gained, I will go on to visions and revelations from the Lord. I know a man in Christ who fourteen years ago was caught up to the third heaven. Whether it was in the body or out of the body I do not know, God knows. And I know that this man, was caught up to paradise and heard inexpressible things, things that no one is permitted to tell. I will boast about a man like that, but I will not boast about myself, except about my weaknesses. Even if I should choose to boast, I would not be a fool, because I would be speaking the truth. But I refrain, so no one will think more of me than is warranted by what I do or say, or because of these surpassingly great revelations."[124]

In the culmination of this section of the letter, Paul got to the heart of his own deeply personal experience of struggling with weakness and his discovery of the source of all his strength being in Christ.

"Therefore, in order to keep me from becoming conceited, I was given a thorn in my flesh, a messenger of Satan, to torment me. Three times I pleaded with the Lord to take it away from me. But he said to me, 'My grace is sufficient for you, for my power is made perfect in weakness.' Therefore, I will boast all the more gladly about my weaknesses, so that Christ's power may rest on me. That is why, for Christ's sake, I delight in weaknesses, in insults, in hardships, in persecutions, in difficulties. For when I am weak, then I am strong."[125]

With the burden discharged in his heart for the Corinthians, Paul was almost ready to finish the letter. His final remarks were a mixture of warnings, challenges, exhortations and a promise. "Here I am, ready to come to you this third time.

"Finally, brothers and sisters, rejoice! Strive for full restoration, encourage one another, be of one mind, live in peace. And the God of love and peace will be with you. Greet one another with a holy kiss. All God's people here send their greetings."

Tychicus put down his stylus and expected Paul to pick it up and write something in his own hand. He turned to look at Paul who was sitting on a chair beside him. Paul sat there in silence, his eyes closed for some minutes. No one spoke. They all recognised the presence of God was filling the room. No one wanted to move or lose the moment. Finally, Paul spoke.

"May the grace of the Lord Jesus Christ, and the love of God, and the fellowship of the Holy Spirit be with you all."[126]

CORINTH THIRD VISIT
AD 56

CHAPTER XXIV

Now that winter had passed, Paul wanted to stay a few months longer in Macedonia visiting Thessalonica and Berea and then pressing westwards as far as Illyricum. The final letter written to the Corinthians was complete and copies had been made as usual. Paul wanted to send the letter as soon as possible, so it would be received in Corinth prior to his going to Corinth later in the year.

Titus would carry the letter accompanied by Tychicus and a slightly nervous Timothy. Timothy's last visit to Corinth, like Paul's, had been difficult. Even though three years had passed, it was a painful memory for him. He was glad his two good friends would be with him this time.

They set off with the letter and a number of other copies of Paul's correspondence with the believers in Asia and Macedonia. Erastus had asked for copies to be sent when he was with Paul in Ephesus and Paul had agreed. As they parted, Paul assured them he would make his way to Corinth in a few months, certainly before winter at the end of the year.

After they left, Paul spent a few more days with Lucas and the rest of the community in Philippi before setting out for Thessalonica. Epaphroditus and Aristarchus accompanied him on the journey. They passed through Amphipolis and visited with the believers in the small city before taking the direct road to Thessalonica. It was a comparatively short journey, which they completed in four days. Aristarchus was thrilled to be back in his home town. Secundus and Silas were overjoyed to see Paul again. Jason opened up his home to them so they could rest and be cared for. Five years had passed since Paul was last with them, and then his brief visit had been interrupted by the attack on Paul initiated by Matthias from Jerusalem.

Much had happened since then. The community under Silas' careful guidance had grown and was now meeting in a number of homes across the city and there were also groups in some of the outlying districts in the countryside. Paul shared with them his plan to remain in the northern part of Macedonia and to take the road west into Illyricum. He hoped to travel as far as Apollonia on the west coast of the province. Epaphroditus spent some days getting to know them in Thessalonica before returning to re-join Lucas in Philippi. Aristarchus, Secundus and Silas joined Paul on his journey west passing through Berea and reconnecting with Sopater in the city.

The weeks turned into months and early in the autumn Paul returned from Illyricum to Berea with his travelling companions. Silas and Secundus went back to Thessalonica with a request by Paul for Jason to accompany him on his journey south to Corinth. When he arrived, Paul and Jason along with Aristarchus set off for Corinth having told the Bereans they hoped to return in the spring. They took the overland route south through the eastern part of Macedonia passing Mount Olympus on their left. It was a long journey taking over three weeks. The route bypassed Athens as Paul was eager to reach Corinth before the onset of the inclement winter weather.

Descending to the narrow isthmus that connected southern

CORINTH THIRD VISIT AD 56

Achaia with the north, they saw the city come into view. There was some apprehension in Paul's heart as he approached the city. He remembered the extremely painful visit he had made over three years before. Even though he knew things had radically improved and Titus and Timothy were already in the city, nonetheless the old fears stirred in his heart. As they approached the walls of the city, he saw the amphitheatre where he had tried to speak to a gathering of the believers and how it had ended in ignominy and disappointment. He was trusting this visit would be different.

They entered the city and went straight to Gaius Titius Justus' house. Gaius and his family were overjoyed to greet Paul again and meet his two friends. Gaius immediately sent messengers off to the various leaders of the community around the city to announce Paul's arrival. Over the next few hours many happy reunions took place. The first to arrive was Chloe and Timothy who was lodging with her. Timothy was very happy and relaxed, and Paul knew straight away all was well. Titus and Tychicus arrived with Erastus and Archaicus. Soon Gaius' house was full of people all eager to greet Paul. The evening turned into a party as food was brought out and friends reconnected. It continued late into the evening as they plied Paul with questions and news. Eventually, Gaius insisted everyone leave and give Paul time to rest.

As Paul lay down on his bed in the guest room, his heart was full of joy and thanksgiving. He remembered how long ago, soon after he had arrived in Corinth for the first time, Jesus himself had spoken to him. He had said, "Do not be afraid. Keep on speaking, do not be silent. For I am with you, and no one is going to attack and harm you, because I have many people in this city." As he thought about these encouraging words, he knew they were true. Indeed there were many people in the city who were believers. Slowly, his eyes closed and he sank into a deep peaceful sleep.

Over the next few days Paul spent time meeting and talking with the various people who made up the family of believers in Corinth. He felt they had truly become a family. Many of the struggles and issues that plagued them in recent years had been resolved or at least were well on the way to being healed. The leaders, Gaius, Chloe, Sosthenes, Erastus, Crispus and others were maturing in wisdom and their knowledge of God the Father. Their love and passion for Jesus was deeply heart-warming. They were filled with the Spirit and their times of worship when they gathered to break bread and remember Jesus' death were full of encouragement and inspiration. There was a flow of life as each brought their contributions to the collective times of worship as Paul had encouraged them to do in one of his letters.

Paul knew he did not need to spend very long in the city. His plan was becoming clearer. He wanted to take the substantial collection back to Jerusalem as soon as the worst of the winter was over. He planned to sail in the spring to Syria and from there go to Jerusalem. At the same time, he was increasingly sensing his work in Achaia, Macedonia and the eastern Provinces of Asia, Pamphylia, Cilicia and Syria was done. His heart continually looked to the west, to Rome and beyond to the far reaches of the Empire, even to Spain. In the same way Antioch had been a springboard for his first missionary journeys and Ephesus had been the hub of much of his ministry around the Aegean Sea, so he began to see Rome as the next centre for his ministry.

He found himself thinking a lot about the believers in Rome. He knew many of them personally. His relatives, Andronicus and

CORINTH THIRD VISIT AD 56

Junia were in Rome. They were recognised as apostolic by the wide group of apostolic leaders of which he was one. He knew Aquila and Priscilla were in Rome, and he heard their tentmaking business had prospered and now spanned Rome, Corinth and Ephesus. Others had gone to Rome. Young Apelles, the ex-male prostitute from Corinth was there. He had settled well into the household of Narcissus according to Chloe. He thought of Epenetus, the first convert in Ephesus. The former slave had accompanied Julia Lavinia, Onesiphorus' widowed mother when she was sent to Rome with Antonia Domitilla. Paul was anxious about them and eager to hear news of them. Many others he had come to know over the years were now in Rome. It seemed to him his destiny was also to follow one of the many roads leading to Rome at the centre of the Roman world.

Paul drew the team around him into the way he was thinking.

"I would advise you to consolidate the collection into smaller coins of higher value in order to make its transportation to Jerusalem easier," said Erastus. "If you want I can handle this as I have easy access to a variety of coins in the city treasury."

He gathered it all together and converted all the sesterces and denarii into gold aurei. Paul was happy to leave the administration of the collection to Erastus.

"What worries me is the weight of this gold will be too much for one man to carry. It will need to be shared. You will need a number of men to accompany you to Jerusalem," Erastus told Paul.

Paul was beginning to think about writing to the believers in Rome partly to introduce himself and his message to them but also as a preparation for moving his base of missionary activity to Rome.

Chloe and Gaius and others of the local leaders came to Paul one morning with a suggestion for him to consider and pray about. Chloe shared what they were thinking.

"Over the years we have known you, we have heard you speak and teach on many occasions. We also have your letters to us and we have read the ones you have sent to Galatia, Thessalonica and other places. However, we have many new believers among us now, most of whom have never met you or heard you teach. We know you will only be here for a few months and then will go on to Jerusalem and eventually Rome." She paused and looked at the others who nodded their encouragement for her to continue.

"Go on," said Paul. "What do you have in mind?"

"We would love you to take time to teach the people what is at the heart of your message. What you consider the good news to be. Also, to use this to add to what you have already told us about living as sons and daughters in this world. How do we live as sons according to the Spirit and not in our old way of living?" said Chloe.

"Remember, we had the challenge about how the grace of God is not something which gives us freedom to live as pagans as the unbelievers do. It still keeps coming up especially among the new converts," said Crispus.

"Then there is also the issue of us Jewish believers," said Sosthenes, "and where the Torah and the Law of Moses fit into the gospel. Since those Judaisers and so-called super apostles came, it has left lots of questions in people's minds."

"What sort of questions specifically?" asked Paul.

"What happens to the Jews who consciously reject Jesus? Will the people of Israel be saved in the end? Has God's purposes for them changed now that Jesus has come? Questions like that," answered Sosthenes.

"Not just easy questions then," laughed Paul. "As you suggest, let me consider and pray about it."

The next day was the first day of the week, the day following the Sabbath. This had become the day when the believers tried to gather together. They would meet on and off throughout the day, with people coming and going as and when their work and family commitments allowed. For many who were slaves, and not free to come and go as they pleased, they arrived after dark. People brought food to share and often times they would remember the death of Jesus by breaking bread and drinking wine several times throughout the day. The earlier problems of people being greedy with the offer of free food had been resolved long ago. There was a naturalness to this and no embarrassment with the coming and going of people.

Many a time someone would share what was happening in their lives and people would gather around them to pray for them and encourage them. Other times if there was news of someone being sick, some would go to them in their homes or lodgings to pray for them and encourage them. If someone brought a teaching invariably this happened in the evening as there were more people available then. So, what began to form in Paul's mind was for him to bring a series of teachings over a number of evenings for several weeks.

He was also thinking about the possibility of a letter to the believers in Rome. He wondered if what he was planning to teach the Corinthians could be the core of what he wanted to say to the Romans. He approached Timothy and Tychicus with this idea. Tychicus became very excited because he had met a young clerk who was part of the community who was also an amanuensis attached to Erastus' office. His name was Tertius. Everyone in the community spoke highly of him and his skill at writing. Erastus rated him as the best scribe he had ever worked with. "Also, the fastest." Tychicus added, "If you wanted someone to write down what you are saying as you speak, then he is your man. He is not just an amanuensis, he is a notarius," said Tychicus. "Erastus uses him all the time to write down things he needs to record quickly."

"What would he do for us?" asked Paul.

"I thought when you are teaching you will not want to keep stopping waiting for me to catch up. Or stopping every time my stylus breaks. You know how it is. If Erastus is agreeable, Tertius could come to the teaching sessions and write down what you say as you say it. Then the next day or something, you and he could go through it and you could add to it if you wanted, it could form the main part of your letter you want to send to Rome. What do you think?" Tychicus looked very pleased with himself.

"Hmm, will you ask Erastus and see if he is willing to lend his notarius to us?" Paul paced up and down as if trying to visualize this idea in his mind. He stopped and clasped his hands together, beaming broadly at Tychicus. "Yes, I like the sound of that very much."

CORINTH THIRD VISIT AD 56

CHAPTER XXV

The next Sabbath Paul visited the synagogue and was well received even though some of them remembered him and were cautious. He used the day to rest and relax at Gaius' house.

"The weather is turning cold, I wonder if we should try to find a large room in which people could gather to hear you teach, Paul," said Gaius.

"Let me look around and see what I can find," said Erastus. "I know the city well." He came back later looking satisfied. "I have found the ideal place away from the centre and the Forum. It is a large room owned by a man who owes me a favour. It is insignificant enough not to attract attention or cause any questions to be asked."

People started to gather soon after dark on the first day of the week. Oil lamps were lit to give some light and a table was set up so Tertius could take notes as Paul spoke. The room was soon filled to capacity with a complete cross section of the community of believers. Most were slaves and from the servant classes of the city. There were some who very obviously had colourful backgrounds. Here and there sat a wealthier family or individual, but they all mingled quite at ease with one another. There were men and women, young and old. Jewish converts and people from Gentile backgrounds. There were African faces from the south and fair skinned Germanic faces from the north. It was a microcosm of the Roman world. The chatter and laughter filling the room was an indicator of how well they knew each other.

When Paul entered the room, people stopped talking and strained in the semi darkness to get a glimpse of the man they had all heard of. Someone had said he did not cut a very imposing figure in the way Apollos had and this was true. Paul was short and slightly stooped on account of the many beatings he had endured. He was balding and the little hair he had left was grey. His face was rugged and lined. His nose was hooked having been broken many times. Crispus called for quiet and then introduced Paul, briefly telling the story of how Paul first came to Corinth five years before. Then he handed over to Paul.

Paul started by introducing what he wanted to speak about.

"Tonight, I want to talk about the gospel. I make no apology. I am not ashamed of the gospel, because it is the power of God that brings salvation to everyone who believes, first to the Jew, then to the Gentile. For in the gospel the righteousness of God is revealed. This is a righteousness that is by faith from first to last, just as it is written in the Jewish Scriptures: 'The righteous will live by faith'."

So began the teaching that went on for a number of hours over several evenings. Paul talked about the devastating impact ignorance had on the human race as they failed to recognise who God was.[127]

"For since the creation of the world God's invisible qualities, his eternal power and divine nature, have been clearly seen, being understood from what has been made, so that people are without excuse. For although they knew God, they neither glorified him as God nor gave thanks to him, but their thinking became futile and their foolish hearts were darkened. Although they claimed to be wise, they became fools and exchanged the glory of the immortal God for images made to look like a mortal human being and birds and animals and reptiles."[128]

He wanted them to see how this played itself out in the chaos of human relationships and sexuality, and the serious damage this ignorance had caused. "Their women exchanged natural sexual relations for unnatural ones. In the same way the men also abandoned natural relations with women and were inflamed with lust for one another. Men committed shameful acts with other men and received in themselves the due penalty for their error. Furthermore, just as they did not think it worthwhile to retain the knowledge of God, so God gave them over to a depraved mind. They have become filled with every kind of wickedness, evil, greed and depravity. They are full of envy, murder, strife, deceit and malice. They are gossips, slanderers, God-haters, insolent, arrogant and boastful; they invent ways of doing evil; they disobey their parents; they have no understanding, no fidelity, no love, no mercy. Although they know God's righteous decree that those who do such things deserve death, they not only continue to do these very things but also approve of those who practice them."[129]

Paul taught until late into the evening sometimes answering questions people wanted to ask. Finally, as the lamps began to sputter and go out, they finished for the night. The next day Paul sat down with Tertius and Timothy to commence writing the letter to the believers in Rome. Tertius read the notes he had taken during the previous evening's talk. Paul listened. He was very impressed with Tertius' skill as a notarius. Very little needed correction, so he asked Tertius to get a fresh sheet of papyrus and they began the letter.

As he thought about believers in Rome to whom he was writing, he realised there were similarities with many other groups. However, he was aware Rome itself was a unique city. It was the seat of the imperial cult which focused around the person of Caesar who was believed to be a god. All over the empire, temples were being built to the divine Augustus, to Claudius and now there was the Emperor Nero. The language of the cult described the Emperor as Lord, as the bringer of peace and salvation to the world. Paul knew this would collide head on with the language he and the believers across the Roman world were using about Jesus.

Whilst up to this point the opposition he had experienced was primarily from Jews who rejected the thought of Jesus being the Messiah, it occurred to him it might not be too long before the attacks came from the empire.

He knew from Aquila and Priscilla in the early days the community of believers in Rome were mostly from a Jewish background. He also knew Rome had an ambivalent attitude towards Jews. On the one hand Rome gave them freedom to practice their monotheistic faith in their synagogues and even freedom from conscription into the Roman army. On the other hand, they had been expelled from Rome back in the days of Claudius because of disturbances connected with a person the Romans called Chrestus. Paul had heard from Aquila this was in reality Jesus the Christ.

Now his friends were back in Rome and he wondered what the community was like. He knew they had a gathering in their home. He knew Chloe's brother Narcissus had a similar group. Paul wondered if these groups were based around ethnic or former religious connections. He hoped these Roman believers had open hearts towards the people of Israel, whether they were believers or

CORINTH THIRD VISIT AD 56

not. He hoped they would not just write off the Jewish people as irrelevant to the new thing God was doing.

Paul felt as he was yet to visit Rome he needed to introduce himself to them. He described himself as a servant of Christ Jesus who was called to be an apostle and set apart for the purpose of preaching the gospel. He wanted them to know their faith was being spoken about all across the world of the followers of Jesus.

"I constantly remember you in my prayers at all times," he said. "I pray that now at last by God's will the way may be opened for me to come to you. I long to see you so that I may impart to you some spiritual gift to make you strong."

Paul paused for a moment. He did not want to give them the impression he was somehow superior to them, instead he wanted them to know it would be a mutual blessing. He continued,

"This is so we may be mutually encouraged by each other's faith. I do not want you to be unaware, brothers and sisters, that I planned many times to come to you, but have been prevented from doing so until now, in order that I might have a harvest among you, just as I have had among the other Gentiles."[130]

The letter began to flow as Paul picked up many of the themes he had spoken of the night before. He made it clear he was speaking to the 'Jew first'. Paul had been dogged by rumours which had been spread about him by his enemies, accusing him of totally discounting the Jewish existence in this new world. Paul, in writing the "Jew first", countered these attacks on him.

Aware this letter would be read in a city at the heart of the Pagan Gentile world, Paul stood firmly against the idolatry that was at the core of Roman society. As the letter flowed from Paul's heart, he sensed he was being led by the Spirit of God in a way he had not experienced before. From time to time, he paused and asked Tertius to re-read a section. And on more than one occasion, with shock evident in his expression, he would respond, "Did I really just say that?"

Tertius smiled and said, "I didn't miss a word."

For Jewish readers, Paul talked about how a righteousness from God had made itself known through the Law of Moses to which the Law and the Prophets testified. He explained how this righteousness from God came through faith in Jesus to all who believe. Then he said how this applied to all, both Jews and Gentiles.

"For all have sinned and have fallen short of the glory of God, and all are justified freely by his grace through the redemption that came by Christ Jesus."

Paul saw how this legally cleared the believer of the guilt and penalty of sin. Redemption was a gift of God, and not the work of man lest it be something to boast about. It was received by faith. Continuing with his Jewish readers in mind he drew heavily from the life of Abraham to illustrate living by faith.[131]

The teaching during the evenings and the writing during the days merged as Paul poured out his heart by day in the letter to the Romans and by night to the Corinthians. He touched a level of revelation he had seldom experienced at any point before. His friends surrounded him with support and care to protect him from distractions and interruptions. They all knew they were witnessing something unlike anything they had ever seen before.

One evening as the people listened in rapt amazement at his words, Paul paused, looked at them all intently and said, "Therefore,

CORINTH THIRD VISIT AD 56

since we have been justified through faith, we have peace with God through our Lord Jesus Christ, through whom we have gained access by faith into this grace in which we now stand. And we rejoice in the hope of the glory of God. Not only so, but we also rejoice in our sufferings, because we know that suffering produces perseverance; perseverance, character; and character, hope. And hope does not disappoint us, because the love of God has been poured out into our hearts through the Holy Spirit, who has been given to us."[132]

As he spoke these words, a tangible wave of God's love swept across the room. People wept for joy. Others laughed for joy. Everyone was overwhelmed with love from the Father. This was expressed as love for one another as they wept and laughed together, embracing one another.

When he had written to the Galatians, Paul wanted them to see how God's law had been like a schoolmaster who taught them the difference between right and wrong. He took up this theme again and explained to the Corinthians since the law was brought in, as a consequence, sin seemed to increase. Then he added, "But where sin increased, grace increased all the more, so that, just as sin reigned in death, so also grace might reign through righteousness to bring eternal life through Jesus Christ our Lord."[133]

At the side of the room one of the listeners raised his hand to ask a question. Paul nodded his willingness to hear it. "Please, Paul, I have a question that has troubled us here in Corinth. Are you saying we can go on sinning so that grace may increase? Do you mean we can continue in sin because we are not under the law but under grace?"

"*Me genoito*!" exclaimed Paul in the strongest possible terms, "God forbid!" This was one of Paul's favourite exclamations. He often used it when something was absolutely unthinkable. This was the kind of thing so absurd it should not even enter a believer's mind, and so Paul would declare, *me genoito*!

Paul's response to this question was to explain what it meant to be united with Christ. He reminded them that all who were baptized into Christ Jesus were baptized into his death. As a result, they were buried with him through baptism into death in order that, just as Christ was raised from the dead through the glory of the Father, they too may live a new life. Paul very carefully dictated his answer to Tertius so that it was as clear as possible. He finally concluded,

"Therefore, do not let sin reign in your mortal body so that you obey its evil desires. Do not offer any part of yourself to sin as an instrument of wickedness, but rather offer yourselves to God as those who have been brought from death to life; and offer every part of yourself to him as an instrument of righteousness. For sin shall no longer be your master, because you are not under the law, but under grace."[134]

Paul illustrated his argument by using an example they would have all identified with. Corinth had large numbers of slaves who were sex workers attached to the temples of Aphrodite and Apollo. Many of the believers came from this background. This was not unique to Corinth and was found all over the empire. Rome itself was full of slaves attached to various temples. In many a household, the slaves were used for the sexual gratification of their masters. Paul powerfully encouraged them by saying they were no longer slaves to sin but now they had been set free from sin and become slaves of God. Even if in their bodies they had to endure suffering and sexual abuse, in their hearts and in God's eyes they were without condemnation and the benefit they reaped led to holiness, and the result was eternal life. "For the wages of sin is death, but the gift of

God is eternal life in Christ Jesus our Lord," he wrote.[135]

The next evening when Paul gathered with the believers to teach, he wanted to talk about the Law of Moses and its relevance in their life as believers. He spoke personally about his own experience and struggles, describing how all humanity was under the law of sin and death which was at work in their mortal bodies. He'd personally experienced its effects. He also showed how the Law of God given through Moses exposed the nature of sin. He saw this law as good and spiritual because it served to draw mankind to God. But it set up a dreadful internal conflict which he knew only too well.

"I find this law at work. Although I want to do good, evil is right there with me. For in my inner being I delight in God's law; but I see another law at work in me, waging war against the law of my mind and making me a prisoner of the law of sin at work within me. What a wretched man I am! Who will rescue me from this body that is subject to death?"[136]

With extraordinary openness and candour the apostle wrote to the Romans, "I myself in my mind am a slave to God's law, but in my sinful nature a slave to the law of sin."

This honesty opened up a whole new area of revelation that flowed through Paul. For a number of years he had been seeing how the true life of the believer was summed up as being in Christ. He saw all believers as sons of God because of the faithfulness of Jesus. He had written about this in his first letter when he wrote to the believers in Galatia almost seven years earlier. Here again these great truths became his theme. The faithfulness of God exhibited in and through Jesus was a central theme in his thinking and writing. Paul saw as a result there was no condemnation for those who were in Christ Jesus, because through Christ Jesus the law of the Spirit who had given them life had set them free from the law of sin and death.

This was the amazing truth. His listeners in Corinth and readers in Rome would discover through this revelation there was a third law at work in them. This was the law of the Spirit of life that was in Christ, it had cancelled the power and effect of the law of sin and death inherited through Adam. The Law of Moses was powerless to do this because it was weakened by human nature and frailty. God resolved this problem by sending his own Son in the likeness of sinful flesh, as a human being, to be a sin offering. And so the Father condemned sin in the flesh, in order that the righteous requirement of the law might be fully met in them, who do not live according to the flesh but according to the Spirit.

Paul continued, "But if Christ is in you, then even though your body is subject to death because of sin, the Spirit gives life because of righteousness. And if the Spirit of him who raised Jesus from the dead is living in you, he who raised Christ from the dead will also give life to your mortal bodies because of his Spirit who lives in you."[137]

As these words flowed out of him everyone recognised the sacredness of the moment and the depth of the truth Paul was seeing. "For those who are led by the Spirit of God are the children of God. The Spirit you received does not make you slaves, so that you live in fear again. Rather, the Spirit you received brought about your repositioning back into sonship. And by him we cry, 'Abba, Father.' The Spirit himself testifies with our spirit that we are God's children. Now if we are children, then we are heirs, heirs of God and co-heirs with Christ, if indeed we share in his sufferings in order that we may also share in his glory."[138]

Paul's heart leapt as the words tumbled out of his mouth and into their hearts and onto the page through Tertius' hand. He was looking at a far bigger picture than anything he had seen before.

"I consider that our present sufferings are not worth comparing with the glory that will be revealed in us. For creation waits in eager expectation for the sons of God to be revealed. For the creation was subjected to frustration, not by its own choice, but by the will of the one who subjected it, in hope that the creation itself will be liberated from its bondage to decay and brought into the glorious freedom of the children of God."

Paul included himself in this revelation. "We know that the whole creation has been groaning as in the pains of childbirth right up to the present time. Not only so, but we ourselves, who have the first fruits of the Spirit, groan inwardly as we wait eagerly to fully experience being acknowledged as sons and the redemption of our bodies. For in this hope we were saved."[139]

A hand went up as he was talking. Paul stopped and asked the young woman what her question was.

"I hear you saying we are God's beloved children but sometimes I feel so weak. Things are really hard in my life. I am a slave; I have had to face many painful and difficult times. I am forced to do things I hate to do. I hardly know how to pray in these situations." Her voice cracked as tears ran down her cheeks. Many others in the room knew exactly how she felt.

Paul gently went to her and held her in his arms for a moment or two. Chloe came alongside the girl as she sat back down. Paul turned to everyone and began again, "In the same way, the Spirit helps us in our weakness. We do not know what we ought to pray for, but the Spirit himself intercedes for us through wordless groans. And he who searches our hearts knows the mind of the Spirit, because the Spirit intercedes for God's people in accordance with the will of God. And we know that in all things God works for the good of those who love him, who have been called according to his purpose. For those God foreknew he also predestined to be conformed to the image of his Son, that he might be the firstborn among many brothers and sisters. And those he predestined, he also called; those he called, he also justified; those he justified, he also glorified."

Paul paused again and looked around the room. Then he closed his eyes and they knew he was talking with the Father. Every eye was on him. Paul opened his eyes and softly began to speak once more.

"What, then, shall we say in response to these things? If God is for us, who can be against us? He who did not spare his own Son, but gave him up for us all, how will he not also, along with him, graciously give us all things? Who will bring any charge against those whom God has chosen? It is God who justifies. Who then is the one who condemns? No one! Christ Jesus who died, more than that, who was raised to life, is at the right hand of God and is also interceding for us. Who shall separate us from the love of Christ? Shall trouble or hardship or persecution or famine or nakedness or danger or sword? As it is written: 'For your sake we face death all day long; we are considered as sheep to be slaughtered.'

"No, in all these things we are more than conquerors through him who loved us. For I am convinced that neither death nor life, neither angels nor demons, neither the present nor the future, nor any powers, neither height nor depth, nor anything else in all creation, will be able to separate us from the love of God that is in Christ Jesus our Lord."[140]

With these words Paul drew the evening to a close.

CHAPTER XXVI

The writing of the letter became the main focus of Paul's attention in this season. It was winter and the days were short and often cold. There were days too when the sun shone and the sky was blue and the promise of spring was in the air. He started to take daily walks out of the city to stretch his legs and strengthen his muscles for the journeys ahead. His plan was to be in Jerusalem by Passover which was only two months away. He knew he would need to secure passage on a ship from Cenchreae to Caesarea in early spring. He hoped the weather would be settled enough to make the journey without yet another shipwreck. Carrying the offering to Jerusalem was also his concern. He did not want it to sink to the bottom of the sea like an offering to Poseidon. On one of his walks he went as far as the port and met the leaders of the believers in the city. They had been coming to his teaching sessions up in Corinth so he knew them quite well. This day he met Phoebe, a businesswoman who was one of these leaders, and had lunch with her in her house.

"When do you think you will have finished your letter to the Roman believers?" she asked.

"Not long now," replied Paul. "I want to answer some questions that keep coming up about Israel and why they have not accepted the truth about Jesus being the Messiah. Also some practical things about how we live as sons of God. Maybe a week or so at the most. Why do you ask?"

"You know I have a business and from time to time I go to Rome to ensure what we produce here in Achaia is what is required by the merchants I trade with," said Phoebe. "Last year, I lost two ships. One to a storm and one disappeared after landing at Ostia. I think someone stole it and its cargo. I am going with some of my men to try to find out what happened. Anyway, I am due to go as soon as the weather improves and ships start sailing more frequently. I have chartered a cargo ship for my latest merchandise and want to personally escort it to Rome. I was going to suggest, if you like, I could carry your letter to Rome and ensure it gets to our brothers and sisters there."

Paul was delighted with this news and the offer to take the letter. He readily agreed with her plan. Then he added, "If you hear of any ships going east to Caesarea can you let me know?"

After lunch, Paul walked back up the road to Corinth alone. He saw three men rounding a bend and coming down the road. They slowed and stood in the road to block his way, glaring at him.

"Hello, friends," said Paul, "what do you want of me?"

"We know you, you blasphemer. We know who you are and how you have been deceiving the people of Israel in this city," said one of them aggressively. He took a step towards Paul with his knife drawn. Realising he was in great danger, Paul stepped back. At that moment a small detachment of soldiers came up alongside, and the officer in charge caught sight of the knife which was being hidden. "Everything all right here?" he asked.

"Yes, everything is now very fine," said a shaken Paul. "May I join

CORINTH THIRD VISIT AD 56

you in the last part of the journey to Corinth, Officer?"

The three thugs quickly moved away and let them go. One turned back and shouted at Paul. "You were lucky this time, but not next time."

When Paul returned to Gaius' house, he told them what happened. Erastus was called and together they all agreed Paul needed to be vigilant and not go off on his own anymore. The incident soured the atmosphere for them. They realised Paul's movements were being watched, and as he had spoken publicly of his plans to go to Jerusalem by sea, he was in danger again.

They decided to finish the teaching sessions within a week and make sure Paul was never alone. The next session was due the following evening and Paul had already decided to talk about the Father's plan for his people Israel. Meeting these Jewish men on the road had stirred many thoughts in Paul's heart, not least the longing he had for all of Israel to be saved.

As they all gathered the next evening, this was his theme. He linked it with much of what he had said previously and it was part of the great theme of God's faithfulness in this case to Israel.

He began, "I speak the truth in Christ. I am not lying, my conscience confirms it through the Holy Spirit, I have great sorrow and unceasing anguish in my heart. For I could wish that I myself were cursed and cut off from Christ for the sake of my people, those of my own race, the people of Israel." He said that they had so much promised to them, sonship, glory, the covenants; they had received the law, the temple worship and the promises. They had the Patriarchs, and from them was traced the human ancestry of the Messiah, Jesus the son of God. Yet the tragedy was they had not accepted the gracious kindness of God. The sadness and longing in Paul's heart was evident as he spoke.

"What then shall we say? That the Gentiles, who did not pursue righteousness, have obtained it, a righteousness that is by faith; but the people of Israel, who pursued the law as the way of righteousness, have not obtained their goal. Why not? Because they pursued it not by faith but as if it were by works. They stumbled over the stumbling stone." To Paul, the stumbling stone for the Jews was Jesus.[141]

He continued, "Brothers and sisters, my heart's desire and prayer to God for the Israelites is that they may be saved. For I can testify about them that they are zealous for God, but their zeal is not based on knowledge. Since they did not know the righteousness of God and sought to establish their own, they did not submit to God's righteousness. Christ is the culmination of the law so that there may be righteousness for everyone who believes."[142]

Paul knew the issue for everyone was Jesus. Whether Jew or Gentile, "If you declare with your mouth, 'Jesus is Lord,' and believe in your heart that God raised him from the dead, you will be saved. For it is with your heart that you believe and are justified, and it is with your mouth that you profess your faith and are saved. As Scripture says, 'Anyone who believes in him will never be put to shame.' For there is no difference between Jew and Gentile, the same Lord is Lord of all and richly blesses all who call on him, for 'Everyone who calls on the name of the Lord will be saved.'"[143]

Paul used a time-honoured rhetorical style, posing questions and emphatically responding with his favourite expression, 'Me genoito!' God forbid, or absolutely not!

"I ask then. Did God reject his people? Absolutely not! Again, I ask. Did they stumble so as to fall beyond recovery? God forbid."

For Paul, as a Jew he had to face the challenge of what happens when Israel rejects the fulfilment of all God's promises in the coming of Jesus the Messiah. Finally, he paused and recognised that what he was saying was in reality a mystery. There was not an answer that could be understood with the mind, it was perceived by revelation in the heart. He continued, "I do not want you to be ignorant of this mystery, brothers and sisters, so that you may not be conceited. Israel has experienced a hardening in part until the full number of the Gentiles has come in, and in this way all Israel will be saved."

These great and unfathomable mysteries undergirded all truth. As the evening drew to an end he declared,

"Oh, the depth of the riches of the wisdom and knowledge of God! How unsearchable his judgements, and his paths beyond tracing out! Who has known the mind of the Lord? Or who has been his counsellor? Who has ever given to God, that God should repay them? For from him and through him and for him are all things. To him be the glory forever! Amen."(144)

The next day Paul and Tertius reviewed the teaching of the previous evening. Paul asked him to re-read a section here and there rewording what he had said. It was a carefully balanced part of the letter. It all hinged around the central statement of the Lordship of Jesus. Paul was a master of literary style and in these passages he carefully employed a chiasm which was a mirroring of statements in order to draw the reader to the central truth. God had eternally planned to have a family of sons and daughters who were marked by the confession that Jesus is Lord. This reflected the hymn like words he had written to the believers in Philippi a year or so before concerning Jesus. God had exalted him to the highest place and gave him the name above every name. At the name of Jesus every knee should bow, and every tongue acknowledge that Jesus Christ is Lord, to the glory of God the Father.[145]

One final evening was planned and the hall was packed as word got out this would be the last session. Every seat was filled. People crowded on the floor and filled the doorways. Paul stood as a diminutive figure at the front of the large gathering. Yet in many ways he was a colossus. The things he had been sharing were faithfully recorded by Tertius and were unlike anything the world had heard before. The anointing on Paul and the revelation he was bringing thrilled the ears of the hearers in the same way it would the eyes of the readers once the letter was sent. Paul remembered the words Jesus had spoken to him when he met him on the road to Damascus twenty-five years earlier.

"I have appeared to you to appoint you as a servant and as a witness of what you have seen of me and the things I will show you. I will rescue you from your own people and from the Gentiles. I am sending you to them to open their eyes and turn them from darkness to light, and from the power of Satan to God, so that they may receive forgiveness of sins and a place among those who are sanctified by faith in me." [146]

On this final night Paul wanted to show them how the good news transforms believers and the behaviour that results from such a transformation. "Therefore, I urge you, brothers and sisters, in view of God's mercy, to offer your bodies as a living sacrifice, holy and pleasing to God, this is your true and proper worship. Do not conform to the pattern of this world but be transformed by the renewing of your mind. Then you will be able to test and approve what God's will is, his good, pleasing and perfect will." Paul got to the heart of the matter straight away. This transformation he described as a renewing of your mind.[147]

The resulting new way of thinking would impact every part of their lives in Christ. In the way they served among the community of believers and how they used their God given gifts. It would change their relationships with everyone in the world also.

"Love must be sincere. Hate what is evil; cling to what is good. Be devoted to one another in love. Honour one another above yourselves. Never be lacking in zeal, but keep your spiritual fervour, serving the Lord. Be joyful in hope, patient in affliction, faithful in prayer. Share with the Lord's people who are in need. Practice hospitality. Bless those who persecute you; bless and do not curse. Rejoice with those who rejoice; mourn with those who mourn. Live in harmony with one another. Do not be proud but be willing to associate with people of low position. Do not be conceited. Do not repay anyone evil for evil. Be careful to do what is right in the eyes of everyone. If it is possible, as far as it depends on you, live at peace with everyone. Do not take revenge, my dear friends, but leave room for God's wrath, for it is written: 'It is mine to avenge; I will repay,' says the Lord. Do not be overcome by evil but overcome evil with good."[148]

As Paul said these things, he thought of the men he had met on the road who had threatened him. He was speaking to himself as much as he was speaking to the Corinthians in front of him or the Romans who would read the letter when they received it. He had shown them this renewal of the mind takes place after the heart had been captivated by the faithfulness of God in Christ. He was not about to replace the Mosaic Law with a new set of rules and regulations, instead it would be by living in the grace of God according to the law of the Spirit that he had already mentioned. Paul said they would know almost instinctively what God wants of them. To the extent they have been set free from sin, they as believers were no longer bound to sin. Believers were free to live in obedience to God and love everybody.

Paul said to them, "Let no debt remain outstanding, except the continuing debt to love one another, for whoever loves others has fulfilled the law. The commandments, 'You shall not commit adultery,' 'You shall not murder,' 'You shall not steal,' 'You shall not covet,' and whatever other command there may be, are summed up in this one command: 'Love your neighbour as yourself.' Love does no harm to a neighbour. Therefore, love is the fulfilment of the law."[149]

Many practical instructions followed this encouragement to live in love. The daily challenges between them as a result of their different cultures and backgrounds could be resolved by living from a place of love. "May the God who gives endurance and encouragement give you the same attitude of mind toward each other that Christ Jesus had, so that with one mind and one voice you may glorify the God and Father of our Lord Jesus Christ. Accept one another, then, just as Christ accepted you, in order to bring praise to God."[150]

Paul knew he had almost finished what God had given him to say to the Corinthians. Finally, he stopped speaking and looked at them. He smiled at them like a father would at his children. His heart was filled with love for them. He concluded by summing up all he had said over the course of these evenings.

"For I tell you that Christ has become a servant of the Jews on behalf of God's truth, so that the promises made to the patriarchs might be confirmed, and moreover, that the Gentiles might glorify

God for his mercy. May the God of hope fill you with all joy and peace as you trust in him, so that you may overflow with hope by the power of the Holy Spirit."[151]

The evening came to an end. The room was filled with tremendous love towards Paul and to God.

Crispus stood and thanked Paul for what he had imparted to them. He also announced as a community they were gathering money to be sent to Jerusalem for the poor there, and they were going to gather gifts for Paul and his team who were going with him to Jerusalem so that they would have the funds they needed for the journey. There was a loud murmur of agreement from everyone.

The next morning as he sat with Tertius, Paul added some quotations from the Law of Moses, the Jewish prophets and the sacred Jewish writings to underline how it had always been God's intention to include the Gentiles in his great saving plan of bringing all mankind back into his family.

He added, "As it is written: Therefore, I will praise you among the Gentiles; I will sing the praises of your name. Again, it says, 'Rejoice, you Gentiles, with his people.' And again, 'Praise the Lord, all you Gentiles; let all the peoples extol him.' And again, Isaiah says, 'The Root of Jesse will spring up, one who will arise to rule over the nations; in him the Gentiles will hope.' May the God of hope fill you with all joy and peace as you trust in him, so that you may overflow with hope by the power of the Holy Spirit."[152]

Paul felt the bulk of what he had wanted to say to the Roman believers was complete. What was left to say was more about his ministry and hopes for them.

"I have written you quite boldly on some points to remind you of them again, because of the grace God gave me to be a minister of Christ Jesus to the Gentiles. He gave me the priestly duty of proclaiming the gospel of God, so that the Gentiles might become an offering acceptable to God, sanctified by the Holy Spirit."

He told the Romans that he had proclaimed the good news about Jesus all the way from Jerusalem to Illyricum to the north west of Macedonia and that it was his desire to press westward to Rome and beyond to Spain. He wrote,

"I hope to see you while passing through and to have you assist me on my journey to Spain, after I have enjoyed your company for a while. Now, however, I am on my way to Jerusalem in the service of the Lord's people there. For Macedonia and Achaia were pleased to contribute for the poor among the Lord's people in Jerusalem."

His concern for his safety was always in the back of his mind and he asked them to pray for him. "Pray that I may be kept safe from the unbelievers in Judea and that the contribution I take to Jerusalem may be favourably received by the Lord's people there, so that I may come to you with joy, by God's will, and in your company be refreshed."

Finally, Paul wanted to greet many in Rome who he knew personally. "I commend to you our sister Phoebe, a servant of the church in Cenchreae. I ask you to receive her in the Lord in a way worthy of his people and to give her any help she may need from you, for she has been the benefactor of many people, including me.

"Greet Priscilla and Aquila, my co-workers in Christ Jesus. They risked their lives for me. Not only I but all the assemblies of believers among the Gentiles are grateful to them. Greet also the community that meets at their house.

"Greet my dear friend Epenetus, who was the first convert to Christ in the province of Asia." The list went on.

"Greet Andronicus and Junia, my relatives who have been in prison with me. They are outstanding among the apostles, and they were in Christ before I was." Other names were added as Paul's mind roved across the communities he had established.

Then at the very end of the letter, he sent greetings from many people in Corinth who had connections with the believers in Rome.

"Timothy, my co-worker, sends his greetings to you, as do Lucius, Jason and Sosipater, my fellow Jews."

Tertius interrupted Paul at this point. "Paul, can I send a greeting too?"

"Of course," said Paul.

"I, Tertius, who wrote down this letter, greet you in the Lord."

Gaius and Erastus who were with Paul that morning also spoke up. "Us too," they both said. Paul went on,

"Gaius, whose hospitality I and the whole church here enjoy, sends you his greetings. Erastus, who is the city treasurer, sends you greetings."[153]

They all watched Paul as he finished dictating. As was his custom he closed his eyes and waited. Then he opened them and said, "Tertius, please add one last thing for me."

Tertius took up his stylus once more.

"Now to him who is able to establish you in accordance with my gospel, the message I proclaim about Jesus Christ, in keeping with the revelation of the mystery hidden for long ages past, but now revealed and made known through the prophetic writings by the command of the eternal God, so that all the Gentiles might come to the obedience that comes from faith, to the only wise God be glory forever through Jesus Christ! Amen."

MACEDONIA AND ASIA
AD 57

CHAPTER XXVII

The letter was finished. It was the longest Paul had ever written. He spent a couple of days re-reading it and making a few minor adjustments. After he was satisfied, several copies were made which would be dispatched to other groups of believers where Paul was known. Tertius gathered a small team to make the copies. The believers in Corinth knew Paul would soon leave and there was sadness at the realisation they may not meet one another again for a very long time. Paul sent a message to Phoebe at the port to secure a ship for his passage to Caesarea. He met with Erastus and finalised the conversion of the collection into gold coins so it would be less bulky for the trip.

In the evening, Phoebe came up to Corinth from Cenchreae greatly agitated and went straight to Gaius' house looking for Paul. She found him with a number of the leaders.

"Brothers, there is bad news," began Phoebe. "My people have been organising a ship for you at the port, and they have uncovered a plot to kill you. There are men in the port who have been asking about you and trying to discover which ship you would be taking. They have been paying money for information. One of my men heard them talking with the captain of the vessel we have found for you going to Caesarea. They saw money exchanged and heard them talking about ensuring you do not arrive. We think it is extremely dangerous to attempt to return to Jerusalem by sea."

Erastus took charge of the situation straight away as they talked. "You must stay here in the house and not go out Paul. It seems you will have to travel overland to Jerusalem via Macedonia and Ephesus and then take a ship from the other side of the Aegean."

"I so wanted to be in Jerusalem for Passover this year. It seems it will not be possible," said Paul. "It is so much slower going by land, but I agree it is safest and wiser. We must leave as soon as we can." He turned to Phoebe. "How soon do you leave for Rome?"

"Two days. Can I take the letter with me now so it can be delivered?"

"Of course. Tertius will prepare it for you. It is quite bulky I'm afraid. We have a leather carrying case prepared for it."

A few hours later Erastus returned to Gaius' house.

"Now, your trip north, Paul, I have arranged transport for you as far as Thessalonica. There is a military unit travelling north tomorrow. I know the commander and he has agreed to escort you and your companions to Thessalonica. They will ensure your safety. I have arranged horses for you all and a pack mule. When you get to Thessalonica or Philippi sell the animals and it will help fund your onward journey."

The plans quickly came into place and Paul made ready to leave Corinth. They all gathered in Gaius' house one last time for a meal together. There was a sadness at the parting but an excitement because they all believed it was the beginning of a new day for the spread of the good news. Gaius had decided to join Paul on the journey along with Timothy and Tychicus. Titus was to remain in

Corinth and await news of Paul's trip to Rome with the hope of joining him at some point. Another traveller joined them, Trophimus from Ephesus who had been in Corinth and was returning home. Jason also would accompany them back to his home in Thessalonica. Six of them set off from Corinth. Erastus and Archaicus, Crispus, Sosthenes, Chloe and many others walked with them to the city gate. They gathered around and prayed laying hands on each one to bless them and asking the Father to watch over them. The military unit was already moving off, so Paul and his companions mounted their horses and followed. (154)

Ten days later they were in Thessalonica. For Paul and Timothy, it was particularly good to be with Silas again. They sold the horses but decided to keep the mule for the time being. They were joined in Thessalonica by Sopater who came over from Berea. Along with Aristarchus and Secundus from Thessalonica, the three of them joined them on the mission to take the collection to Jerusalem. There were now eight of them representing the various groups of believers who had contributed to the collection.

They travelled on to Philippi where the believers welcomed them warmly. Lydia and Epaphroditus hosted them all. Paul decided to stay a few days in Philippi at Lydia's house as it was the Jewish Festival of Unleavened Bread. The main group went ahead on the overland route and agreed to go as far as Troas and await Paul's arrival. Lucas stayed in Philippi with Paul in order to accompany him to Troas. After the Passover, Paul and Luke, as he was affectionately called, went to the coast to Neapolis and took a ship to Troas. What should have taken just two days turned out to be five as the winds were against them. Paul prayed that he would not add another shipwreck to his list.

They all met up again in Troas, and it was decided that everyone needed a rest after the journey so they stayed for a week.

The believers in Troas were delighted to have so many visitors and wanted to make the most of their stay. Carpus asked Paul if he would be willing to speak to the community when they next gathered, and he readily agreed. A large room on the third floor of a city tenement was their usual meeting place. They began with a meal in the evening. Eutychus was particularly happy to see Paul again and he spent a very busy day helping his mother prepare food for the group. They broke bread together and remembered the sacrifice of Jesus. When Paul spoke his heart was full of the things he had written to the Romans and talked beyond midnight.

Lucas later recorded the events of the evening. There were many lamps in the upstairs room where they were meeting which made it hot and stuffy. Eutychus was sitting on a window ledge. As Paul talked on and on, Eutychus nodded off into a deep sleep. Suddenly he fell sideways out of the window. Everyone ran downstairs to find him lying dead in the street. Paul went down, threw himself on the young man and put his arms around him. "Don't be alarmed," he said. "He's alive!"

Everyone gasped as the boy opened his eyes and looked surprised at them all. Eutychus was taken upstairs; this time he was seated on a stool while people crowded around and looked at him.

"What are you all looking at?" he asked.

"Are you sure you are alright, son?" asked Carpus.

"I'm fine, father, honestly. But I'd love something to eat."

They gave him some food and he tucked in as if nothing had happened.

"I think he should go home to bed," said Paul.

His mother took him home greatly relieved. Paul, in the meantime, continued where he left off, talking until daylight. He had so much to say that was fresh in his heart.[155]

It was time to move on from Troas and Paul wanted to leave in the morning. He had been speaking all night and after a brief sleep took an unusual step. He sent all of his group down to the harbour to get a ship and sail around the headland to Assos. He, however, said he wanted to walk to Assos over land. Lucas and Timothy offered to walk with him, but he was insistent he wanted to take the long walk alone. It was as if Paul wanted to take the day to have some time alone with his God. For weeks and weeks, he had been with people who surrounded him with love and support. They stopped trying to insist and let him go alone. They took the collection with them as it would have been too heavy and too risky for him to have taken it.

Paul was facing a major transition in his life which was full of danger and challenge. He had virtually fled from Corinth because of the plot. He knew he may encounter opposition in Jerusalem. He wondered if his 'thorn in the flesh,' Matthias would be there, if indeed he was still alive. Paul last heard of the man's whereabouts following the riot in Ephesus. He knew Matthias had been one of the fermenters of trouble when the riot broke out.

Paul plodded up the road and over the hills to Assos. He was physically tired having poured out what was in his heart in Troas. His mind was full of fears and anxieties, yet his heart was increasingly at peace. He remembered his words to the Romans and prayed in the Spirit as he walked, allowing the comforting love of the Father to suffuse his whole being.

He stopped at the top of a hill from which he could see Assos down on the coast. He saw a tiny sail heading towards the harbour. Paul stood there, his arms outstretched and his head looking towards heaven. He said aloud, "I know in all things, Father, you are working together for my good. I love you and I know I am called according to your purpose. Father, you are for me. Who can be against me? No one! In all these things I am more than a conqueror because you love me. I am convinced that neither death nor life, neither angels nor demons, neither the present nor the future, nor any powers, neither height nor depth, nor anything else in all creation will be able to separate me from the love of God that is in you my Lord Jesus."

He continued downhill and soon was at the port. As planned the boys were waiting for him on the quayside. They were relieved to see him as they had been concerned about his decision to walk.[156]

They all boarded and set sail south down the coast first to Mitylene on the eastern shore of the island of Lesbos. The next day the ship arrived off Chios. The day after it crossed over to Samos, and on the following day arrived at Miletus, a port to the south of Ephesus. Paul had decided to sail past Ephesus to avoid spending time in the city because he was in a hurry to press on to Jerusalem and get there by the day of Pentecost. He wondered if Matthias was still in the area. However, he wanted to see Epaphras and Onesiphorus and the other leaders. Discovering the ship would be staying three days at Miletus to take on more cargo, he commissioned a rider to take a message to the Ephesian leaders to let them know he was in Miletus. He encouraged them to come if they could. He knew it would take them at least a day to get to the port.

Amazingly, they came late the next day having hurried as fast as they could. They had borrowed a wagon and horses that speeded up their journey. They all met together near the quay where the ship was moored. It was a wonderful reunion for many of them. Paul wanted to talk to them knowing this may well be the last time he would see them.

When they arrived, he began to share what was in his heart. They had plenty of time to talk together. Paul reminded them how he had lived among them, serving the Lord in tearful humility and facing all manner of attacks from Jewish opponents. He remembered how he taught them declaring to both Jews and Greeks to repent and have faith in Jesus.

He went on to tell them his plans to go to Jerusalem led by the Spirit, not knowing what would happen when he got there. He told them everywhere he had been he was warned prophetically by the Holy Spirit that prison and hardships were facing him.

"However, I consider my life worth nothing to me," he said. "My only aim is to finish the race and complete the task the Lord Jesus has given me, the task of testifying to the good news of God's grace."

He urged them to keep watch over themselves first and foremost and then over the flock of which the Holy Spirit had made them overseers.

"Be shepherds of the gathered assembly of the people of God, which he bought with his own blood," said Paul. He continued the picture of being shepherds and warned them of the danger of savage wolves attacking the flock. He added even from among their number, men would arise and distort the truth in order to draw away disciples after them.

"So be on your guard! Remember that for three years I never stopped warning each of you night and day with tears.

"Now I commit you to God and to the word of his grace, which can build you up and give you an inheritance among all those who are sanctified. I have not coveted anyone's silver or gold or clothing. You yourselves know these hands of mine have supplied my own needs and the needs of my companions. In everything I did, I showed you that by this kind of hard work we must help the weak, remembering the words the Lord Jesus himself said: 'It is more blessed to give than to receive.'"

When Paul had finished speaking, he knelt down with all of them and prayed. They all wept as they embraced and kissed him. What they were most saddened by was his statement that they would never see him again.[157]

A sailor arrived from the ship announcing its imminent departure, so they accompanied Paul and his group to the ship. With great difficulty, they tore themselves away from each other on the quayside.

The ship raised its sail and put out to sea and taking advantage of the fresh wind sailed straight to Kos. The next day they went to Rhodes and from there to Patara. They found a ship crossing over to Phoenicia, boarded and set sail. After sighting Cyprus and passing to the south of it, they sailed on to Syria. They landed at Tyre, where the ship unloaded its cargo.

They found a group of believers in Tyre and stayed with them for a week. As they gathered to worship and pray together someone prompted by the Spirit urged Paul not to go on to Jerusalem. When it was time to leave, all of them, including their families accompanied them down to the beach where they all knelt and prayed for them before they boarded the boat again.[158]

JERUSALEM AD 57

CHAPTER XXVIII

The group continued their voyage from Tyre and landed at Ptolemais, where they met with the believers and stayed with them. Leaving the next day, they sailed on to Caesarea. They disembarked and Paul was very moved to put his feet on the soil of Israel once more. Going into the city they made their way to the home of Philip who had been one of the early leaders in Jerusalem. Lucas was excited to meet him as he had heard of the stories of Philip's exploits in the early days.

Philip had four unmarried daughters who were gifted with spiritual insights and would often prophesy. The girls were delighted to welcome so many unmarried young men into their home. In the ensuing days, many stories were told and news shared. Philip recounted his activities in Samaria then continued,

"I met an Ethiopian official once, somewhere on the road to Gaza in the south of Judea. He was riding in the back of his chariot on his way back to Ethiopia. It was extraordinary, he was reading from a copy of Isaiah he had picked up in Jerusalem. He had no idea who he was reading about. It's a long story, but I told him it was Jesus. I ended up baptising him in a water hole." Philip chuckled at the memory. There was an affinity between Paul and Philip. They both desired Jews and Gentiles to hear the good news about Jesus.

Paul discovered Philip had known Stephen. Paul told how he held the cloaks while Stephen was stoned. His eyes filled with tears as he remembered the event twenty-five years earlier. He went on to tell Philip about his vow to crush and wipe out the followers of Jesus. Memories came flooding back to Paul as he contemplated going up again to Jerusalem. He wondered if his collection had been an attempt to compensate for what he had done all those years before. Yet the willingness of the Gentile believers to contribute had calmed and assuaged his apprehensions.

A few days after their arrival, a man called Agabus came down from Judea. Paul had met him sixteen years before when he came to Antioch. Agabus was known to carry a prophetic gift. Years before his prophecy led to Paul visiting Jerusalem with Barnabas bringing gifts from the believers in Antioch to the needy in Jerusalem. It occurred to Paul history was repeating itself. Agabus was delighted to see Paul again but he was also serious. He went over to Paul, took Paul's belt off and then tied his own hands and feet with it and said, "The Holy Spirit says, 'In this way the Jewish leaders in Jerusalem will bind the owner of this belt and will hand him over to the Gentiles.'"

Agabus did not add anything else to the prophetic sign. He did not say, "Don't go!" He left it with Paul. The whole group went silent. This added to the concerns others had already expressed all along the journey back to Jerusalem. Finally, they could hold back no longer. One after another, they urgently pleaded with Paul to reconsider. They suggested he stay at Philip's house and they would take the gift to Jerusalem. Everyone urged Paul not to go up to Jerusalem. Paul's reaction was typical. He had made up his mind.

"Why are you weeping and breaking my heart? I am ready not only to be bound, but also to die in Jerusalem for the name of the

Lord Jesus." Nothing anyone could say would dissuade him and they all gave up. Finally, it was Philip who spoke for them all. "The Lord's will be done."

Soon after this, they started the journey up to Jerusalem. Some of the believers from Caesarea accompanied them as far as the home of Mnason, where most of them were to stay while they were in the city. This man was originally from Cyprus and like Philip was one of the early 'Followers of the Way' as they still liked to call themselves, but he was also familiar with the customs of the non-Jews in Paul's group.[159]

News of their arrival in Jerusalem spread rapidly among the believers and they were received very warmly. Paul was delighted to visit his younger sister and her family. Word was sent to James of Paul's arrival and his desire to meet him and the other leaders. None of the apostles were in Jerusalem as they had scattered all over the empire and beyond with the message of Jesus. The next day Paul and his companions went to see James. All the local leaders were present. Paul greeted them and introduced the delegates from the cities where he had evangelised. One by one they presented their bags of money they had brought. Paul told them what God had done among the Gentiles through his ministry.

The 'elders', as they liked to be called, began to give thanks to God in a half-hearted way. They seemed to have something else more important on their minds and they quickly changed the subject. They only to wanted to talk about what was happening among them.

"Have you noticed, brother, how many thousands of Jews have believed, and all of them are zealous for the law?"

This was the description of a community dominated by a pharisaical approach to the message of Jesus. The elders then got to the main point.

"We have been informed you teach all the Jews who live among the Gentiles to turn away from Moses, telling them not to circumcise their children or live according to our customs."

The words were thrown down before Paul as an accusation. There was no attempt to discuss or hear Paul's reaction to this claim. Instead, they continued in what had clearly been a premeditated agenda on their part.

"What are we to do? They will certainly hear you have come. Now do what we tell you. There are four men with us who have made a vow. Take these men, join in their purification rites and pay their expenses, so they can have their heads shaved. Then everyone will know there is no truth in these reports about you. It will show you yourself are living in obedience to the law. As for the Gentile believers, we wrote to them long ago they should abstain from food sacrificed to idols, from blood, from the meat of strangled animals and from sexual immorality."

Paul and his companions were staggered by this. It seemed to be driven by fear. It sought only to address the symptoms of the problem rather than the root. Paul had consistently addressed the error of the problem wherever he spoke and in all of his letters. Yet here in Jerusalem they were only concerned with keeping the peace and being seen to follow Mosaic laws.

Paul was deeply disappointed and discouraged as he went back to Mnason's house. Paul wrestled all night with how to respond. In his letter to the Romans he had so carefully addressed the issue and yet here in Jerusalem they didn't want to hear what he had to say. He

JERUSALEM AD 57

wondered if the pain of twenty-five years ago was still playing itself out at a very deep level in all their leaders, most of whom would have remembered. He was hurt they had assumed he was a rich man and he could pay the expenses of the purification rites, especially after they had received such a big gift. All manner of feelings and reactions swirled through Paul's mind.[(160)]

When morning came Paul had made a decision. He told his companions he had decided to honour the Jerusalem elders and go along with their plan. He knew their plan was to exploit this action to prove he kept the Law.

"But you don't keep the Law, Paul!" said an astonished Timothy. "I see you honour it and you are ready to identify with your Jewish brothers. But they are just using you, Paul!"

Paul was on the horns of a dilemma. After a while he answered,

"I do hear what you are saying, Timo, but can I remind you of something I wrote a while ago in one of my letters to the Corinthians? It was something like, to the Jews I became like a Jew to win the Jews. To those under the law I became like one under the law, though I myself am not under the law so as to win those under the law. To the weak, I became weak to win the weak. I have become all things to all people so that by all possible means I might save some. I do all this for the sake of the gospel, that I may share in its blessings."

They listened and recognised again it was impossible to dissuade Paul when his mind was made up even if it was an error of judgement in their opinion.

Later that day having given his friends instructions to stay out of the way, avoid getting into trouble and to keep well clear of the temple area, Paul went back to James and the elders. They cautiously welcomed him and sent him off with the four men wanting to conduct their purification rites and purified himself along with them. Then he went to the temple to give notice of the date when the days of purification would end and the offering would be made for each of them. This necessitated he remain in the Temple precincts the whole seven days. Paul consoled himself in thinking he would be able to teach these four men a better way while he was with them.

Completely unknown to Paul he had stepped right into a trap. His coming to Jerusalem had galvanised his enemies. They suggested to the elders the plan to get Paul into the Temple for a week to demonstrate his obedience to the Law. He would be on his own away from his friends and they could move against him. The elders had no idea of their real intention.

On the evening of his fourth day in the Temple, Paul was walking slowly around the colonnades of the outer courtyard of the Temple precincts. Deep in thought, he did not notice anything around him. Suddenly in the gathering darkness, two men jumped him from behind and forced a hood over his head. Paul was not strong and could not fight them off. They dragged him down some steps into an underground corridor. He heard a door being opened and then felt himself being roughly pushed into a room. He fell on the floor and lay there wondering what was about to happen. There was no sound. He smelt oil lamps but also a fetid stink filled his nose. It was the smell of sickness, almost of death itself. He thought he must be in a prison. One of the men who had abducted him picked him up and he felt himself placed on a stool.

Then a voice spoke. "So here you are! My nemesis!"

The hood was pulled off Paul's head, and he blinked and tried to focus on the speaker. He could barely make out where the voice came from. Across the room the man spoke again to Paul's abductors. "Leave us."

Paul became accustomed to the light in the room and could make out the figure of a man lying on a bed in the corner of the room. He was clearly sick and Paul located the source of the miasma filling the room. His body was covered in suppurating sores.

"I am sorry you were brought here rather roughly. As you can see, I could not come to you. Don't you recognise me? Don't you know my voice? No, of course you don't. Yet you and I have followed each other for years."

"Matthias!" said Paul suddenly recognising him.

"Yes, indeed! It is I!" Matthias was silent as he let this realisation sink in. "I don't suppose you remember when or where we first met, do you?"

"No," said Paul.

"Typical," said Matthias. "As usual, you are obsessed with your great mission and everything revolving all around you. Well, I will tell you where we met."

He paused as he tried to raise himself a little on the bed. Paul started to stand in order to assist him. "Don't touch me," said Matthias as every move he made seemed to cause pain.

"We met in this very room long ago. It was used then as a prison cell. The High Priest used it to keep people who had been arrested in your persecution of the Followers of the Way of Jesus. Do you remember it now? You regularly came here."

Paul's mind filled with memories of those terrible days of persecution long ago.

Matthias continued. "I was here with my young brother. I was a Pharisee like you, but I had become a follower of Jesus. My brother was no more than fifteen years old. We were kept here along with some others for several days. No food just a bucket of filthy water. People became sick and one old woman died. We put her in the corner over there just next to where you are sitting right now." Matthias started to cough and Paul picked up a cup that was beside the bed and gave him a drink.

"You never did that for any of us back then." Matthias' weak voice was full of bitterness.

"Matthias, I had no idea—"

"Shut up! I am not finished yet. You came here one day. You stood in that doorway in your full robes as a Pharisee. You had two men with cudgels with you. You demanded we renounce our faith in Jesus. You said you would release us if we denied him. Not one of us did that. The more you demanded, the stronger we all became and the angrier you became. You took off your prayer shawl and took the cudgel from one of your thugs. Then you grabbed my brother by his hair and forced him to his knees. You twisted his hair and made him look at you. 'Deny, you little runt!' you screamed right into his face."

Matthias stopped as his voice choked. "I can hear those words ringing in my ears. He did not deny, he simply looked at you and said, 'Nothing you can say will make me deny my Lord Jesus after all he has done for me.' With that, you started to beat him. You turned his face to pulp. Finally, you stopped. I remember you sweating and gasping for breath as you stood over him. You screamed at him, 'Deny him.' I heard his weak broken voice say, 'I cannot, but I forgive you.'

"My brother died in my arms that day. He may have forgiven you, but I never have. I vowed that day I would get even with you."

There was a heavy silence between them. Paul could feel the pain in Matthias' words.

"We were released some weeks later. No one knew why. Then after some months, we heard you had converted and also were a follower of Jesus. Easy for Jesus to forgive you but not so easy for those of us you had abused. I met you in Antioch many years later and tried to speak to you, but you didn't even recognise me. What's more, you were infecting the followers of Jesus with all this Gentile contamination of being one in Christ. I knew God had given me a call to oppose you and bring people back to the true faith and follow Jesus as Messiah by keeping the law of Moses. Well, you know how that has gone.

"Here we are years later and your way is gaining ground. We who have been faithful to the Law of Moses and the teaching of Jesus are being pushed aside. You even bring money from the Gentiles. Is that to bribe us? Is it to assuage your conscience, Paul?"

Paul was astonished by Matthias' reaction and pain.

"May I speak?" Paul asked.

Matthias' silence was a tacit approval of his request.

"I cannot ever undo the terrible wrong I inflicted on you, your family or your brother or any of the others I hurt and abused in my ignorance back then. What I did was dreadful. I have grieved over my actions many times. But God our Father has forgiven me and I have committed my life to serving him. I am not trying to do things to gain forgiveness. It is his wonderful gift to me that I truly did not deserve. All my life I have tried to serve him out of love and gratitude." Paul looked at Matthias.

"Now sitting here with you, I see how the pain of my actions has blighted your whole life. My words can never heal those wounds. All I ask is for your forgiveness." Matthias broke into a spasm of coughs. After he stopped Paul continued.

"I heard one of Jesus' stories recently about forgiveness. It involved a man who was forgiven a great debt but who refused to forgive someone who owed him. As a result, he ended up in prison and spent the rest of his days being tortured. The point of the story is we who have been forgiven so much by God are to forgive others who have sinned against us. If we don't, we end up in a prison of our own making tortured by our own unforgiveness. We become locked in our own bitterness and pain. Jesus doesn't want us live like that, he longs for us to forgive from our hearts and be free."

Paul let these words sink in.

"Easy for you to say," said Matthias.

"No! It's not easy for me to say! I have had an attitude of unforgiveness towards you, Matthias. Your vendetta towards me has followed my steps ever since those days in Antioch. You have been like a thorn in my foot. Every step I take, you have pained me. I have lost count of the number of times I have been whipped or beaten because of you and your schemes. But I have learnt to not hold this against you. So, it is not easy for me to say. There have been times when I would happily have seen you dead. I confess that to you and I have confessed it to God. Now as I look at you lying there, I can see you are close to death. What my heart feels is love for you, godly sorrow at your condition. I want to bless you and see you free not just from physical pain but also from the deep wound in your heart. Can I pray for you now?"

Matthias' eyes hardened. "No! Leave me. I have said what I wanted to say to you. Just leave me." He turned his face away from Paul and shuffled over onto his side, groaning as he did so.

Paul stood and went to the door. He turned back and looked at Matthias.

"I forgive you, my brother, and I bless you to find peace."

He quietly shut the door behind him and started to walk down a corridor. From back in the room he heard a terrifying howl of anguish and sobbing. Paul's eyes filled with tears. He went back to the door, placed his hand on the door and prayed, "Father, fill this room with your love and peace and healing."

The plan of the Jerusalem elders to show Paul was not a law breaker backfired badly. Two days after his encounter with Matthias, some Jews from the province of Asia spotted Paul in the temple. They saw him with the four men who were doing their ritual purifications and jumped to the conclusion he had brought Gentiles into the sacred precincts of the Temple having previously seen Trophimus in the city with Paul. They stirred up the whole crowd, shouting, "Fellow Israelites, help us! This is the man who teaches everyone everywhere against our people and our law and this place. And besides, he has brought Greeks into the temple and defiled this holy place."[161]

People came running from all directions. Seizing Paul, they dragged him from the temple, shutting the temple gates and started to beat him up. High up on the walls of the Antonia Fortress which overlooked the Temple precincts, Roman soldiers spotted the commotion. They quickly informed the commander of the disturbance. He summoned the guards and went down to the crowd. Seeing the commander and his soldiers coming, the rioters stopped beating Paul.

The commander arrested Paul and had him bound. He demanded to know who he was and what he had done. Some in the crowd shouted one thing and some another. The commander could not get at the truth because of the uproar, so he ordered Paul be taken into the barracks. The violence of the mob was so great, the soldiers had to carry him on their shoulders. The crowd followed shouting, "Get rid of him! Kill him."

As the soldiers were taking Paul into the barracks, Paul asked the commander, "Let me speak to you."

"You speak Greek! Aren't you the Egyptian who started a revolt and led four thousand terrorists out into the wilderness some time ago?"

Paul answered, "No, not at all, I am a Jew, from Tarsus in Cilicia. Please let me speak to the people."

The commander realising it was a case of mistaken identity permitted Paul to speak. Paul stood on the steps and called for their attention. When they were all silent, he said to them in Aramaic: "Brothers and fathers, listen to my defence." When they heard him speak to them in Aramaic, they fell silent.

"I am a Jew, born in Tarsus of Cilicia, but brought up in this city. I studied under Gamaliel and trained in the law of our ancestors. I was just as zealous for God as any of you are today. I persecuted the Followers of the Way to their deaths, arresting them and throwing them into prison as the high priest and the Sanhedrin can testify. I even obtained letters from them to their associates in Damascus and went there to bring these people as prisoners to Jerusalem to be punished." This was fresh in Paul's mind after having talked with Matthias, and he went on explain how he had become a follower of Jesus.

"About noon as I came near Damascus, suddenly a bright light from heaven flashed around me. I fell to the ground and heard a voice say to me, 'Saul! Saul! Why do you persecute me?' "

Paul told them how he met the risen Jesus that day and the commission given to him. He felt it was important to explain that his companions saw the light but did not recognise the voice of the one speaking to him. He explained how a man named Ananias came to see him who was a devout observer of the law and highly respected by all the Jews living in Damascus. He then described how he was prayed for and was able to see again. He told them Ananias said,

"The God of our ancestors has chosen you to know his will and to see the Righteous One and to hear words from his mouth. You will be his witness to all people of what you have seen and heard. And now what are you waiting for? Get up, be baptized and wash your sins away, calling on his name."

Paul did not mention his time in Arabia but picked up the story when he returned to Jerusalem some years later. He described an incident when he was praying in the temple and heard the Lord speaking to him and telling him to leave Jerusalem because people would not accept his testimony about him. At this point, Paul told the crowd the Lord specifically told him to go to the Gentiles.

As soon as Paul mentioned his call to preach to the Gentiles the crowd became very angry and shouted, "Rid the earth of him! He's not fit to live!"(162)

The commander seeing the situation was getting out of hand took Paul into the Antonia Fortress and commanded his soldiers to flog and interrogate him. As he was being stripped and stretched out to be flogged Paul said to the centurion,

"Is it legal for you to flog a Roman citizen who hasn't even been found guilty?"

"This man is a Roman citizen," the centurion hastily told to the commander.

"Tell me, are you a Roman citizen?" asked the commander.

"Yes, I am."

The commander was alarmed and wanted to find out exactly why Paul was being accused by the Jews. He kept Paul in prison overnight and the following day he ordered the chief priests and the Sanhedrin to come to him. When they arrived, he brought out Paul and had him stand before them. He told Paul to explain himself to them.

"My brothers, I have fulfilled my duty to God in all good conscience to this day." At this, the high priest Ananias ordered those standing near Paul to punch him on the mouth.

Then Paul said to him, "God will strike you, you whitewashed wall! You sit there to judge me according to the law, yet you yourself violate the law by commanding that I be struck!"

"How dare you insult God's high priest!" shouted one of the Council.

"Brothers, I did not realise he was the high priest; I would not have spoken evil about the ruler of your people if I had known." Then Paul, knowing some of them were Sadducees and others Pharisees, shouted out, "My brothers, I am a Pharisee, descended from Pharisees. I stand on trial because of the hope of the resurrection of the dead."

This was a master stroke because immediately a dispute broke out between the Pharisees and the Sadducees. The assembly was divided between Sadducees who did not believe in resurrection, nor angels or spirits, and Pharisees who believed in all these things. There was a great uproar, and some of the teachers of the law who were Pharisees stood up and argued vigorously.

"We find nothing wrong with this man," they said. "What if a spirit or an angel has spoken to him?"

The dispute became so violent the commander was afraid Paul would be torn to pieces by them. He ordered his soldiers to take him away and bring him back into the Fortress.[163]

Paul was taken to a cell in the Antonia Fortress and was permitted to send a message to his sister and her family who lived close to the Temple area to let them know he was safe and alive. He was anxious about what would happen next and found it difficult to sleep. As he lay on a pallet on the floor of his cell, he felt a presence in the room with him. He was filled with a sense of peace and comfort. He knew it was Jesus himself standing next to his bed.

Then the voice he recognised so well spoke gently to him,

"Take courage! As you have testified about me in Jerusalem, so you must also testify in Rome." Paul's heart was at peace and he went to sleep.[164]

In the city there was no peace. A group of Jews including the

Asian Jews from Ephesus gathered in the temple and formed a conspiracy against Paul. They bound themselves with an oath not to eat or drink until they killed him. Over forty men were involved in this plot. They went to the chief priests and the elders and told them of their plans which required the Sanhedrin asking the Roman commander to have Paul brought to them on the pretext of wanting more accurate information about his case. Their plan was to kill him on the way there.

Matthias was breathing weakly. He was close to his end. He had been awake much of the night. In his fitful sleep, he imagined Jesus had come to him or was it a dream, he didn't know. In this dreamlike experience and he sensed Jesus speak to him, "Matthias, I want you to be at peace. You know what to do." When he woke, he pondered this dream. Soon after this one of his friends came with food for him. This man excitedly told him of the plot to kill Paul. "By this time tomorrow, he will be dead," he said. "Then you will be able to rest in peace, Matthias. Is there anything else I can get for you?"

"Yes, there is something you can do for me. There is a woman in the city who washes my clothes for me. Can you ask her to come to me today? It is very urgent."

Matthias gave him details of where the woman lived. An hour later, there was a knock at his door and a young teenage boy came in.

"My mother sent me. She said you would give me things to take to her to wash," said the boy.

"Tell me, boy, do you have an uncle who has recently come back to the city?" asked Matthias.

"Yes, sir," said the boy looking worried, "My uncle Paul, but he is in prison."

"Now listen very carefully, I need you to take your uncle a very important message. Do not go home, go straight to the Fortress. Take this basket of bread and tell the guard you have food for him. Is that clear?"

"Yes, sir."

"Then you must tell him there is a plot to kill him. Forty men are plotting to kill your uncle. The Sanhedrin are requesting the Commander to have him sent to them. He will be attacked tomorrow on the way to the Sanhedrin by these men. It is essential you get the message to him today. Is that clear?" Matthias' breath was shallow and his voice failing.

"Now go, boy, don't delay." He lay back on the bed and closed his eyes. His breathing became even shallower and then stopped.

Thinking he was sleeping the boy quietly left the room.

He ran as fast as he could out into the street clutching the small basket of bread. Arriving at the Fortress he banged on the door used by those bringing food to the prisoners. He told the guard he had bread for the prisoner Paul and was let in. Within a few minutes he was standing in Paul's cell.[165]

"Uncle, I have bread for you." He was out of breath and very agitated.

"Calm down, lad, and tell me whatever is the matter," said Paul. "Is all well with your mother?"

The whole story tumbled out. Paul knew who had sent the message. He needed to act fast and called the centurion. "Take this young man to the commander; he has something very important to tell him."

The commander took the boy by the hand, drew him aside and asked, "What is it you want to tell me?"

Paul's nephew told the commander everything.

The officer acted immediately. He told the boy to say nothing to anyone, and then called two of his centurions and arranged to have Paul moved that evening to Caesarea. He wrote a letter to the Governor Felix explaining the whole situation.

It all happened very quickly. In less than twenty-four hours, Paul was escorted from Jerusalem under guard and taken to Herod Agrippa's palace in Caesarea to await trial. His life had been saved by the one he least expected.

The middle years of Paul's ministry ended and his journey to Rome was about to begin.[166]

DRAMATIS PERSONAE

All the characters below appear in the story and this glossary relates to their connection with Paul in the book. Fictional characters are also included for reference and clarity.

ANTIOCH

Barnabas

His name means "son of encouragement." He was a Levite from Cyprus who was known for his generosity. He vouched for Paul's character when some were suspicious of his conversion. He served the rapidly growing number of believers in Antioch and as numbers grew he sought the help of Paul, who was living in Tarsus. He was sent out as an apostle and evangelist with Paul traveling with him on his first missionary journey to Cyprus. He later separated from Paul due to a disagreement over John Mark (Acts 4:36, 9:27, 11:22 - 30, 12:25, 13, 14, 15; I Corinthians 9:6; Galatians 2:1, 9, 13; Colossians 4:1).

Silas

Silas was a Jewish Christian living in Jerusalem, who was considered a prophet. He went with Paul and Barnabas to Antioch. After the disagreement between Paul and Barnabas, he teamed up with Paul on his second missionary journey travelling through Galatia westward. He shared hardships with Paul as they visited Philippi, Thessalonica, and Berea. He stayed in Berea for an extended period to aid the fledgling church, then re-joined Paul in Corinth. Almost nothing is known of Silas after the second missionary journey. The last mention of him, around 65 A.D. states that he delivered Peter's first epistle "to the elect strangers scattered in Pontus, Galatia, Cappadocia, Asia, and Bithynia" (Acts 15:22 - 40, 16:19 - 29, 17:4 - 15, 18:5; I Thess. 1:1; II Thess. 1:1; II Corinthians 1:19; I Peter 5:1; 1 Peter 1:1).

Titus

Titus was a Gentile convert to Christianity who was one of Paul's most trusted companions. He is not mentioned at all in Acts. He first appears with Paul when he accompanies him and Barnabas to Jerusalem. During Paul's extended stay in Ephesus, he is sent to Corinth to handle the growing distrust and hostility toward the apostle. He meets up again with him in Macedonia to report their respect for him has been restored. Paul, after he is freed from his imprisonment in Rome, reconnects with Titus to give him instructions regarding the believers on Crete (Titus 1:4 - 5). Titus was loyal to the apostle to the end, evangelising Dalmatia and Illyricum during his final stay in Rome before martyrdom. Tradition states Titus died sometime after he turned ninety (Gal. 2:1, 3; II Cor. 2:13, 7:6, 13 - 14, 8:6, 16, 23, 12:18, 13:14; Titus 1:4, 3:15; II Timothy 4:10).

John Mark

John Mark, the cousin of Barnabas, was a Jewish convert and writer of the Gospel named after him. His mother, called Mary, owned a house in Jerusalem with a large upstairs room. Mark travelled with Barnabas and Paul on their first missionary journey but left them when they got to Perga. Barnabas wanted to give Mark another chance and take him on the next journey, however, Paul refused to do so. Their disagreement was so serious that they separated. Years later, Paul reconciled to Mark. While in prison, the apostle sent a greeting from Mark to the church at Colossae. Paul also told Philemon that he considered Mark a fellow labourer. Around 64 to 65 A.D., Peter wrote that Mark was with him during his evangelism of "Babylon", which may have been code for Rome. In the last letter to Timothy, written in perhaps 67 A.D., Mark is listed as one of the few remaining people loyal to the apostle. Paul encouraged his friend to bring Mark to Rome "because he is helpful to me for the ministry of the Word" (Acts 12:12, 25, 15:37 - 39; Colossians 4:10; Philemon 1:24; I Peter 5:13; II Timothy 4:11).

Manaen

Manaen is described by Luke as one of several prophets and teachers in the church at Syrian Antioch (Acts 13). Nothing more, biblically, is known about him except that he grew up with Herod the tetrarch. I have assumed he may have been wealthy (Acts 13:1).

LYSTRA

Timothy

Timothy was born in Lystra, the son of a Gentile father and a Jewish mother. Although his mother's lineage made him a Jew, he was not circumcised at birth. This situation was later rectified by Paul. He first met Paul during his second missionary journey visit to Lystra. He accompanied him on most of his second missionary journey. He was with the apostle during his first imprisonment in Rome. Timothy was Paul's most trusted and closest friend, and he treated Timothy like a son. Paul believed he was the only person he could trust to care for the churches with the same heart he possessed. The notation found at the end of I Corinthians credits Timothy with helping to copy the epistle. Timothy is also credited, in the endnotes of the book of Hebrews, with delivering this epistle to its destination. Timothy, unlike many others, stayed faithful to Paul until the very end of his life. II Timothy, the last letter the apostle wrote, shows the faith and love he had for his friend and fellow labourer (Acts 16 to 20; I Thess.1:3; II Thess. 1:1; I Cor. 4:6; II Cor.1:1; Romans 16:21; Hebrews 13:23; Philippians 1:2; Colossians 1:1; Philemon 1:1; I Timothy 1:6; II Timothy 1:1).

Lois

Lois was the mother of Eunice and the grandmother of Timothy. Together they taught Timothy the Old Testament Scriptures from an early age. Paul commends the faith of the two women and their role in shaping the destiny of his beloved fellow labourer in the gospel (II Timothy 1:5).

Eunice

Eunice was the mother of Timothy, Paul's traveling companion. She was a Jew by birth who married a Gentile. The family lived in Lystra. She later converted to Christianity along with her mother Lois (II Timothy 1:5).

DRAMATIS PERSONAE

JERUSALEM

Peter, Simon Peter, (Cephas)

Peter was one of the original twelve apostles. He wrote two letters in the New Testament. He and Paul met three times during their ministries. When Paul, journeyed to Jerusalem in 36 A.D. he stayed with Peter for fifteen days. When Paul, Barnabas and Titus went to Jerusalem in 49 A.D. for the council, Paul talked with Peter and some of the other apostles. Soon after this, Peter visited Antioch. During the first part of his visit, Peter readily mixed and ate with both Jewish and Gentile converts. When believing Pharisees visited from Jerusalem who believed Gentiles should adopt Jewish religious practices, he changed his behaviour. Peter's behaviour put him on a collision course with Paul, who was called to be the apostle to the Gentiles. Paul publicly rebuked him. In Peter's second letter written around 66 A.D, he acknowledged the truth written in Paul's letters and considered them on the same level of inspiration as Scripture (Galatians 1:18, 2:7 - 14; I Cor. 1:12, 3:22, 9:5, 15:5; II Peter 3:15 – 16).

Nicodemus

A Pharisee and a member of the Sanhedrin. He visited Jesus by night when Jesus told him of the need to be born again. He speaks up for Jesus before the Sanhedrin. The final mention of Nicodemus is when he takes part in the preparation for the anointing and burial of the body of Christ. There can be little doubt that he became a true disciple. I have assumed that he was a disciple by the day of Pentecost. He is considered to be a saint by the Roman Catholic and the Eastern Orthodox churches (John 3:1 - 21, 7:50, 19:39).

James

The half-brother of Jesus along with Jude, Joses and Simon. James, as well as his brother Jude, wrote New Testament books named after them. Paul writes that James, Jesus' brother, had a personal resurrection encounter with Jesus. Paul, after spending three years in Arabia, met James when he visited Jerusalem. Paul talked with James who presided over the Jerusalem conference in 49 A.D. Paul presumably met him in Jerusalem at the end of his second missionary journey, and then again at the end of his third missionary journey and before his arrest (Matthew 13:55, Mark 6:3, Galatians 1:19; Acts 12:17, 15:13, 21:18; I Corinthians 15:7; Galatians 1:19, 2:9, 12).

Matthias

A fictional character introduced into the story to personify the continual dogging of Paul by the Judaisers who some considered to be "his thorn in the flesh."

ROME

Claudius Caesar

Emperor reigning from 41 to 54 A.D. His last wife was Agrippina the Younger, a great granddaughter of Augustus. Soon after becoming Emperor, he issued an edict re-establishing the rights of Jews to keep their "ancient customs" without being hindered (Antiquities of the Jews, Book 19, Chapter 5, Sections 2 - 3). Although Jews were granted the right to practice their beliefs under the Emperor, their numbers became so great in Rome that they were forbidden to assemble. Evidence suggests that the regular disturbances caused by

Jews in the city led to the edict banishing them from the capital. In Claudius 25, Suetonius refers to the expulsion of Jews by Claudius and states, "Since the Jews constantly made disturbances at the instigation of Chrestus, he expelled them from Rome." It was this expulsion that impacted Aquila and Priscilla. Over time, however, the Jews and Christians returned to the city (Acts 11:28, 18:2).

Pallas

Marcus Antonius Pallas (died AD 62) was a prominent Greek freedman and secretary during the reigns of Claudius and Nero. His younger brother was Marcus Antonius Felix the procurator of Judea during Paul's imprisonment in Caesarea.

Andronicus

Paul records that Andronicus, who lived in Rome, had been a Christian longer than he had. He also mentions Andronicus was of note among the apostles. Based on these statements, I have placed Andronicus and his wife Junia in Jerusalem at the beginning of the Church who were visitors from Rome (Acts 2:11 -12). The language suggests Andronicus may have been one of Paul's relatives (Romans 16:7).

Junia

Junia, whose name follows Andronicus indicating she is his wife, is a woman greeted in the last chapter of Romans. According to Paul, she had been a Christian longer than he had. He also mentions that she along with her husband had been in prison like Paul. Romans 16 also states Junia was "of note among the apostles." In the story, I place both husband and wife as having an apostolic ministry in Rome (Romans 16:7).

Julia

Julia is one of many Christians in Rome greeted in the letter to the Romans. Nothing else is known of her. In the story, I place her as the mother of Onesiphorus (Romans 16:15).

Narcissus

Narcissus is greeted, as well as his entire household in Rome, in Paul's letter to the Romans written from Corinth. Nothing more is known about this person. In the book, I place him as the brother of Chloe from Corinth and to whose household she sends Apelles (Romans 16:11).

TROAS

Lucas (Luke)

Luke was a Gentile convert who wrote the Gospel that bears his name and is the author of the Acts of the Apostles. Interestingly, he never mentions his own name anywhere in Acts. Although his role in the church's early history was important, he is only referenced by name three times in the New Testament. He is affectionately referred to as "the beloved physician" by Paul. Luke travelled with Paul on parts of his second and third missionary journeys. He also accompanied the apostle from Caesarea to Rome in 60 A.D. Luke is again with Paul in 67 A.D. during his final imprisonment in Rome (Colossians 4:14; II Timothy 4:11; Philemon 1:24).

Eutychus

Eutychus was a young man who, after falling asleep listening to

Paul preach in Troas, fell out a window and died. The apostle went immediately to him and after stretching himself on the young adult, he was miraculously healed and brought back to life! In the story, I make Carpus his father (Acts 20:9 – 10).

Carpus

Paul requested something special from Timothy just before his martyrdom. He asked, "When you come, bring the cloak that I left in Troas with Carpus, and the scrolls, especially the parchments." In the story, I have made Carpus the father of Eutychus (2 Timothy 4:13).

PHILIPPI

Lydia

Lydia was a prosperous businesswoman who sold purple dye. She was originally from Thyatira, a city in the Province of Asia. The dye's rarity in nature, along with the time and effort it took to collect it, made it a highly prized and expensive commodity sought by kings and rulers. Lydia may have been visiting Philippi when Paul and Silas arrived in the city. After hearing the apostle preach, not only was she baptized but her entire household as well. She became Paul's first convert on the continent of Europe. Lydia was a generous and hospitable woman who insisted Paul and Silas stay in her Philippi residence (Acts 16:14 - 15, 40).

Drusilla

Fictional name for the slave girl who was a fortune teller healed by Paul (Acts 16:16 – 18).

Clement

Clement was considered a co-worker in the gospel by the Apostle Paul and specifically mentioned as having his name written in the Book of Life. Origen, a third century A.D. theologian, believed this Clement became the leader of the Church in Rome whose writings among others form part of a group known as the Apostolic Fathers (Philippians 4:3).

Epaphroditus

Epaphroditus was sent by those in Philippi to deliver financial support, clothes and other necessities to the apostle while he was a prisoner. He was a leader in the Philippian church who Paul described as a "fellow soldier" in spreading the gospel and serving the church. Epaphroditus, while attending to Paul's needs in prison, got so sick that he almost died. The apostle commended him to the Philippians for this selfless act and willingness to place his own life at risk for the cause of Christ. After Epaphroditus' recovery, he was sent back home to deliver the letter Paul had written to the Philippians (Philippians 2:25 - 30, 4:18, 23).

Euodia

Euodia was a prominent woman living in Philippi, where the church first took root among the city's women (Acts 16:13 - 15). Paul, in his letter to the church, asked her and Syntyche, another Christian woman, to settle their differences. Both of them had helped him in the work of the gospel (Phil. 4:2 – 3).

Syntyche

Syntyche was another woman living in Philippi. Paul, in his letter to the church, asked her and Euodia, to settle their differences. Both of them had helped Paul in the work of the gospel. It is unknown what the nature of their disagreement was (Acts 16:13 – 15; Philippians 4:2).

THESSALONICA, BEREA, AND ATHENS

Jason

Jason was a Jewish convert living in Thessalonica. He hosted Paul and Silas when they stayed in the city. When the Jews in Thessalonica caused a riot due to rejecting the gospel, they stormed Jason's house looking for Paul and Silas. When they could not be found, the mob dragged Jason and some brethren in front of the city's rulers. They were soon freed, however, after they posted bail. Jason also sent his greetings from Corinth to Roman Christians through the epistle sent to Rome (Acts 17:5 - 9; Romans 16:21).

Aristarchus

Aristarchus was a Thessalonica Christian who was likely a Jewish convert to Christianity. He visited Paul in Ephesus. During the riot he was seized by an angry mob toward the end of Paul's long stay in Ephesus. He ended up in prison with Paul in Ephesus (Acts 19:29, 20:4, 27:2; Col. 4:10; Philemon 1:24).

Secundus

Secundus was a native of Thessalonica. He accompanied Paul on the last leg of his journey that took him through Macedonia to Asia after leaving Corinth. It is unclear if Secundus went with him on the remaining part of the trip to Tyre and ultimately Jerusalem (Acts 20:4).

Sopater

Sopater, described as the son of Pyrrhus, lived in Berea and travelled with Paul during his third missionary journey. He accompanied the apostle on his eastward journey through Macedonia to Asia. It is unclear if he went on the remaining part of the trip to Tyre and Jerusalem (Acts 20:4).

Dionysius the Areopagite

Dionysius is one of only two people specifically named as having converted to Christianity during Paul's brief evangelism of Athens. Dionysius was likely a prominent citizen of Athens and a member of the Areopagus, the Athenian Supreme Court (Acts 17:34).

Damaris

Damaris is one of only two people listed as having converted to Christianity during Paul's brief visit to Athens. Luke may have recorded her name due to her being an important or noteworthy person (Acts 17:34)

CORINTH

Priscilla (Prisca) and Aquila

Aquila was born in the Roman province of Pontus. He, along with his wife Priscilla, were Jews who converted to Christianity. As a couple they frequently travelled with Paul. Like Paul, they were tentmakers and met him on his first visit to Corinth. The couple had previously resided in Rome but were expelled along with other Jews and Christians by the Emperor Claudius Caesar. Priscilla's name is often listed before her husband Aquila's name. This may be an indication that she had a stronger personality than her husband or because she was of a higher status socially. Priscilla and Aquila accompanied Paul after he left Corinth and went with him to Ephesus. They stayed in the city when Paul continued his journey to Jerusalem. It is after he left that they met Apollos, an eloquent man whose knowledge they completed by telling him about Jesus. The couple resided in Ephesus long enough to meet Paul again when he returned to the city. When Paul wrote his letter to Corinth from Ephesus, he sends greetings from the couple and commended their selfless sacrifices for the brethren. The couple stayed loyal to Paul to the very end when many others abandoned him. In his last letter to Timothy before his death, he saluted them and their tireless efforts for the gospel (Acts 18:2, 18, 26; II Cor. 16:19; Romans 16:3 - 4; II Timothy 4:19).

Stephanas

Stephanas and his family are described as being the earliest converts to Christianity in the province of Achaia. They were also some of the few people Paul personally baptized in Corinth. Stephanas, as well as Fortunatus and Archaicus, visited Paul in Ephesus during his extended stay in the city (I Corinthians 1:16, 16:15, 17).

Crispus

Crispus was an educated Jewish man who was the leader (ruler) of Corinth's synagogue. He, along with his household, became

Christians during Paul's eighteen month stay in the city. Crispus was one of the few people in Corinth personally baptized by the apostle (Acts 18:8; I Corinthians 1:14).

Gaius (Titius Justus)

There are possibly two individuals named Gaius connected to Paul. One is described as Gaius from the city of Derbe (Acts 19:29, 20:4), who accompanied Paul during his third missionary journey. Towards the end of Paul's extensive visit of Ephesus, whilst visiting the city, he was seized by a mob stirred up by those whose businesses were suffering due to the gospel's impact. He was released by the city's senior administrator. The other man named Gaius lived in Corinth. Many scholars identify his full name as Gaius Titius Justus who was converted through Paul's preaching and was one of only two Corinthians personally baptized by the apostle. He made his home, which was next to the synagogue, available to Paul as a place to preach from on the Sabbath. On Paul's third visit to Corinth, Gaius provided a place in Corinth for the apostle to stay during this visit. He greeted their brethren in Rome in the final chapter of the letter to the Romans written by Paul.

My conclusion for the purposes of the book is the two may have been one and the same person. The Gaius of Corinth could have originally come from Derbe (Acts 18:7, 19:29, 20:4; II Cor. 1:14 Romans 16:23).

Sosthenes

The first mention states that a man named Sosthenes was the chief ruler of a synagogue in Corinth. He was likely the replacement for Crispus, the previous ruler, who had converted to Christianity after hearing Paul preach. After the Proconsul Gallio refused to hear the charges brought against Paul by angry Jews, the Greeks beat up Sosthenes. The second time Sosthenes is mentioned is in the opening statement of I Corinthians. Written from Ephesus, Paul greets those in Corinth and links his greeting with Sosthenes who is with him, presumably having come to visit him with news of the situation in Corinth (Acts 18:17; I Corinthians 1:1).

Gallio

Lucius Junius Gallio was a Roman senator and brother of the Roman writer Seneca. Towards the close of the reign of Claudius, Gallio was appointed Proconsul of the newly constituted senatorial province of Achaea of which Corinth was the capital. He was referred to by Claudius as "my friend and proconsul" in an inscription found at Delphi circa 52AD. Gallio was appointed the new Proconsul during Paul's first visit to Corinth. After assuming his position, the city's Jews dragged the apostle before him with the accusation that he was, "persuading men to worship God contrary to the law." Gallio abruptly refused to hear the case made against Paul. He was so irritated that a religious disagreement, and not a Roman law related matter, was brought before him that he drove the Jews from his presence! (Acts 18:12, 14, 17).

Erastus

The name of Erastus is recorded three times in the New Testament. It is unclear, however, whether all these references are to the same person. I have concluded they are. In the Letter to the Romans written from Corinth, Erastus is described as the city treasurer who sends greetings to the Romans. He visited Paul during his extended stay in Ephesus and was sent by him along with Timothy ahead into

Macedonia to help encourage the churches in the area. The final time the name Erastus is used is in II Timothy, where it is stated he was living in Corinth at the time of the letter (Acts 19:22; Romans 16:23; II Timothy 4:20).

Archaicus

Archaicus was a Christian who lived in Corinth. Along with Stephanas and Fortunatus, he made the trip from the city to Ephesus during Paul's stay. They probably brought with them a letter with questions for the apostle to answer. In the story, I have made him a freedman of Erastus (I Corinthians 16:17).

Fortunatus

Fortunatus was a Christian in Corinth. He travelled to see the apostle in Ephesus during his stay in the city (I Corinthians 16:17).

Sosipater

Sosipater was a Jewish Christian who joined Timothy and others in Corinth in sending their greetings to believers in Rome (Romans 16:21).

Apelles

Apelles is one of the many Christians in Rome referenced in the last chapter of Romans. Paul knew of his conversion and describes him as having been tested and found faithful. In the story, I place his conversion in Corinth, and then he is encouraged to go to Rome by Chloe (Romans 16:10).

Chloe

Chloe was a woman whose household informed Paul about the divisions and arguments taking place in the Corinthian church. This suggests she was a householder and woman of influence in Corinth (I Corinthians 1:11).

Phoebe

Phoebe was a female leader in the church at Cenchreae, which was the eastern port of Corinth. The church there may have been independent from the Corinthian church. Paul commends her help not only to him but also to the rest of the church. He took advantage of Phoebe traveling to Rome to have her deliver his letter to the Romans. He requests the church in Rome assist her in whatever way she needed when she arrived (Romans 16:1 – 2).

Tertius

Tertius is the person who wrote down the Letter to the Romans dictated to him by Paul. He sends greetings to his fellow Christians living in the empire's capital. He is presumably one of the Christians in Corinth (Romans 16:22).

Trophimus

Trophimus, a Gentile convert to Christianity, was one of a people who accompanied Paul on his return trip from Corinth to Jerusalem. Trophimus' arrival in Jerusalem was noticed by some of the city's Jews who knew he was not Jewish. When Paul visited the temple, the Jews thought he was bringing him into the temple, an act that was strictly forbidden. Their mistake, coupled with their already existing hatred of the gospel, was the catalyst for a riot that got the apostle arrested by the Romans (Acts 20:4, 21:29; II Timothy 4:20).

EPHESUS

Apollos

Apollos was a Jew from Alexandria in Egypt and a gifted orator with an extensive knowledge of the Old Testament Scriptures. He arrived in Ephesus just after Paul left for Jerusalem at the end of his second missionary journey. He met Aquila and Priscilla who filled in the gaps in his understanding of the gospel. He then left for Corinth. There, his teaching and debating skills earned the church's respect and thwarted the attempt by some Jews to prove that Jesus was not the Messiah. Apollos' evangelistic efforts were so effective that Paul considered him a fellow labourer in the gospel who complemented his own work. He was in Ephesus when Paul was there writing his first letter to the Corinthians. Some scholars suggest he may have been the author of the Letter to the Hebrews (Acts 18:24, 19:1; I Corinthians 1:12, 3:4 - 6, 22, 4:6, 16:12; Titus 3:13).

Onesiphorus

Onesiphorus was a Christian who lived in Ephesus. He greatly aided the Apostle Paul during his first visit to the city. In the story, I connect him to Paul on a ship going from Corinth to Ephesus. I imagine him to be the son of one of Ephesus' Asiachs. I create a fictitious father called Cassander and a mother called Julia Lavinia. Paul specially commends Onesiphorus for tracking him down and visiting him during his second imprisonment in Rome. Onesiphorus frequently refreshes the apostle and is not ashamed of his chains, unlike so many others who abandon him (II Timothy

1:16 - 18, 4:19).

Demas

Paul initially considered Demas a fellow labourer in the gospel. He was in Ephesus during Paul's imprisonment. A few years later, however, in his last letter to Timothy, Paul laments that Demas forsook him to pursue what the world had to offer (Colossians 4:14; Philemon 1:24; II Timothy 4:10).

Demetrius

Demetrius was a wealthy and important Ephesian silversmith who made his fortune by selling idols. He, and his fellow craftsmen, made small shrines, idols themed around the pagan goddess Diana also known as Artemis. Demetrius, fearing the gospel would continue to negatively affect his business, stirred up other tradesmen in Ephesus to oppose Paul (Acts 19:24, 38).

Epenetus

Epenetus was one of the first converts in the province of Asia. It is unknown whether or not Paul's preaching led Epenetus to become a Christian, but he is greeted by Paul in his Letter to the Romans (Romans 16:5).

Alexander

Alexander was a Jew who Ephesian Jews tried to use to quell a riot. The uproar was caused by a local silversmith named Demetrius determined to stop Paul and his teachings from adversely affecting Ephesus' well-known idol making businesses. Alexander's efforts failed to calm the riotous crowd (Acts 19:33).

Hymenaeus

Hymenaeus was an Ephesian Christian. He plays a minimal role in the story but becomes more significant later. Paul later turned him over to Satan so that he would repent. Hymenaeus had shipwrecked his faith through the rejection of his conscience (I Timothy 1:20; II Timothy 2:17 – 18).

Tychicus

Tychicus was from the province of Asia, possibly Ephesus. In his letter to the Ephesians and to the Colossians, Paul calls Tychicus a "dear brother and faithful servant in the Lord." In both Ephesians and Colossians, Paul indicates that he is sending Tychicus to them in order to encourage them. Along with Onesimus, he took Paul's letter to Colossae. Later references in Paul's letters to Timothy and Titus show that Tychicus was again with Paul after the appeal to the emperor had resulted in him regaining his freedom in Rome. The apostle wrote to Titus, who was in Crete in charge of the churches there, that he intended to send either Artemas or Tychicus to him to take the oversight of the work of the gospel so that Titus might be free to come be with the apostle at Nicopolis. Paul sent Tychicus to Ephesus. As Timothy was in charge of the church in Ephesus, the coming of Tychicus would set him free, so as to enable him to set off at once to re-join Paul at Rome (Acts 20:4; Ephesians 6:21; Colossians 4:7; II Timothy 4:12; Titus 3:12).

Marcus Junius Silanus (AD 14-54)

He was the Roman Proconsul governor of the Province of Asia with his residence in Ephesus. His mother was the great-grand-daughter of the emperor Augustus. As a member of the imperial family, Silanus could therefore be considered a possible candidate for the succession. His establishment would be referred to as Caesar's Household and he would be entitled to a detachment of the Praetorian Guard. He became consul in 46 AD and served as proconsular governor of Asia. Silanus did not survive the death of the Emperor Claudius. The historian Tacitus hints Silanus was assassinated by consuming mushrooms doused with a dose of poison said to have been administered at the instigation of the emperor's fourth wife, Agrippina the Younger, another descendant of Augustus. She feared Silanus would avenge his brother's death, of which she was the perpetrator. As with Claudius, poison was the means to Silanus' end. The writer Dio Cassius records that she sent Silanus the same poison which she gave her late husband Claudius. Tacitus informs us that the lethal drug was administered by a Roman of the Equestrian class named Publius Celerius, with the aid of a freed slave named Helius. The pair committed the crime openly in Ephesus, and the Province of Asia eventually prosecuted Celerius for this deed; moreover, according to Tacitus, Nero saw to it that the prosecution was delayed to such an extent that Celerius died of old age.

Publius Celerius

A Roman of the Equestrian class from Rome sent by the Emperor Nero's mother, Agrippina to Ephesus to poison the Proconsul Silanus.

Apollonius - Fictional character

I have imagined him as a relative of Philemon and Apphia in Colossae who is an Asiach (Acts 19:31).

DRAMATIS PERSONAE

COLOSSAE

Epaphras

Epaphras lived in Colossae and was considered a faithful fellow servant of Christ by Paul. The apostle commends him to the church as someone who was always praying for their spiritual wellbeing. Epaphras not only spearheaded the spreading of the gospel in Colossae but also in nearby Laodicea and Hierapolis. At the time of the writing of Philemon, he was a fellow prisoner with Paul in Ephesus. I have imagined him to be a relative of Philemon (Colossians 1:7, 4:12; Philemon 1:23).

Philemon

Philemon, a friend and helper of Paul, was a Christian living in Colossae. He hosted a church in his home. A slave owned by Philemon named Onesimus stole from him then fled to Ephesus. While he was in the city, he found Paul. The Letter to Philemon is a personal letter from Paul to him hoping to convince him to forgive the wrongs committed by Onesimus (Philemon 1:1).

Apphia

Apphia is a woman greeted as "our beloved" by Paul in his opening remarks to Philemon. Some biblical commentaries speculate, without proof, that Apphia may have been the sister or wife of Philemon. I have written her as his wife (Philemon 1:2).

Archippus

Archippus is greeted as "our fellow soldier" by Paul in his opening remarks to Philemon. Archippus is mentioned by Paul in connec-

DRAMATIS PERSONAE

tion with Philemon and Apphia and the church that meets in their home. I have concluded from this that they are a family. I have made him Philemon and Apphia's son. In Colossians, Paul challenges Archippus to devote himself to the ministry that he has received in the Lord (Colossians 4:17; Philemon 1:2).

Onesimus

Onesimus lived in Colossae. He was an educated slave of Philemon, a Christian who was a friend and helper of Paul. He ran away from Philemon. Paul hints that he robbed his owner and then fled. After leaving his owner he made his way to Ephesus and found the place where Paul was under arrest. Although Paul wanted Onesimus to stay with him, he sent him back to Philemon and hoped he could convince his friend not only to forgive any wrong done by Onesimus but also to treat him as a fellow brother in the faith. Onesimus and Tychicus together delivered the Letter to the Colossians. Onesimus also wrote down Paul's words that became the Letter to Philemon. It is possible both letters were delivered at the same time since Philemon lived in Colossae (Colossians 4:9; Philemon 1:10).

Nympha

Nympha was a Christian woman who lived in Laodicea. Paul greets her, and those who gathered at her home to worship God. I have made her a sister to Apphia in Colossae (Colossians 4:15).

CAESAREA

Philip the Evangelist

Philip the Evangelist was an early Jewish convert to Christianity. His exemplary character in the early church was such that he was selected, as well as six others, to serve as a deacon. Philip, later in his life, married, lived in Caesarea, and was the father of four daughters who possessed the gift of prophecy. Philip and Paul met face to face when the apostle, nearing the end of his third missionary, stayed several days at his house in Caesarea. After his stay, Paul proceeded to Jerusalem (Acts 6:1 – 6; Acts 21:8).

Agabus

Agabus, who lived in Jerusalem, was a prophet who had two of his prophecies recorded which affected the life and ministry of Paul. The first prophecy proclaimed to the church in Antioch warned of a severe worldwide famine. The second prophecy spoken roughly sixteen years later at Caesarea predicted to Paul that he would be arrested in Jerusalem and turned over to the Romans (Acts 11:28, 21:10).

Mnason

Toward the end of the third missionary journey Mnason accompanied Paul on his trip from Caesarea to Jerusalem. Mnason, a native of Cyprus, had been a Christian for many years. Paul and company, upon their arrival in Jerusalem, stayed in Mnason's house (Acts 21:16).

BIBLICAL REFERENCES

A NIGHT AND A DAY IN THE OPEN SEA

(1) II Cor. 11:26
(2) II Tim. 1:16 - 18, 4:19

CHAPTER I

(3) Acts 26:4 - 11
(4) Acts 26:12 - 18
(5) Acts 9:26 - 30
(6) Acts 11:19 - 21
(7) Acts 11:22 -24.
(8) Acts 11:25 - 26
(9) Acts 12:25 - 13:4
(10) Acts 13:13
(11) Acts 13:13 - 14:28
(12) Acts 15:1 - 2
(13) Acts 15:2 - 3, Gal. 2:1 - 10
(14) Acts 15:4 - 29
(15) Acts 15:30 - 35
(16) Gal. 2:12
(17) Gal. 2:11 - 21

CHAPTER II

(18) Acts 26:9 - 11
(19) Acts 15:36 - 39

CHAPTER IV

(20) Rom. 16:7
(21) Acts 2:1 - 40

CHAPTER V

(22) Acts 18:2 - 3
(23) II Cor. 11:25
(24) II Cor. 1:2 - 4

CHAPTER VI

(25) Acts 15:40 -41
(26) Acts 16:1 - 2
(27) Gal. 2:1 - 5
(28) Acts 16:1 - 3

CHAPTER VII

(29) Acts 16:5 - 6
(30) Acts 16:7 - 8
(31) Acts 16:9 - 10

BIBLICAL REFERENCES

CHAPTER VIII

(32) Acts 16:11 - 12
(33) Acts 16:13 -15
(34) Acts 16:16 -18
(35) Acts 16:19 - 24
(36) Acts 16:25 - 39

CHAPTER IX

(37) Acts 17:1 - 4
(38) Acts 17:5 - 9
(39) Acts 17:10 - 15
(40) Acts 17:13 -15
(41) Acts 17:16 - 34

CHAPTER X

(42) II Cor. 12:7 - 8
(43) Acts 18:2 - 4
(44) I Cor. 1:14 - 17

CHAPTER XI

(45) I Thess. 3:6 - 7
(46) I Thess. 4:13 - 18
(47) I Thess. 5:16 - 28

CHAPTER XII

(48) Acts 18:6 - 8

(49) Acts 18:9 - 10
(50) Acts 18:12 -17
(51) Rom. 16:23 -24

CHAPTER XIII

(52) II Thess. Chps. 1 - 3
(53) Rom. 16:10, 11
(54) Jeremiah 3:19
(55) Acts 18:18, Rom 16:1

CHAPTER XIV

(56) Acts 18:19 - 21
(57) Acts 18:24 - 26
(58) Acts 18:27 - 28

CHAPTER XV

(59) Acts 18:22
(60) Acts 13:1
(61) Acts 18:23
(62) Col. 4:12 - 17, Phm. 1:1-2
(63) Acts 19:1

CHAPTER XVI

(64) Acts 19:11 -12
(65) Rom. 16:5
(66) Acts 19:2 - 7

BIBLICAL REFERENCES

(67) Acts 19:8 - 10
(68) I Cor. 5:9 - 10
(69) II Cor. 8:10
(70) II Cor. 6:14 - 7:1
(71) I Cor. 1:10 - 12, II Cor. 11:5
(72) I Cor. 16:17, I Cor. 7:1
(73) I Cor. 16:5 - 24, I Cor. 4.17

CHAPTER XVII

(74) I Cor. 6:9 - 11
(75) I Cor. 1:26 - 31
(76) I Cor. 2:1 - 5
(77) I Cor. 4:14 - 17
(78) Mark 14:22 - 25
(79) I Cor. 11:23 - 26
(80) I Cor. 13:1 - 13
(81) I Cor. 16:1 - 4
(82) I Cor. 16:19 - 24.
(83) II Cor. 2:1, II Cor. 13:2 - 4
(84) II Cor. 11:25

CHAPTER XVIII

(85) II Cor. 2:1 - 4, 7:8, 12
(86) Acts 19:13 - 17
(87) Acts 19:18 - 20
(88) Acts 19:22
(89) Acts 19:23 - 27
(90) Acts 19:28 - 41
(91) Phil. 1:12, Phm. 1:23

CHAPTER XIX

(92) Phil. 1:1 -2
(93) Phil. 1:12 - 14
(94) Phil. 2:1
(95) Phil. 2:19 - 2
(96) Phil. 2:25 - 30
(97) Phil. 4:1 -3
(98) Phil. 4:10 - 20
(99) Phil. 4:21

CHAPTER XX

(100) Col. 1:9 - 23
(101) Col. 2:6 - 17
(102) Col.4:7 - 18
(103) Phm. 1:1 - 25

CHAPTER XXIII

(104) II Cor. 2:12 - 13
(105) II Cor. 1: 3 - 8
(106) II Cor. 1:8 - 11
(107) II Cor. 1:15 - 17

(108) II Cor. 1:23 - 2:4
(109) II Cor. 2:5 - 11
(110) II Cor. 2:12 - 13
(111) II Cor. 2:14 - 16
(112) II Cor. 2:17 - 3:3
(113) II Cor. 3:7 - 18.
(114) II Cor. 4:7 - 12.
(115) II Cor. 5:17 - 6:2
(116) II Cor. 6:18
(117) II Cor. 7:2 - 7, 13 - 16
(118) Rom. 15:19
(119) II Cor. 8:16 - 24
(120) II Cor. 9:12 - 15
(121) II Cor. 10:1 - 11
(122) II Cor. 11:5, 13 - 15
(123) II Cor. 11:21 - 31
(124) II Cor. 12:1 - 7a
(125) II Cor. 12:7b-10
(126) II Cor. 13:14

CHAPTER XXV

(127) Rom. 1:16 - 17
(128) Rom. 1:20 - 23
(129) Rom. 1:29 - 32
(130) Rom. 1:8 - 13
(131) Rom. 4:1 - 25
(132) Rom. 5:1 - 5
(133) Rom. 5:20 - 21
(134) Rom. 6:12 - 14
(135) Rom. 6:19 - 23
(136) Rom. 7:21 - 24
(137) Rom. 8:10 - 11
(138) Rom. 8:14 - 17
(139) Rom. 8:18 - 24
(140) Rom. 8:31 - 39

CHAPTER XXVI

(141) Rom. 9:1 - 13
(142) Rom. 10:1 - 4
(143) Rom. 10:9 - 13
(144) Rom. 11:33 - 36
(145) Phil. 2:9 - 11
(146) Acts 26:16 - 18
(147) Rom. 12:1 - 2
(148) Rom. 12:9 - 19, 21
(149) Rom. 13:8 - 10
(150) Rom. 15:5 - 7
(151) Rom. 15:8 - 9
(152) Rom. 15:9 - 13
(153) Rom. 16:1 - 24

CHAPTER XXVII

(154) Acts 20:3 - 4
(155) Acts 20:7 - 12
(156) Acts 20:13 - 14
(157) Acts 20:17 - 38
(158) Acts 21:1 - 6

CHAPTER XXVIII

(159) Acts 21:8 - 16
(160) Acts 21:20 - 25
(161) Acts 21:27 - 29
(162) Acts 21:37 - 22:22
(163) Acts 22:23 - 23:10
(164) Acts 23:11
(165) Acts 23:12 - 16
(166) Acts 23:17 - 35

OTHER BOOKS BY TREVOR GALPIN

Falling from grace into Grace and being caught by the Father. *(2012)*

This book describes Trevor's journey from being a hardworking, wounded, orphan hearted pastor to discovering his true identity as a son of God the Father who is loved unconditionally.

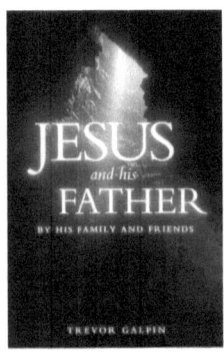

Jesus and His Father by his family and friends. *(2014)*

The revealing of God as Father was the primary ministry of Jesus. He revealed this through conversations with his family and friends. This book is the story of fourteen people who heard Jesus say things about God as a Father as recorded in the Gospels.

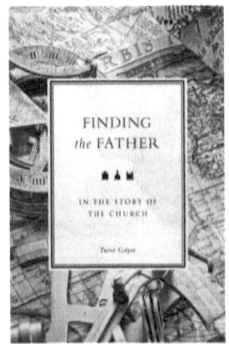

Finding the Father in the Story of the Church. *(2016)*

When Jesus returned to his Father he commissioned his followers to continue his work. This is the story of how the church has tried to do this through 2000 years. It looks specifically at the place the truth about the

Father heart of God has had in the story. Sometimes it was almost forgotten but gloriously has not been lost.

The Story of Paul the Early Years *(2018)*

See the introduction at the beginning of the book for a description of this book which sets the scene for the early part of Paul's ministry up to the end of his first missionary journey and his writing of the Letter to the Galatians.

You can contact Trevor Galpin via his website:
www.trevorlindafhm.com

All the above books are available on **Amazon.com** in paperback, Kindle and the Story of Paul is also an audio book read by Trevor.

www.ingramcontent.com/pod-product-compliance
Lightning Source LLC
Chambersburg PA
CBHW021138080526
44588CB00008B/112